Japan in Transformation, 1952–2000

We work with leading authors to develop the
strongest educational materials in history,
bringing cutting-edge thinking and best learning
practice to a global market.

Under a range of well-known imprints, including
Longman, we craft high-quality print and electronic
publications which help readers to understand and
apply their content, whether studying or at work.

To find out more about the complete range of our
publishing please visit us on the World Wide Web at:
www.pearsoneduc.com

SEMINAR STUDIES   IN HISTORY

Japan in Transformation, 1952–2000

JEFF KINGSTON

Longman

An imprint of **Pearson Education**

Harlow, England · London · New York · Reading, Massachusetts · San Francisco · Toronto · Don Mills, Ontario · Sydney
Tokyo · Singapore · Hong Kong · Seoul · Taipei · Cape Town · Madrid · Mexico City · Amsterdam · Munich · Paris · Milan

Pearson Education Limited
Edinburgh Gate
Harlow
Essex CM20 2JE
England
and Associated Companies throughout the world.

Visit us on the World Wide Web at:
www.pearsoneduc.com

First published 2001

© Pearson Education Limited 2001

ISBN 0-582-41875-5 PPR

British Library Cataloguing-in-Publication Data
A catalogue record for this book is
available from the British Library

Library of Congress Cataloging-in-Publication Data
Kingston, Jeffrey, 1957–
    Japan in transformation, 1952–2000 / Jeff Kingston.
    p. cm. -- (Seminar studies in history)
    Includes bibliographical references and index.
    ISBN 0-582-41875-5 (ppr)
    1. Japan--History--1945- I. Title. II. Series.

DS889.K546 2001
952.04--dc21   00-067849

Set by 7 in 10/12.5 Sabon Roman
Printed in Malaysia

CONTENTS

Introduction to the Series		viii
Author's Acknowledgements		ix
Publisher's Acknowledgements		x
Maps		xi–xii
1.	INTRODUCTION	1
	PART ONE: THE BACKGROUND	7
2.	THE US OCCUPATION OF JAPAN, 1945–52	9
	Enemies to Allies	9
	What Went Wrong?	10
	Democratization	12
	The Reverse Course	13
	The Legacies of Occupation	14
	Hiroshima and Pearl Harbour	17
	PART TWO: ANALYSIS	19
3.	POSTWAR POLITICS	21
	The Yoshida Doctrine	22
	The US–Japan Security Treaty	22
	The 1955 System	23
	The Decline of Radicalism	27
	The Changing Logic of Japanese Politics	27
	Corruption	30
	The Shadow Shogun	31
	Sagawa Kyubin	33
	Political Reform	33
4.	THE ECONOMIC MIRACLE	36
	The Development State	36
	Favorable Factors	37
	Adversarial Trade	41
	A Dual Economy	42
	Shock Absorbers	43
	Growth as Ideology	43
	The Setting Sun	43

5. JAPAN AND ASIA: PAST AND PRESENT   45
    A Lingering Legacy   45
    Atonement and War Guilt   47
    Textbooks and Masochistic History   49
    Comfort Women   50
    The Nanking Massacre   51
    Contemporary Ties   53
    Multilateral Participation   55
    The Future   56

6. JAPANESE SECURITY   58
    The US–Japan Alliance   58
    The Reactive State   60
    Transforming Japan's Security Posture in the 1990s   61
    A Normal Nation   63
    North Korea (DPRK)   64
    People's Republic of China   65
    Lingering Taboos: Article Nine and the Three Non-nuclear Principles   65

7. WOMEN IN JAPAN   68
    Women and Work   69
    The Labor Force Periphery   70
    The Wage Gap   72
    Education   73
    Recruitment   74
    Low Birth Rate   75
    The Birth Control Pill   76
    Sexploitation   77

8. THE DEMOGRAPHIC TIME-BOMB   79
    Family-based Elderly Care   80
    Public Policy   82
    Nursing Care Insurance   83
    Pension and Medical Care Solvency   85
    Reform   86
    The Labor Shortage   87

9. PARADIGM SHIFT IN THE 1990s   90
    A System that Soured   90
    The Changing Employment Paradigm   92
    Restructuring   93
    Transformation, Deregulation and *Gaiatsu*   95
    The Unraveling Nexus   98
    A Compelling New Logic   99
    A New Frontier   103

10. JAPAN AT THE CENTURY'S END   104
    The Lost Decade   104
    The Emperor's Death   104
    The Burst Bubble   105

The Binge   108
Hangover   108
Aum Shinrikyo (Supreme Truth Cult)   110
The Kobe Earthquake   112
Nuclear Mishaps and Misgivings   114
Symbols that Divide   116
Social Mores and Delinquency   116
Discrimination   118

PART THREE: ASSESSMENT   **121**

11. IN RETROSPECT   123
    Transformation?   126

PART FOUR: DOCUMENTS   **129**

Chronology   190
Glossary   195
Prime Ministers since 1952   200
Who's Who   201
Bibliography   205
Index   215

INTRODUCTION TO THE SERIES

Such is the pace of historical enquiry in the modern world that there is an ever-widening gap between the specialist article or monograph, incorporating the results of current research, and general surveys, which inevitably become out of date. *Seminar Studies in History* is designed to bridge this gap. The series was founded by Patrick Richardson in 1966 and his aim was to cover major themes in British, European and world history. Between 1980 and 1996 Roger Lockyer continued his work, before handing the editorship over to Clive Emsley and Gordon Martel. Clive Emsley is Professor of History at the Open University, while Gordon Martel is Professor of International History at the University of Northern British Columbia, Canada, and Senior Research Fellow at De Montfort University.

All the books are written by experts in their field who are not only familiar with the latest research but have often contributed to it. They are frequently revised, in order to take account of new information and interpretations. They provide a selection of documents to illustrate major themes and provoke discussion, and also a guide to further reading. The aim of *Seminar Studies in History* is to clarify complex issues without over-simplifying them, and to stimulate readers into deepening their knowledge and understanding of major themes and topics.

AUTHOR'S ACKNOWLEDGEMENTS

I am especially indebted to Machiko Osawa and Yutaka Mataebara and thank them for their sustained patience, generosity, encouragement and wise insights. Ochan and Rhubarb have been best friends during this project and also deserve credit for indulging and distracting me.

I am also grateful for the comments, advice, inspiration, assistance and insights of the following people who are all duly absolved: Junko Akama, Mike and Marie Therese Barrett, Tom Boardman, Mary Brinton, Roger Buckley, Kyle Cleveland, Gerald and Midori Curtis, David and Noriko Campbell, Greg Davis, George Deaux, Philip Evanson, Philip Everson, Carol Gluck, Jon Gomon, Ivan Hall, Hiroshi Hamaya, Laura Hein, Velisarios Kattoulas, Atsushi Maki, Gordon Martel, James Morley, Jack Mosher, Akiko Okitsu, Robert Orr, Jr., Donald Richie, William and Sue Roff, Masako Sakata, Murray and Jenny Sayle, Fritz Schmitz, Kurumi Sugita, Stephen Talasnik, Kazuko Tanaka, Tradd Thomas, Hisashi Urashima, Shinya Watanabe, Herschel Webb, Robert Whiting, Charles Worthen and William Young. This book also owes much to my students and colleages at Temple University Japan.

At my publishers I would like to thank Heather McCallum, Verina Pettigrew and Sarah Bury for shepherding the manuscript through the process with patience and efficiency.

PUBLISHER'S ACKNOWLEDGEMENTS

We are grateful to the following for permission to reproduce copyright material:

Columbia University Press for extracts from *The Columbia Guide to Modern Japanese History* by Gary Allinson © 1999 Columbia University Press; The Feminist Press for an extract from 'Pornographic culture and sexual violence' by Kuniko Funabashi in *Japanese Women: New Feminist Perspectives on the Past, Present and Future*; Kodansha International Ltd for an extract from *The Straitjacket Society* by Masao Miyamoto; Melus for an extract from 'Multiethnic Japan and the monoethnic myth' by Stephen Murphy-Shigematsu in *Melus*, 18:4 (Winter 1993); New York Times for extracts from the articles 'Why Japan has been right to wonder about the pill' by Francis Fukyama in *New York Times*, 9.6.99 and 'Japanese call '37 massacre a war myth, stirring storm' by Howard W. French in *New York Times*, 23.1.00; and Mainichi Shimbun for the photographs comprising the plate section.

Though every effort has been made to trace the owners of copyright material, in a few cases this has proved impossible and we take this opportunity to offer our apologies to any copyright holders whose rights may have been unwittingly infringed.

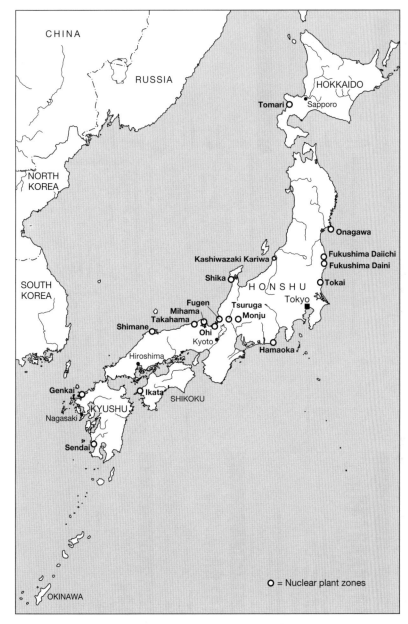

Map 1   Sites of nuclear power plants

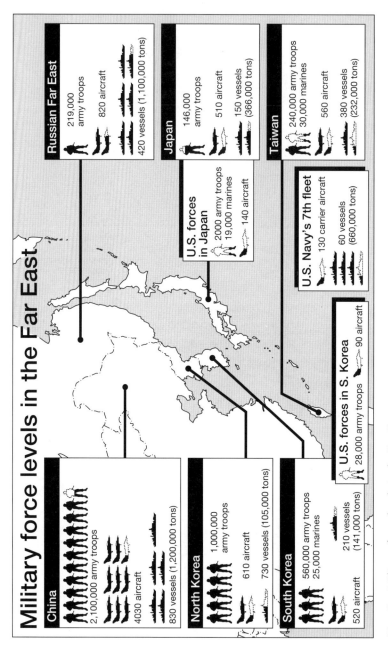

Map 2 Military force levels in the Far East

CHAPTER ONE

INTRODUCTION

This book covers the second half of the twentieth century in Japan, a period of tumultuous change that has transformed the way Japanese view their world and act in it. This ideological transformation has been driven and reinforced by institutional changes, economic development, political ferment and the dynamic tension between prevailing norms and shifting realities. Transformation has been experienced, rejected, embraced and reviled, leaving no corner of the archipelago, nor any sector in society, unaffected. This does not mean that there are not substantial elements of continuity, for societies are not nearly as abruptly decisive as light switches; change is incremental, cumulative and always includes considerable overlap between old and new. The past continues to resonate powerfully in the present and old verities linger, influencing attitudes, inclinations and patterns of behavior. And yet, the past and these verities are fading under the onslaught of time, modernization and the inexorable change inherent in a dynamic society. The human condition conjures up a variety of descriptions, but stasis is not one of them.

The concept of time figures prominently in the way a historian analyzes a society. Choosing a span of time to study involves a choice about what to include and exclude since historical processes tend to respect our concept of time no more than they do national borders. Framing this study between the years 1952 and 2000 is not intended to cut this period off from its antecedents nor its consequences. The end of the US Occupation in 1952 and the beginning of a new millennium are arbitrary dates in the sense that historical processes cannot be neatly packaged. For many Japanese who reckon dates based on the imperial system (*gengo*), this study begins in Showa 27 (the twenty-seventh year of Emperor Hirohito's reign) and ends at Heisei 12 (the twelfth year of Emperor Akihito's reign). Nonetheless, usually in Japan the twentieth century is divided between the prewar and postwar periods, thus for Japanese the periodization proposed here might seem eccentric. The notion of history as merely a collection of names, dates, events and watersheds to be memorized is not inspiring precisely because it ignores the issue of how the processes of history work themselves out over time in a continuous, dynamic and cumulative manner. Time also confers perspective on change. This study is being written and read while the processes under examination continue to evolve. Thus, any assessment made and understanding conveyed is preliminary and provisional, straining credulity by the act of considering history while it is still happening. Studies of the distant past give the historian the advantage of orderly perspective while those of the recent past and present can convey both an appealing and confusing immediacy. This book is an attempt to chart the tides of change at a time when they appear to be running faster than ever before, spilling over the banks and outside the channels that leaders and policy-makers planned. This book aims to elucidate the tension between change and continuity, and suggest some overall patterns of transformation and what they portend for the future. Such a task is ambitious and humbling.

Students of history can learn much from examining and comparing the intended and unintended consequences of choices and policies made by people and how these are affected by the given institutional arrangements, and political and economic conditions. The complex interweave of historical forces and factors does not lend itself to easy assessments. Students of history need to train their senses to analyze not only what happened, but also to grasp what did not happen and why. Historians are acutely aware that History with a capital H does not exist. Those who chronicle and interpret the past are all guilty of selectivity in what they focus on and what they push to the side. Omissions, emphasis and interpretations reflect an inherent subjectivity. Students of history need to hone their critical thinking skills to engage and question the material presented, reading between the lines and in the margins, and considering the sources used, ignored and those that do not even exist. As Graham Swift points out, history 'is that impossible thing: the attempt to give an account, with incomplete knowledge, of actions themselves undertaken with incomplete knowledge' (in *Waterland* (London: Picador), 1992: 93–4 [originally published in 1983]). Good history will stimulate thinking and raise as many questions as it answers. Why is history important? I do not think that it is a question of learning about the mistakes of the past to avoid repeating them, although this would not be an unwelcome outcome. Cicero perhaps best summed it up as an exercise in self-cultivation and maturity by suggesting, 'Not to know what happened before you were born is always to remain a child.' At a minimum, history is the basis for being an informed and judicious observer of the world in which one lives.

Understanding contemporary Japan is important for everyone because of its global reach and the closer and sustained interactions between countries and people that characterize the world in the twenty-first century. It is a leading nation economically, technologically, strategically and in terms of its cultural influence. Explaining Japan is especially difficult because perhaps more than with other countries, knowledge of Japan too often relies on, and remains blinkered by, misleading stereotypes. There is a rich history of orientalism among foreign observers that has fostered a tendency to focus on what is exotic, mysterious, surreal or odd. Images of Japan around the world frequently remain fixed in time and it is not rare to see magazine cover stories on modern Japan depicting a *geisha*, a *sumo* wrestler, a *samurai*, or a militaristic rising-sun flag. These are aspects of Japan that have become familiar by repetition, but they tend to obscure and ignore how much change has occurred in modern Japan. For example, one frequently hears how conformist the Japanese are, but one needs to question such trite characterizations. As in other societies, many Japanese are conformist and in many cases groups dictate individual behavior to a great extent. However, conformity is not unique to Japan and group or peer pressure remains powerful in most societies. One also needs to distinguish between public behavior (*tatemae*) and private feelings and attitudes (*honne*). For many Japanese, *tatemae* is essentially common sense, doing what is proper and expected, but this should not be confused with *honne*. Here too, their behaviour differs little from people elsewhere who also do what is expected of them in public. Paradoxically, it is possible for Japanese to express their individuality and assert themselves within their conformity. If one plays by the rules sufficiently, one can get away with quite a bit of individualism and society will look the other way. In reading Japan, it is essential for the observer to look beyond the first impression, to remain skeptical about what one thinks he or she knows about it and always recall that sweeping generalizations are a lazy way out in a diverse and changing society of 125 million people. This is a society with a tremendous capacity for change and growing tolerance of diversity, and the advent of the twenty-first century is a perfect period to witness this dynamism at work.

The postwar era has been a time of miraculous economic success for Japan and has seen a vast improvement in the lives of most Japanese people. At the time Japan lay in smoldering ruins in 1945, who would have guessed the amazing recovery from war devastation, and the material progress that ensued? Japan at century's end certainly has its share of social ills, economic problems, political corruption, and spiritual anomie, but these do not diminish how much has been accomplished in improving living and working conditions in such a brief period of time. The real miracle in Japan is how many have shared in the fruits of progress and how few have been left in the wake of development. As in other industrialized societies, the costs of progress have been high, taking a toll on the environment, the family and the sense of community. The repercussions of progress have challenged society in many ways and in doing so have stoked a healthy introspection and a relatively high level of self-criticism. Over the years, the troubles of society have been the impetus for citizens to pursue political activism and seek improvement in the status quo. One of the great changes between Japan in the 1950s and 1990s is the attitude and sense of mission held by growing numbers of ordinary citizens who are now engaged in non-governmental, non-profit and other organizations trying to increase accountability, transparency and myriad other reforms. The radical activism of the 1950s and 1960s has given way to a more centrist, pragmatic and popular activism, working through the status quo rather than trying to topple it, meaning that the agenda of change is more incremental and less dramatic and polarizing.

Since the oil shocks of the 1970s, there has been more concern about the fragility of what has been achieved and concerns about balancing the need to change in order to survive and the desire to protect those who would be the losers from such changes. The political economy of Japan has thus featured a dynamic tension between the forces of transformation and the beneficiaries of the status quo. Japan's material success has sparked diversity and new sources of power that have gradually eroded the status quo. There is greater economic, political and cultural space for the expression of diversity and this is having an impact on the pace and nature of transformation. Intensified interaction with the outside world is also reinforcing this trend. Japan is thus becoming a far more complex society with more options and choices and less certainty. This is a troubled time as people try to cope with the destabilizing and disconcerting ramifications of change as it ripples through society. It is also a time when the currents of change are welcomed by those who have been stifled by a relatively rigid system. The system that has brought so much prosperity to so many since World War II is now blamed for many contemporary problems. Despite the emerging consensus favoring a wide-ranging set of reforms to address evident problems, there is much less certainty on how to navigate these uncharted waters. It is thus a time when pressures for change are building while action is limited.

It is important to bear in mind that symptoms of change do not necessarily mean that change is happening. While the rest of the world has admired the Japanese educational system, the government, business and citizens have criticized a system that they believe has curtailed creativity and needs to change. They have been demanding change for some three decades, but the evident reforms remain muted. This example is not meant to deny the forces of change, but rather to sensitize students to their sometimes glacial pace. Other aspects of socio-economic change may move with the ferocity of an avalanche while some familiar features of the landscape slowly mutate, remaining recognizable but distinctly different.

In focusing on transformation, this book emphasizes the consequences and outcomes of trends, choices, policies and actions in the initial decades of the period under study relevant to selected themes. Here we consider the influence of the US Occupation (Chapter Two), postwar political changes (Chapter Three), factors favoring the economic miracle (Chapter Four), Japan's relations with Asia (Chapter Five), security (Chapter Six), the changing situation of women (Chapter Seven), the implications of a rapidly aging society (Chapter Eight), the restructuring of corporate Japan (Chapter Nine) and a variety of themes in the 'lost decade' of the 1990s (Chapter Ten) that help define what kind of society Japan is becoming. Many important aspects of Japanese history and social change cannot be included in this short study. In focusing on the recent past and ongoing transformation relevant to courses on contemporary Japan, the initial decades of this period are primarily considered as antecedents to ongoing developments in institutions, relations and patterns of behavior. This volume is intended to give students of Japan an introduction to contemporary Japan and to examine what is changing, why these changes are happening and what they portend.

PART ONE　　THE BACKGROUND

CHAPTER TWO

THE US OCCUPATION OF JAPAN, 1945–52

ENEMIES TO ALLIES

An important story of the Occupation concerns how the US and Japan were able to transform their bitter rivalry into a close alliance, sometimes resembling friendship. During the Pacific War (1941–45), the propaganda machines of both nations demonized and dehumanized the enemy to an extraordinary extent. Each side committed atrocities, but focused only on those committed by the other, and citizens on both sides of the Pacific were conditioned to expect the worst from each other (Dower, 1986b). The Japanese had seen their major cities reduced to ashes by extensive conventional bombing and firebombing. The twin tragedies of Hiroshima and Nagasaki in August 1945 brought an abrupt end to what has been called a 'war without mercy', but the decision to surrender was opposed by military leaders until the Emperor intervened and broke a deadlock among his senior advisors. Japan's fifteen year rampage through Asia was finished, in the end claiming the lives of an estimated 3 million Japanese and over 15 million Asians, mostly in China. Japanese brutality in war, including mistreatment of prisoners-of-war (POWs), generated sentiments favoring retribution and punishment. It was in this inhospitable climate that US troops landed in Japan and began the Occupation.

The Occupation was a well-planned operation aimed at demilitarizing and democratizing Japan. The US arranged for the repatriation of some 7 million Japanese scattered around the rubble of empire throughout the Asian theater, an operation that taxed the logistical capacity of the US military and added to the already large problems of unemployment and food and housing shortages. Upon returning home, the troops were demobilized and sent home with a train ticket and a bag of rice.

The demilitarization of Japan meant the elimination of the armed forces. This was seen to be a guarantee that Japan would not again embark on military adventurism. In the first two years of the Occupation purges of thousands of officers, bureaucrats and industrialists blamed for the war were a further hedge against a revanchist threat. Democratization was also seen to guarantee Japanese pacifism by eliminating the concentration of power exercised by a small elite prior to and during the war. By spreading power within the government and among all citizens, including voting rights for women, and by supporting a robust press and unions, the Supreme Command of the Allied Powers (SCAP) was attempting to inoculate Japan from the scourge of militarism. US policies in the Occupation are best understood in the context of what people at that time thought had been the sources of Japan's descent into militarism.

WHAT WENT WRONG?

There are competing schools of thought when it comes to explaining what went wrong in Japan during the 1930s and 1940s. Some scholars trace the problem to the Meiji Constitution of 1889. They argue that the absence of checks and balances within the government and the concentration of broad discretionary powers in the office of the Emperor created a distorted system. The advisors of the Emperor could wield the power and authority of the Emperor to promote their agenda without having to accommodate the usual debate and compromise characteristic of a parliamentary system of democracy. During the Meiji period (1869–1911), these powers were used to transform Japan and promote modernization under the slogan 'fukoku kyohei' ('rich nation, strong military'). Scholars generally credit the Meiji Emperor's advisors with using these powers wisely, but given the unchecked, discretionary powers of government concentrated in the executive, the potential for the abuse of power, authoritarianism and radical swings in policy carried ominous potential. In this system, the military exercised *de facto* veto power because it could block the formation of a cabinet. The rising fortunes of the military based on victory over China in 1895 and Russia in 1905, combined with its decisive political power in forming cabinets, facilitated the emergence of military-dominated governments in the 1930s.

The Great Depression that started in 1929 in the US and soon spread around the world became a catalyst for Japanese militarism. The sharp decline in world trade caused by protectionist policies had a devastating impact on the Japanese economy, hitting the majority of Japanese still living in the countryside especially hard. The dislocation in rural areas dependent on the export of silk involved the familiar cycle of indebtedness, loss of land, growing class disparities and often the selling of daughters into prostitution. Many of Japan's military officers were farm boys who were angered at the ineffectiveness of the government in bringing relief to their country brethren. In addition, they were disenchanted with the corruption and excess displayed by leading industrialists and politicians. In this turbulent time of socio-economic upheaval, the military engaged in assassinations and other acts of intimidation against government officials, often in the name of the Emperor (but without his support). Young military officers were committed to purifying Japan by imposing greater discipline and rooting out the corrupt excesses of capitalism and the vacillation of party politics. Some scholars have described this as fascism, but there were significant differences from developments in Germany and Italy where Hitler and Mussolini rose to power.

The Taisho era (1912–25) was a heady period for Japanese internationalism and democracy. There is general agreement that Japan became disenchanted with the post-World War I international system because it seemed weighted to the advantage of the Western-directed status quo and relegated Japan to the second tier of nations. Since Japan's aspirations were to modify that status quo to its advantage, and there were scant signs that the leading powers were inclined to accommodate these aspirations, national interests seemed to dictate that Japan steer a more confrontational course. The roots of Japan's alienation from the international system are long and complex, but it is safe to argue that racism and double standards played a key role. Japan's moderates had little to show for their efforts at working within the international system, prompting criticism of those efforts and highlighting the insults and sacrifices Japan was seen to be enduring at the hands of the Western powers. The Japanese invasion of Manchuria in 1931 and its withdrawal from the League of Nations in 1933 over criticism of this invasion marked Japan's transformation from supporter to challenger of the international system. The militarist hardliners succeeded in taking over Japan's foreign policy, steering it on a collision course as they escalated expansion into China, especially after 1937.

Reischauer (1977) has suggested that Taisho democracy was going well until it was hijacked by the militarists in the 1930s, arguing that Japan was on the trajectory of modernization until this process was derailed by a relatively small group of ultra-nationalists. Those sympathetic to his view argue that the Occupation was an effort to revive democracy and return Japan to the modernization trajectory. Others argue that the Taisho democracy was an illusion doomed to fail because of the structural flaws of the Meiji Constitution that favored the emergence of authoritarianism. Proponents of this view dismiss the 'hijacking' theory and point out that the shift towards ultra-nationalism and imperial expansionism enjoyed broad media and popular support (Young, 1998). Blaming a small group of fanatics, they argue, tends to exonerate the Japanese people from responsibility for Japan's expansionist rampage in Asia and overlooks sustained public enthusiasm for such policies. These differing interpretations of what went wrong are connected to the ongoing debate over continuity and transformation between contemporary and wartime Japan. Did SCAP remake wartime Japan or, in making common cause with the existing conservative elite, did it accommodate a certain degree of continuity unimaginable in occupied Germany?

DEMOCRATIZATION

MacArthur and his advisors exercised a decisive influence on the nature of democracy in Japan. Confident in victory and, 'With a minimum of rumination about the legality or propriety of such an undertaking, the Americans set about doing what no other occupation force had done before: remaking the political, social, cultural, and economic fabric of a defeated nation, and in the process changing the very way of thinking of its populace' (Dower, 1999: 78). Perhaps the boldest initiative was in writing the new Constitution in 1946 and compelling its acceptance by the Japanese Diet. It is often considered the greatest achievement of the Occupation and has never been amended since being promulgated in 1947. The Emperor was forced to renounce his divinity and was stripped of all political power. Interestingly, his support for the new Constitution proved critical in winning its acceptance among the public. Sovereignty was vested in the people and the prewar aristocracy lost its privileged status. Women were given the right to vote and indeed, the rights of women as specified in the Constitution are perhaps some of the most progressive in the world. In reality, these ideals have remained elusive. The new Constitution specifies and guarantees a total of thirty-one civil and human rights, clearly responding to the widespread trampling of these rights under the Meiji Constitution.

The new Constitution is based on the British system of parliamentary supremacy rather than the American system of checks and balances between the respective branches of government. The Constitution promotes the autonomy of the judiciary and a Supreme Court was established with the power of determining the constitutionality of laws, although it has demonstrated little enthusiasm for exercising this power of review.

Article Nine of the postwar Constitution aimed at imposing pacifism by prohibiting Japan from maintaining armed forces and obliging it to renounce the right of belligerency [*Doc. 1*]. Although the language is clear and the intentions of the legislation were spelled out in Diet interpolations in 1946, since the early 1950s the Self-Defense Force (SDF) has existed and Japan now has the third-largest defense budget in the world. The constitutionality of the SDF has been challenged, and some lower court decisions have determined the SDF to be unconstitutional, but the higher courts have consistently affirmed the constitutionality of the SDF. This position rests on a convoluted and obtuse interpretation of the wording in the article. This constitutional sleight of hand is the source of considerable and ongoing political debate in Japan, judicial decisions and government pronouncements notwithstanding (see Chapter Six).

SCAP also promoted democracy by promoting land reform in the countryside and a strong union movement that drew inspiration from the New Deal reforms under the Roosevelt administration during the 1930s. Union organizers, including many communists, were released from jail and legislation protected their right to establish unions. Given the miserable working and living conditions prevailing in the aftermath of war, the unions grew rapidly and became more radical in their demands and tactics.

The early months of the Occupation were a time of grand efforts at socio-economic reforms based on a belief that Japan needed to be transformed in order to exorcise the demons of militarism. Right-wing militarists and alleged sympathizers were purged from government service and banned from elected office. The powers of the police were restricted and centralized authority was abolished. The educational curriculum was modified to eliminate vestiges of imperial ideology and central government control over the educational system, including textbooks, was curtailed. The conservative landlord class was targeted with the land reform aimed at redistributing land in favor of the farmers actually working the land. The rural gentry was considered a bastion of conservatism and thus a barrier to democratization; removing their economic clout based on large landholdings and onerous sharecropping arrangements was a strategy to eliminate their political influence.

MacArthur also promoted trust-busting tactics at the expense of the *zaibatsu*, the large family-owned industrial conglomerates that dominated the Japanese economy since the Meiji era. Reports about large-scale pilfering by the *zaibatsu* of public stockpiles of commodities soon after the surrender on 15 August 1945, at a time when ordinary citizens were at the brink of starvation, made a deep impression on MacArthur. In addition, analysts suggested that the *zaibatsu* were willing accomplices of the military and had benefited handsomely from military expansionism and war-related procurements. Breaking up the *zaibatsu* was intended to promote the general policy of deconcentrating power as that was seen to be the major flaw of the Japanese prewar system. The excessive concentration of power, political and economic, was thought to have made it easier for a small coterie of conspirators to hijack national policy for their own ends.

THE REVERSE COURSE

The record of SCAP on democracy after 1947 left much to be desired. The 'reverse course' is the term often used to describe the sudden conservative shift in US Occupation policies. The reverse course was one of the early consequences of the Cold War that was just heating up between the US and Soviet Union (Schaller, 1985). The first salvo involved MacArthur banning a general strike that had been called for 1 February 1947. This signaled the beginning of the end for the radical union movement as SCAP withdrew its support and encouraged the union-busting tactics of Japanese corporations and the government. For the US, in waging a worldwide ideological war, it became imperative that Japan be a success story. Japan was to be a showcase for the superiority of capitalism and the American way. Thus retribution and any reforms that might impede Japan's rapid recovery were shoved to the side in favor of policies that would transform Japan into a 'bulwark of the free world' in Asia. This was also a time when political attitudes in the US were rapidly shifting to the right, meaning that the New Deal-inspired reforms that had initially animated the Occupation were out of favor. It is perhaps difficult to appreciate the sudden swing in the mood of the country, but the rise of McCarthyism and communist witch-hunts were soon central features of the US political landscape and were echoed in US policy in Japan.

The anti-*zaibatsu* efforts of SCAP had little impact because there were very few trustbusters and there were many opponents skillful at defending big business. The Japanese conservative political elite repeatedly warned SCAP that over-zealous reforms of the *zaibatsu* would play into the hands of the communists by slowing economic recovery and prolonging the suffering of workers. Since the Occupation was indirect, meaning that SCAP depended on the Japanese government for implementing its ambitious agenda of reforms, there was ample opportunity for modifying, vitiating and slowing the pace and extent of reform initiatives. They quickly teamed up with American allies, including some large, influential US corporations that had prewar ties with the *zaibatsu* and were concerned that their business interests might be adversely affected (Davis, 1997). They lobbied Congress for support, lamenting the 'left-wing' inclinations of SCAP and pointing out that busting the *zaibatsu* would prolong Japan's dependence on US aid. Thus, the domestic political fallout of the Cold War in the US resonated strongly in Japan. In the end, the *zaibatsu* emerged from the Occupation in modified form as *keiretsu*, bank-centered conglomerates that continue to dominate the Japanese economy.

THE LEGACIES OF OCCUPATION

From 1947, the Japanese government, supported by MacArthur, unleashed a 'red purge' that targeted those Japanese considered to have left-wing views. Union activists, members of the Communist Party, writers and government officials were affected by the purge. The success of the Japanese Communist Party in the 1949 elections, continued labor unrest and Mao's victory in China had hardened attitudes. The resulting infringement on the civil liberties enshrined in the new Constitution certainly reflects badly on the US commitment to the democratic ideals it was espousing and reminded not a few Japanese of the authoritarian system they had endured before and during the war. Certainly most Japanese enjoyed far more freedoms and rights during the Occupation than they had under the militarists, but the use of tactics inimical to democracy cast a cloud over the morality of US leadership. Censorship was also prevalent as SCAP prohibited negative commentary about the Occupation and discussion of the atomic bombings. Ironically, SCAP was nurturing democracy, but was itself unaccountable and could and did act arbitrarily, claiming rights and privileges that put its staff above the law. Moreover, the virtual imposition of a democratic constitution on Japan with little consultation or compromise generates doubts about the nature of Japanese democracy that still resonate today. In order to achieve its goals SCAP sometimes acted outside the law or issued what amounted to edicts in an effort to create a semblance of legality. The suppression of democracy for the sake of democracy proved to be a lasting paradox of the American interregnum [*Doc. 2*].

Dower, the pre-eminent historian of the Occupation, argues that SCAP's neo-colonial revolution from above pursued an agenda of both progressive change and reaffirmation of authoritarian structures of government. It is a telling commentary that, 'while the victors preached democracy they ruled by fiat; while they espoused equality, they themselves constituted an inviolate privileged caste … almost every interaction between victor and vanquished was infused with intimations of white supremacism' (Dower, 1999: 211). While the embrace of peace and democracy may well be the talismanic legacy of the Occupation, the gutting of the union movement, suppression of dissent and ruthless repression during the Cold War-inspired 'Red Purge' left a bitter taste and did little to promote tolerance. The American embrace of the conservative elite in Japan during the reverse course enabled the latter to slow the pace of reform, shift it to the right and consolidate their power; once the Occupation ended in 1952 they were in a position to roll back or dilute many of the reforms.

The US decision not to prosecute Emperor Hirohito for war crimes was controversial at the time because allies and leftists in Japan believed that he should be held accountable for the excesses committed by the Imperial armed forces. (See Bix (2000) for a detailed account of the Showa Emperor's active involvement in waging war and complicity in covering up that role in the postwar era.) The Americans believed that Hirohito was more valuable to their reform efforts alive and free than dead or incarcerated and feared creating a martyr for the nationalist movement. The Showa Emperor went on to become a symbol of Japan's postwar renaissance and is widely credited with playing a constructive role during and after the Occupation. However, the decision to absolve the Emperor of war responsibility rendered the War Crimes Tribunal a meaningless exercise and clouded the entire issue of war responsibility. If the national leader could not be held accountable, others felt justified in also evading their responsibility for what happened since they believed they were acting in his name. Significantly, this meant that few Japanese really confronted their support of Japan's military violence in Asia or the prevailing racist attitudes that had condoned it.

Japanese remain ambivalent about the Occupation. It is interesting that Japanese of all political stripes can find something to dislike in the Occupation; those on the left are bitter about the betrayal of the reverse course while those on the right argue that the US went too far in transforming Japan. The policies of democratization and demilitarization were generally welcomed at the time and there is still a substantial residue of goodwill emanating from the positive legacies of that period. Older Japanese, who lived during the Occupation, recall the hardships and some unfortunate incidents, but express generally positive impressions about the process of transformation unleashed by SCAP. Certainly the Occupation went better than anyone had anticipated at the time of surrender and the US is credited with enacting policies that benefited most Japanese and laid the foundations for later economic success. In addition, many Japanese were relieved that the American Occupation bore no resemblance to Japan's often brutal occupation of China and Southeast Asia during the war. It is perhaps one of the most benign and non-punitive occupations in history, an extraordinary achievement given the level of hostility between the US and Japan at the end of the war.

The Occupation helps explain why American influence is so strong in Japan and why Washington looms so large in the mindset of Tokyo. The patterns of relationships developed during the Occupation have lingered too long; many Japanese slide easily between resentment and respect for the US because they chafe at the unequal relationship, but are reluctant to dispense with the security of American tutelage. Even a half-century after the Occupation ended, neither nation has yet to come to terms with the past and forge a new relationship free from the biases of the ruler and ruled experience that permeates this shared history.

Conservative Japanese frequently trace many of Japan's current social problems back to the Occupation. They see women's legal equality, the end of the patriarchal *ie* system, educational reforms, the new Emperor system, demilitarization, etc., and a vague process of Americanization as harmful to the Japanese social fabric. In 1998, one of the largest grossing films produced in Japan was *Pride*, an epic hagiography focusing on Prime Minister Hideki Tojo and the injustice of the Tokyo War Crimes Tribunal that led to his death by hanging. Certainly the proceedings of the tribunal ignored due process and they serve as compelling evidence of American hypocrisy and victor's justice. However, the popular press and right-wing writers tend to portray the Japanese defendants solely as victims of biased legal proceedings without examining the question of whether they in fact committed war crimes. In Japan as elsewhere, the present is usually projected on to the past in ways that tend to do history little service.

HIROSHIMA AND PEARL HARBOR

Japanese and Americans look back at their shared past through the images conjured up by two catastrophic events. Pearl Harbor, what President Roosevelt described as the 'Day of Infamy', remains shorthand for sneaky treachery. Many Americans draw on this memory of victimization to vindicate their subsequent actions and to ascribe undesirable national characteristics to the Japanese. By focusing on the single event, there is no need to examine the preceding process of polarization between the two nations that began back in 1853 when Commodore Perry arrived in Japan with an armada and demanded that Japan sign an unfavorable treaty of commerce with the US. In the subsequent nine decades, there are numerous instances of American actions that were provocative, insensitive and punitive. So it is folly to examine Pearl Harbor in a historical vacuum and to portray the US as an innocent victim of an inexplicable outrage. There is plenty of blame to share on both sides of the Pacific for the outbreak of war.

Similarly, when Japanese recall the war it is usually to dwell on their own suffering. Hiroshima has become a symbol of Japan's victimization during the war. Unfortunately, the lure of victimization has tended to obscure Japan's role as victimizer and how its own suffering was a consequence of its actions and choices. The victims of Japanese aggression remain faint images in the official history. There are signs of improvement, however. The haunting exhibits displayed at the Peace Memorial Museum in Hiroshima previously presented the atomic bombing in a historical vacuum, with no attempt to explain how or why this tragedy occurred. Now, dioramas provide enough historical background for visitors to realize that this was not some inexplicable natural disaster. These efforts to provide a more balanced view have not been replicated throughout Japan and sadly failed in 1995 when the Smithsonian Museum in Washington, DC staged a watered-down exhibit about the atomic bombings that described the events leading up to the detonation of the bombs, but nothing of their terrible aftermath (Hein and Selden, 1997). Clearly, the past still lingers in the present and both nations have only begun to come to terms with the tragedies of their shared past. The consequences remain an undercurrent in dealing with current frictions that flare up between these allies.

CHAPTER THREE

POSTWAR POLITICS

Postwar politics in Japan has been marked by the dominance of the conservative Liberal Democratic Party (LDP) since its formation in 1955. Scholars often refer to the Iron Triangle or Ruling Triad to describe the nexus of political power involving big business, the LDP and the government ministries. There is considerable debate among political scientists about which of the three is dominant in forging the policy agenda and how and why they exercise their power as they do. The strong state model suggested by Johnson (1982) has been challenged in recent years by those who argue that the state is not as autonomous and dominant as his analysis of the role of the Ministry of Trade and Industry (MITI) in guiding rapid economic growth in the postwar period suggests (see Richardson 1997 for a comprehensive critique). Calder (1991) suggests a model of 'crisis and compensation' in which the LDP initiates policy reforms in response to critical political pressures. Ramsayer and Rosenbluth (1993) argue that the LDP plays a key mediating role in balancing competing interests and agendas in a manner that allows the LDP to influence outcomes. Broadbent (1998) argues that big business has been dominant in the postwar period, supporting various measures and compromises that sustained LDP hegemony and thus its own interests. Journalists such as von Wolferen (1989) argue that Japan is characterized by an absence of a locus of power, explaining why there is so much evident policy drift on the important issues. Fallows (1994), another influential journalist, portrays a powerful and predatory neo-mercantilist state using trade as a weapon of domination. Even such a brief survey of the vast relevant literature indicates that there is considerable disagreement on the basic questions, and little consensus on what it all means. Politics conveys different meanings when viewed from the commanding heights, the streets, or out in the rice paddies, and is embedded with varying perspectives. Certainly Japan is an interesting and complex advanced capitalist industrialized democracy and here only a few important themes and issues are introduced to give a general sense of political currents during this era.

THE YOSHIDA DOCTRINE

The Yoshida Doctrine was the eponymous policy stance of Prime Minister Shigeru Yoshida (1946–47, 1948–54) regarding Japan's rearmament. Back in 1946, the US had insisted on Article Nine in the Constitution, which prohibited Japan from maintaining military forces. However, with the outbreak of the Korean War in 1950 and the escalating tensions of the Cold War, Washington reversed its position and began pressuring Japan to rearm. There was no enthusiasm in Japan for reviving the reviled and discredited military. In fact, the Japanese were proud of their 'Peace' Constitution and were adamant about not caving in to US demands. Prime Minister Yoshida rejected the US pressure, arguing that Japan could ill afford to squander its scarce resources on rebuilding its military power. He astutely played on the Cold War concerns of the US, arguing that Japan could make a greater contribution by demonstrating the superiority of capitalism; Japan was a showpiece for the free market, democratic model espoused by the US. He told the US Secretary of State John Foster Dulles that public opinion in Japan would not tolerate the creation of a military force big enough to have any significant security value. Thus the Yoshida Doctrine meant that Japan would focus on economic growth and rely on the US for its security.

As will be discussed in Chapter Six, as a price for ending the US Occupation, the Japanese government did have to agree to create a small army, the National Police Reserve, of a projected 300–350,000 troops. This became the nucleus for today's Self-Defense Forces (SDF). However, as Michael Schaller argues, 'Yoshida worked to sabotage the program. Even Japanese conservatives cited economic, political and philosophical objections to direct rearmament. It would, they feared, elicit tremendous opposition at home, rekindle anxiety among Japan's wartime victims, isolate the nation from its Asian neighbors, and defy the letter and spirit of Article Nine of the new constitution' (Schaller, 1985: 293). In addition, as the Korean War raged on, many Japanese feared that the US would demand Japanese soldiers also fight on the peninsula. For these reasons, the Japanese government dragged its feet on complying with US demands that it contribute more to its own security.

THE US–JAPAN SECURITY TREATY

The 1951 San Francisco Treaty brought an end to the American Occupation in 1952 and was dubbed the 'Peace Treaty' even though the Soviet Union and the People's Republic of China refused to sign it. The Soviets saw the settlement as the handiwork of the US and, as such, supportive of US strategic interests in the region. The terms of the settlement provided for the retention of US base facilities and a US–Japan

Security Treaty linked to American Cold War objectives and signaled that Japan had not achieved unfettered independence [*Doc. 3*]. As Buckley notes, the security relationship became the leading source of tension between Tokyo and Washington: 'The greatest difficulty facing the Eisenhower administration and successive conservative cabinets in Japan during the 1950s was undoubtedly the issue of the security treaty and its possible modification. All other problems in US–Japan relations between the San Francisco peace settlements and the eventual revision of the security pact in 1960 pale into insignificance against this running sore' (Buckley, 1999: 50). The security treaty and the continued American military presence also became a focus of domestic political confrontation. Street demonstrations against the US bases and the security alliance persisted throughout the 1950s, culminating in the crisis of 1960 when the security treaty was revised and extended. This provoked huge demonstrations and eventually the cancellation of President Eisenhower's planned visit. Certainly the security issue was one of the main cleavages in Japanese politics during the 1950s and 1960s, pitting America's conservative allies in the government against their leftist opponents.

Protests erupted again with the renewal of the Security Treaty in 1970 as students viewed it as symbolic of Japan's complicity in the Vietnam War and as a betrayal of fellow Asians (Havens, 1987). Critics pointed out that Japan was used as a staging ground for US military action and the government had virtually no influence over the use of military facilities based on Japanese soil. In this sense, Japan was being involved in overseas conflict and could potentially be putting its own peace and security at risk. During the 1980s and 1990s, the protests against the security alliance that had dominated bilateral relations in the postwar era receded behind the recriminations and ill-will generated by growing trade imbalances. Japan's economic success pushed security off the political radar screen and rendered trade tensions the main focus of trans-Pacific ties.

THE 1955 SYSTEM

The 1955 system is a reference to the conservative, one-party-dominated political system that prevailed in Japan from 1955 to 1993. In 1955 two conservative parties merged to create the Liberal Democratic Party (LDP). This party held power continuously until 1993 before being ousted by a coalition government representing all of the political parties except the Communist Party and the LDP. In 1994, however, the LDP returned to power in a coalition government and remains the largest and most dominant party in Japan. LDP dominance of Japanese politics has fostered the image of a one-party democracy (Pempel, 1990).

The defining feature of the 1955 system was the tension between conservative and progressive political forces. Progressive in this context meant the Marxist and radical left political culture that prevailed in trade unions and among the members of the Japan Socialist Party (JSP), the largest opposition party in Japan until its demise in the mid-1990s. The LDP was formed in 1955 in response to the growing unity and strength of the left and efforts to pursue a 'class struggle' supported by Sohyo (the General Council of Trade Unions of Japan), Japan's largest union organization at that time.

The 1950s and 1960s witnessed bitter ideological battles in Japan between supporters of the progressive agenda, led by the JSP, and the coalition of conservative forces rallying around the LDP. The LDP was a champion of conservative causes and ideology. It stood for overturning many of the reforms initiated during the American Occupation, including an overhaul of the Constitution and a revival of certain features of the prewar political system. (However, the LDP stood for close ties with the US, a stance opposed by the JSP.) These efforts to roll back the American reforms were opposed by progressive forces, provoking widespread strikes, media protests and periodic Socialist boycotts of the Diet.

The LDP enjoyed the support of the middle classes, represented by farmers, merchants, owners and employees of family businesses and small manufacturing concerns. The JSP represented the modern sectors of rapidly developing Japan, attracting unionized blue-collar workers, white-collar 'salarymen' and generally younger, well-educated urban voters. Back in the late 1950s the LDP seemed to represent a shrinking, backward-looking, tradition-bound constituency, but one of the interesting stories of Japanese politics is how the LDP managed to reinvent itself to become a party with broader appeal. The JSP, meanwhile, pursued policies and promoted an ideological agenda that became increasingly irrelevant and unattractive to Japanese voters. Perhaps the highpoint of the Socialists' political fortunes came with the mass street protests in 1960, opposing the renewal of the Security Treaty. The JSP evolved from a position of relative strength as the vanguard of progressive forces and the leading opposition party to a renamed party, the Socialist Party of Japan (SPJ), that had virtually disappeared by the late-1990s.

The LDP is composed of factions (*habatsu*) that date back to its establishment in 1955. The factions are made up of varying numbers of LDP Diet politicians and serve as the unit within the LDP for distributing party and ministerial posts. Factions are not necessarily issue-focused – most serve to enhance the status and bargaining power of individual members and to provide access to pork-barrel projects and campaign funds. The LDP leadership needs to balance factional rivalries, ensuring that each gains from being inside the party. Managing intra-factional politics is ultimately the job of the prime minister who serves concurrently as the party president. Although there have been high-profile defections from the LDP over the years, such cases are rare because the party is a powerful vehicle for delivering what politicians need to remain in power and party leaders have been adept at balancing interests despite lingering intra-factional feuds and personal antagonisms.

In the wake of the divisive political battles over the revision of the US–Japan Security Treaty and the ousting of Prime Minister Nobusuke Kishi (1957–60), Prime Minister Hayato Ikeda (1960–64) redirected party efforts and public attention to his ambitious economic agenda, the income doubling plan (see George Packard (1966) for a full discussion of this dramatic period). This was a program aimed at fostering rapid economic growth based on regional development initiatives. Aside from the enormous success of this program, the flow of central government money to regional and local authorities created a distribution apparatus that enabled the LDP to expand its power base via lucrative pork-barrel projects. LDP members maintained *koenkai* (personal support associations in their electoral district) which became mechanisms for channeling massive public works projects and industrialization initiatives to the local electoral districts and thus a key factor in election campaigns. Politicians who delivered were returned, making them ever more dependent on their factions since factions served as the basis for allocating the flow of funds and concessions within the LDP and thus the government (Curtis, 1999).

This focus on pork-barrel politics has had a devastating impact on the environment, as wetlands are paved over, rivers and coastlines are concreted, dams are built where they are not needed, and roads and train lines are constructed to nowhere. As a result Japan has the highest per capita cement consumption in the world. With 10 percent of the nation's workforce engaged in construction, and given the opportunities for raising campaign funds due to the nature of the *dango* (rigged bidding system for public works contracts), it is not surprising that the government lavishes a considerable budget on this sector. However, in the *dokken kokka* (construction state), it is astonishing to realize that construction-related spending in Japan exceeds the Pentagon's nearly $300 billion annual budget by a considerable margin, especially in recent years as the government has tried to counter the ongoing recession with additional public works spending. Corruption is rife and collusion involves politicians, bureaucrats, businessmen and the underworld. The huge burden of public works spending means that future generations will be paying off the accumulated debts for many mega-projects that they neither need nor desire. Lamenting these construction boondoggles, Gavan McCormack asserts that, 'too much of the energy, capital, and skills of the Japanese people had been appropriated, mobilized, and focused in a political economy of exploitation, both human and material, that ultimately exhausted both the people and their environment' (McCormack, 1996: 64). But for the LDP, infrastructure projects solidified the foundations of its power, offering cement in exchange for support. This has been, and continues to be, the logic of the *dokken kokka*.

During the 1970s, the LDP reinvented itself as a catch-all party that was able to offer a vision that had broad appeal beyond its traditional constituencies. Ideology was downplayed in an effort to retain power. The LDP has been identified as the party of the status quo and has had enormous success in convincing voters from all social strata that their interests were tied to that status quo. Rather than emphasizing the policy issues that divided society, the LDP promoted economic recovery and growth, reviving the Meiji era quest for catching up with and overtaking the West. This emphasis on economic progress has been dubbed 'GNPism', an ideology that brought disparate groups together to work for the common goal of development. Overtaking the West had an appeal for a nation still reeling psychologically from the catastrophic defeat in war and humbling Occupation.

The LDP was also adept at adopting opposition issues and integrating them into its own party platform. As the public and media grew concerned about the environmental costs of rapid industrialization, the LDP took the lead in promoting policies aimed at addressing these concerns. The 1970 'Pollution Diet' passed tough environmental laws in response to growing public outrage over the environmental and health costs of economic growth. Soon after, there was a series of victories for pollution victims, including the Minamata sufferers born with severe birth defects from mercury poisoning caused by a local chemical plant. According to Broadbent (1998), big business and the LDP cooperated on cleaning up water and air pollution as a means of shoring up the legitimacy of the LDP and preserving a political order favorable to business interests. As popular agitation spread, the costs of not responding outweighed the costs of neutralizing critics by taking meaningful action. He describes the rapid improvement in air and water in the 1970s, far surpassing similar efforts in other industrialized nations, as the second 'miracle' in postwar Japan and gives much of the credit to the 'voluntary' compliance of the business community. Yet, the environmental agenda remains daunting and much still needs to be done. Many victims of various forms of pollution have not yet received redress and even some of the Minamata victims have still not received compensation or support. In addition, discoveries in the late 1990s of very high concentrations of dioxins and polychlorinated biphenyls (PCBs) in vegetables, mothers' milk and waterways have raised alarms. It is also worrisome that Japanese farmers use the most pesticides per hectare in the world.

In broadening its base of support, the LDP also tackled other quality of life issues, for example improving the welfare system and government services that helped attract support in urban constituencies. Thus, by selectively embracing progressive issues, the LDP significantly broadened its base of support beyond its traditional strongholds and in so doing weakened the opposition. By virtue of its stranglehold on the government, the LDP could rightfully claim to be the party with solutions, making small adjustments to the status quo and demonstrating enough flexibility on the issues to preserve the essential interests and features of the status quo.

THE DECLINE OF RADICALISM

The decline of radical political activity in Japan since the 1970s mirrors the demise of the Socialist Party. Society overall seems to be turning more conservative and supportive of the status quo. It is ironic that a society known for harmony (*wa*) and consensus (*goi*) has a rich tradition of postwar protest. Labor agitation in the late 1940s and 1950s belies contemporary assertions about a benevolent, patron–client tradition of management–labor relations (Garon, 1987; Gordon, 1998). In addition to student protests in the 1960s and 1970s, the environmental movement also marked a period of often exuberant assertion of the democratic rights bestowed on the Japanese people in the new Constitution. Since then, through isolation, marginalization, cooptation and classic divide-and-rule tactics, the government has succeeded in using methods of soft control to dampen radical political movements. The violent street protests over the US–Japan alliance of the 1960s have given way to a resigned acceptance. The Chukakuha (Red Army Faction) that led campus protests in the late 1960s amidst the Vietnam War, carried out terrorist attacks both in and outside Japan and spearheaded opposition to Narita International Airport has disappeared from the political landscape. Campus politics are quiescent and in 1999 the final parcel of land needed to build Narita's long-awaited second runway was finally sold by a farmer who had held out for a quarter of a century. Most Japanese seem unaware now that Narita had once served as a powerful political symbol of the left's opposition to the government's heavy-handed ways.

THE CHANGING LOGIC OF JAPANESE POLITICS

To understand the changing logic of Japanese politics it is useful to consider the pillars of the 1955 system. As Curtis argues:

> There were four crucial pillars supporting the '55 system. One was a pervasive public consensus in support of policies to achieve the catch-up-with-the-West goal. A second was the presence of large integrative interest groups with close

links to political parties. The third was a bureaucracy of immense prestige and power. And the fourth was a system of one-party dominance. Just to list these features of the '55 system is to indicate how profoundly Japan changed in the 1990s. All of these pillars of policy making had either weakened or crumbled. (Curtis, 1999: 39)

By the 1990s Japan had caught up with the West, the large integrative interest groups (such as unions) were no longer so unified or close to the parties, the bureaucracy's reputation was in tatters due to a series of widely publicized corruption scandals and one-party dominance had given way to LDP-led coalition governments. In addition, policy issues that animated the 1955 system were no longer compelling or divisive. When the Socialists joined the LDP in a coalition government in 1994, it was clear that the ideological divide no longer mattered. As a price for gaining a taste of power, the Socialist Party abandoned its opposition to the existence of the Self-Defense Forces, the US–Japan Security Treaty, nuclear power, the national anthem and the national flag – issues that had once been emotive and defining. The principles that instilled loyalty in the party faithful through years of opposition had been discarded, a watershed that spelled the end of the JSP as a significant political force.

The LDP and Socialists commanded 91 percent of the vote in the 1958 elections, but by 1986 these two parties controlled only 67 percent of the vote, indicating how much the political landscape had changed. The cleavages that marked Japan in the 1950s and 1960s no longer existed. The class-based appeals of the JSP did not resonate in a polity where consistently more than 90 percent of the people perceive themselves as belonging to the middle class. By the early 1970s, the JSP's self-destructive factional infighting and failure to promote an agenda in tune with the changing realities of the political landscape reduced its share of the popular vote to about 20 percent. The LDP also featured factional disputes, but these were managed relatively smoothly. In addition to coopting the policy agenda of the opposition and the various *jumin undo* (issue-oriented activist move-ments), the LDP oversaw a period of rapid economic growth combined with a relatively equal distribution of the fruits of that growth. The explosive growth of the middle class and relatively small income disparities was the real 'miracle' of Japan's rapid postwar recovery. In the absence of class, ethnic, religious, regional or social cleavages, life became difficult for opposition political parties. Extremist views held scant appeal for a people who were experiencing rapid improvement in their lives. The LDP derived its legitimacy from its economic stewardship and growing numbers of Japanese identified their interests with those of the status quo. Any party that tried to emulate the catch-all appeal of the LDP faced the problem of presenting itself as a needed and viable alternative.

The end of the Cold War in 1989 further accelerated the trend towards diminishing the importance of ideology in Japanese politics. The battle lines, already blurry, grew even more opaque. By abandoning its principles, the Socialist Party was perhaps bowing to the inevitable but in doing so it alienated the core of its constituency and has all but disappeared as a significant political force.

Perhaps one of the most important developments in the 1990s has been the emergence of a significant number of 'floating voters', meaning those voters who have no ties to a particular party. This phenomenon has introduced an element of volatility and unpredictability in Japanese elections. The implications for parties are not certain, but Japan has gone from being a nation with high voter participation to one with levels of participation roughly equal to the US, a democracy where the right to vote is sparingly exercised. It is possible that the spate of scandals and the poor image of politicians in the media has fanned voter alienation. In addition, campaigns in Japan are uninspiring, with candidates criss-crossing their districts in sound trucks only blaring their name, occasionally stopping to give staid stump speeches featuring little interaction with the public. In the old days, strong community cohesion meant that local leaders could mobilize and 'deliver' the vote, but this cohesion has declined. Voters used to vote out of a sense of obligation to a politician or a local lieutenant who had rendered service to his district in terms of government projects or concessions and made the rounds of weddings and funerals. At these frequent gatherings, politicians are expected to make sizeable donations that cumulatively can add up to more than eight times their official income, generating pressures to raise considerable additional funds to spread around the constituency. But the political machines seem to be less powerful, and the Diet is grudgingly adopting campaign finance reform that promises to diminish the role of large corporations in bankrolling campaigns. This is seen as a positive sign for democracy, but public skepticism runs high that meaningful change will result.

The dismal 1990s has been a time akin to the *bakumatsu* period prior to the Meiji restoration in 1868. Everybody knows (and knew) that it is well past time for change and that the existing system is part of the problem. Everybody wants change and is waiting for it to happen. And everyone wants change that will be minimally disruptive to their lives. What is fascinating about the 1990s is the strong popular sentiment for reform and the failure of the most vociferous and ambitious reformers at the polls. In an abstract way everyone supports reform and discarding an obviously sclerotic system, but inside the voting booth voters have been more pragmatic and less inclined to support changes in a system that has delivered for so long. Voters are not yet prepared to accept the uncertainties and risks associated with navigating uncharted waters. As Japan enters the twenty-first century, the public seems more inclined to support incremental change than sweeping transformation. The patterns and practices of the past are fading, but in a gradual and measured manner that seems odd given the prevailing sense of anxiety and urgency. Dire times may require dire measures, but in Japan the dynamics of transformation involve an emphasis on minimizing social dislocation at the expense of a rapid, far-reaching implementation of the reform agenda. This inclination may diminish the positive consequences of reform by delay and dilution, but the negative fallout of far-reaching, dramatic reform has been avoided. The key challenge in the early twenty-first century will be whether or not Japan can enjoy the same degree of success in reinventing and reinvigorating the nation as it did during the Meiji era and the US Occupation. The potential consequences of Japan's demographic time-bomb discussed in Chapter Eight make success far from a sure thing.

Curtis argues that the public is now more inclined to hold their representatives accountable than in the past and is less tolerant of malfeasance and incompetence. The spirit and habits of democracy have taken root and it is a far cry from the Occupation days when Prime Minister Yoshida made a pun out of the Japanese pronunciation of 'democracy', quipping perhaps apocryphally, 'demo kurushii' (but it hurts). At that time the political elite was suspicious of observing much more than the form of democracy and distrusted the masses. The conservative elite was compelled by the Americans to embrace democracy, but then made the most of the opportunity. Now, the pillars and practices of the 1955 system are fading away, creating a transition period of uncertainty. The public mood, in Curtis's view, is conservative rather than revolutionary, more wary and less passive than in the past. The setbacks of the 1990s have generated a national mood of gloom and pessimism, but he suggests that Japan's high level of social capital and cohesion, in combination with a more responsive, transparent and accountable political system, is the basis for cautious optimism about the future (Curtis, 1999).

CORRUPTION

In all societies political corruption has been a blot on democratic development and Japan is no exception. In prewar Japan, militarists cited widespread corruption as justification for their destruction of the political party system and assumption of power. A vast majority of postwar prime ministers have been implicated in corruption scandals and every decade has featured at least one major scandal beginning with the Showa Denko scandal in the 1940s and continuing with a shipbuilding scandal in the 1950s, a series of scandals in the 1960s that are referred to as the 'black mist' and the Lockheed scandal of the 1970s involving Prime Minister

Kakuei Tanaka (1972–74). In the 1980s and 1990s, the scandals have grown more blatant and the press has played a more aggressive role in exposing the grubby venality of politicians and bureaucrats. The economic bubble in the late 1980s raised the stakes and led to widespread corruption involving astronomical sums. The Recruit (1988) and Sagawa Kyubin (1992) scandals were a sign of the times, confronting the public with the dirty facts of their political system. The existence of corruption among politicians left few people surprised, but the extent of the problem was stunning and unexpected. The extensive involvement of bureaucrats in a variety of influence-buying scandals also challenged public perceptions of their civil servants. The mandarins had always been seen as the best and brightest and as such beyond reproach and untainted by malfeasance. However, once their indiscretions were reported, the public mood turned ugly and the media delighted in revealing the dirty laundry, pettiness, incompetence and other shortcomings of government officials. Public disenchantment with this sordid state of affairs became a significant factor in ending one-party rule and creating momentum for political reform in the 1990s.

The Bad Sleep Well (1960) is a classic movie by Japan's most famous film director, Akira Kurosawa, and it enjoyed a revival of popularity in the late 1980s and 1990s because its focus on the nexus of corruption involving politicians, bureaucrats, big business and the *yakuza* (organized crime syndicates) proved to be an enduring theme (Whiting, 1999). As press reports in the 1990s detailed the latest corruption scandal, Kurosawa's mordant black-and-white film seemed to paint a disturbing but accurate portrait of a society that had lost its bearings and values. In the race for growth and emphasis on material gains, there is a wistfulness in the film about the emptiness and crassness of a society where the line between right and wrong had grown blurry and ethics had been sacrificed. It is not lost on the public that the men on the take in the film are not brought to justice and that the men who strive for justice fail and suffer for their efforts. In 1999, *Kinyu Fushoku Retto Jubaku* (Jubaku: The Archipelago of Rotten Money) became a hit film in depicting the same web of corruption as outlined by Kurosawa in a less subtle fashion, showing that the same themes persist despite the changing times.

THE SHADOW SHOGUN

Prime Minister Kakuei Tanaka (1972–74) has been perhaps the most influential Japanese politician in the post-1952 era, playing a dominant role in the national political scene from the early 1970s until his death in 1987. His legacy is synonymous with money politics since his name is always linked with the Lockheed bribery scandal first exposed in Congressional hearings in Washington, DC that led to his ousting from official power. He developed the art of raising funds, selling access and delivering contracts and in the process cobbled together the most powerful faction in the LDP. He tapped the construction industry for funds and rewarded them with generous public works contracts doled out at his bidding. He was the architect of the 'construction state' and made it his business to determine who would benefit from the largesse (McCormack, 1996). He was not university-educated and did not hail from a distinguished political lineage. He was a coarse, bullying, self-made construction magnate who blatantly wielded power, solicited 'contributions' and courted influence, earning the sobriquet 'computerized bulldozer'. Even after he was indicted (1974), prosecuted on corruption charges (1977), and later found guilty (1983), he continued to control the LDP because he had the largest faction and wielded considerable influence over the bureaucrats who made key decisions affecting his 'clients'. His constituents returned him to office anyway. The Nakasone governments in the 1980s were referred to in the media as the Tanakasone administration, reflecting Tanaka's continuing role as the shadow shogun of the LDP. Prime Minister Nakasone deferred to Tanaka in terms of cabinet appointments, and throughout his tenure (1982–87), was dependent on Tanaka's factional support, without which he never would have gained the highest political office in the land (for a full discussion see Schlesinger, 1997).

The Recruit scandal first came to public attention in June 1988. Recruit was a relatively new up-and-coming company with a range of ventures connected with the information industry. It is best known for its job information services, but the scandal involved an as yet unlisted real estate affiliate called Recruit Cosmos. In 1986, unlisted shares of the company were offered at low prices to various influential government officials and politicians, many of whom bought the shares with money lent by Recruit. Once the stock went public, share prices soared and tidy profits were salted away. Public anger mounted as it became apparent that the beneficiaries included a who's who of Japanese politicians, even including figures from the opposition parties. In addition, Recruit purchased millions of dollars of tickets to fund-raising parties for LDP leaders. Prime Minister Takeshita, Finance Minister Miyazawa, LDP Secretary General Abe and former Prime Minister Nakasone are only some of the more famous political luminaries implicated.

Hiromasu Ezoe, the founder and head of Recruit, was trying to purchase influence, connections and favorable decisions on projects or regulations that affected his business ventures. His extensive efforts to rig the system also extended to the bureaucrats whose once high reputation rapidly declined over the ensuing years. The endless exposés and scandals made it glaringly apparent that government officials could be bought. The society that had embraced economic growth at all costs in the 1960s came to confront in the 1990s the consequences of unabashed materialism. It also confronted the strange twists of justice; only one government official was convicted for his part in the Recruit scandal and not until 1999. The who's who of politicians who were implicated in the scandal never were indicted and continued to command Japanese politics. Just as Kurosawa had portrayed Japan in the early 1960s, the bad were still sleeping relatively well.

SAGAWA KYUBIN

Compared to the Recruit scandal, the trucking firm scandal that broke in the summer of 1992 was a blatant, unsophisticated scheme that involved astronomical sums of cash. Over a period of twenty years Sagawa Kyubin had generously donated sums of money – well in excess of official limits to politicians – that dwarfed the Recruit donations. Even a public inured to venality took notice of press reports about a cart piled high with 500 million yen (about $400 million) being wheeled into the office of the LDP's chief fixer, Shin Kanemaru. Later it emerged that Kanemaru had also used Sagawa Kyubin to request the assistance of the *yakuza* to silence some right-wing political activists who were harassing Noboru Takeshita, faction leader, kingmaker and former prime minister (1987–89) in the LDP. The press highlighted a dinner he hosted to express his gratitude to a ranking *yakuza*, also arranged by the trucking firm, to illustrate the confluence of power in contemporary Japan. Kanemaru, a gruff, old-school politician who had teamed up with Takeshita in 1987 to gain control of the Tanaka faction, later was forced to resign from politics as the Sagawa Kyubin scandal triggered a wider investigation into his finances. A raid on his home uncovered a horde of 100 kilograms of gold, 3 billion yen in anonymous bond certificates and stacks of cash – the booty from decades of politics and the largesse of construction firms thankful for the contracts he had arranged, all duly noted in his files.

The Tanaka machine had been taken over by his lieutenants and run with the same brash cash-and-carry approach to politics. The public indignation was offset by political ambivalence and apathy. The Tanaka machine's influence was so pervasive, even involving the opposition, that there seemed to be no viable, untainted alternative. In 1993, however, five months after Kanemaru's conviction for tax evasion, the public decided to 'vote the bums out of office', ending the LDP's stranglehold on power.

POLITICAL REFORM

In 1994 the Diet passed electoral-reform legislation affecting lower-house elections, perhaps the boldest political reform in the post-Occupation era. This was the first change to an electoral system that dates back to 1925, when Japan first introduced universal male suffrage. Under the new system, there is a complicated mix of single-seat constituencies and proportional representation for the lower house of the Diet. The old system featured multiple-seat constituencies, meaning that a number of top vote-getters would be elected from a district. Now, under the new mixed system of voting, voters directly elect only one member from their district.

Electoral reform was propelled by the need of politicians to appear to be responding to public outrage about the extent of corruption scandals. It was the most significant legislation passed by the first non-LDP government for four decades. In addition, the success of the government in delivering economic prosperity had long been its source of legitimacy, but as the recession persisted, public patience with the usual peccadilloes wore thin. In the wake of the Recruit and Sagawa Kyubin scandals, politicians of all political stripes sought to reinvent themselves as crusading reformers. Suddenly everyone called for political reform and the existing electoral system proved a handy target. Many of the ills of the political system were attributed to the electoral system and thus changing it was portrayed as a means of taming corruption, refocusing political debate on the real issues facing society and creating the basis for a two-party system. However, the new electoral system could not meet such lofty expectations and an issues-oriented, untainted two-party system remains an elusive goal. Ironically, the new mixed system of single-seat constituencies and proportional representation, widely thought to favor the LDP, was passed by a governing coalition of smaller parties that had fared well under the prevailing multiple-seat constituency system. In the spirit of reform, they created a system that paved the way for the LDP's return to power and the slippery status quo it represented.

The electoral reform did not address the unequal representation of urban and rural voters. The Supreme Court has ruled that the current system is unconstitutional because urban voters are systematically underrepresented while sparsely populated rural districts are significantly overrepresented. The votes of rural voters count, on average, over twice as much as urban voters in terms of national political representation, but despite the court ruling no election results have been overturned. In general, the LDP has gained from this disparity in voting power because it enjoys the support of farmers who remember who helped them gain ownership of their land during the Occupation-era land reform sponsored by the US and its conservative political allies. In addition, generous agricultural subsidies and pork-barrel public works projects have made the countryside a bedrock of support for the LDP. It is a measure of how much the LDP is willing to do on behalf of its rural constituency that the government nearly scuppered the Uruguay Round of negotiations in 1989 that led to the creation of the World Trade Organization (WTO) due to a determination not to liberalize the politically sensitive rice market. Only after intensive lobbying by the economically far more important business community did the government relent on rice imports.

At the turn of the century, the political world in Japan looks little changed. The LDP is still in power, the government is spending vast sums on public works projects and a geriatric elite seems more concerned about propping up a sclerotic system than in achieving meaningful reform. However, it seems that the public mood is less tolerant of the patterns and practices of the past. The system is discredited and distrusted, government officials are demoralized and policy drift is pervasive and widely criticized. Given the enormous problems facing Japan, there is a sense that the elite is merely rearranging the deck chairs on the Titanic instead of making serious efforts to avert calamity. People wonder what it will take to shake off the enervating inertia.

CHAPTER FOUR

THE ECONOMIC MIRACLE

The economic miracle refers to the spectacular economic growth recorded by Japan during the 1950s and 1960s. Japan rose phoenix-like out of the ashes of war to build a world-class economy. This was certainly not an anticipated or likely outcome. Most of Japan's large cities had been reduced to rubble and its industrial capacity had been decimated by sustained aerial bombing. Adequate housing was in short supply, food was scarce and these problems were aggravated by the return of some 7 million Japanese troops and civilians scattered around Asia. Japan was a nation without capital, raw materials or friends. Survival alone seemed a worthy goal for most Japanese. In 1946, high-level economic planners were looking to the Danish economy as their model for development, indicating that they did not foresee the emergence of an industrial juggernaut (Okita, 1992). What went right?

THE DEVELOPMENT STATE

Chalmers Johnson (1982) argues that the key factor in explaining Japan's economic miracle was the not-so-invisible hands of state-sponsored development [see *Doc. 4*]. According to Johnson, the Ministry for International Trade and Industry (MITI) played the main role in orchestrating economic growth by channeling low-cost loans and extending other benefits to targeted sectors of the economy. This process of picking winners was not infallible, but was often very effective in nurturing the growth of industries in promising areas. At a time when capital was scarce and foreign exchange was strictly controlled, MITI sponsorship had a significant impact. In addition, MITI played a key role in brokering technology licensing deals with US corporations on attractive terms, thus sparing Japanese firms the time and cost of research and development. The government also helped by encouraging cartels to avoid excessive competition and by supporting a variety of protectionist practices that helped reserve the domestic market for domestic producers. MITI and other ministries often exercised control through *gyosei shido* (administrative guidance). This informal approach amounted to strong suggestions about desired actions, policies or results and it was in the best interests of the recipient of such advice to comply or risk facing the troubles that powerful bureaucrats could cause. In this way, the government used its formal regulatory powers sparingly in favor of exercising influence through its informal powers of suasion.

FAVORABLE FACTORS

The media dubbed Japan's rapid recovery from the war and high growth between 1955 and 1973 as the 'economic miracle', but scholars have taken issue with this characterization. This is not to diminish the success, but rather to place that success in historical context. In examining the factors favoring postwar economic growth in Japan it is important to bear in mind that Japan was already a relatively advanced industrialized nation before the war and already possessed advanced technological knowledge. Thus, even though the nation was devastated by the war, Japan could draw on the knowledge and experience that had accumulated since the Meiji drive for modernization in the late nineteenth century. Japan's economic recovery was relatively quick because it had a reservoir of human capital and scientific expertise that enabled it to rebuild.

Institutions and policies mattered a great deal because Japan had little margin for error in its straitened circumstances. During the war the bureaucracy gained extraordinary powers to mobilize the nation's scarce resources in order to deploy them most effectively. Under what is known as the 1940 system, the Japanese economy was tightly managed and planned by the bureaucrats who wielded their powers to maximize Japan's industrial capacity. Under the American Occupation, many of these same bureaucrats continued to exercise power because the Americans ruled indirectly through the Japanese bureaucracy. Johnson argues that SCAP kept this wartime economic system largely intact, conferring extensive regulatory powers on the economic ministries. Through this power over the allocation of resources, the government could and did direct the course and pace of national economic recovery. The men who had maximized Japan's scarce resources during the war were well prepared for and accustomed to the role they played in orchestrating the 'miracle'. Bureaucratic continuity favored rapid growth because of the accumulated institutional expertise in making and implementing economic policies in adverse conditions. It also helped that corporate Japan had also worked within this system and knew the ropes.

In addition to the critical role of the Japanese government, Japan was also blessed with a relatively benign occupation. SCAP played a critical and positive role in creating favorable conditions for growth. Japanese reparations were minimized and early plans to strip Japan of its remaining industrial plant and equipment were scrapped in favor of promoting Japanese growth in accordance with Cold War aims. There was no equivalent to the Marshall Plan that had jump-started economic recovery in Europe because there was little support for using American taxpayers' money to support Japan. Instead, the US stabilized Japanese government finances and fixed the exchange rate at a low level (360 Yen = $1) favorable for exports. The land reform played a critical role in boosting food production and creating a growing middle class of consumers for the products of Japanese industry (Cohen, 1987). The Americans also succeeded in loosening the dominance of the *zaibatsu*, permitting the emergence of some of Japan's leading companies, such as Sony and Honda.

The war procurements by the American military during the Korean War (1950–53) are often credited with pulling Japan out of a dire postwar recession and putting the economy on a steep growth trajectory. Prime Minister Yoshida referred to this estimated $3 billion windfall as a 'gift from the gods' because austerity measures imposed by the US in 1949 had drastically shrunk domestic demand and threatened to stifle recovery. War on the peninsula provided a much-needed stimulus.

Unhindered access to the US market and technology also played a key role in Japan's growth spurt. The US market provided the crucial economies of scale while licensing of US technology on favorable terms saved Japanese companies enormous R&D expenses. US companies were inclined to license their technology because the business operating environment in Japan was not favorable for foreign firms. Restrictions on land ownership, foreign exchange and profit repatriation, in addition to low consumer demand, discouraged most foreign firms from establishing operations in Japan, an outcome that was consistent with the government's protectionist inclinations. In addition, the US government was eager to promote Japan's economic success in order to further its Cold War aims and had a role in expediting the flow of technology to its protégé in the Pacific. It is also true that Japanese firms were quicker to adopt recent technological innovations than their foreign counterparts. Technology that was developed abroad was rapidly disseminated on the plant floor in Japan's factories as they pursued their goal of becoming competitive and overtaking the West.

In this respect, the war devastation proved an opportunity as Japan had to rebuild most of its industrial plant and equipment from scratch. Thus, Japanese industrial plants were, on average, more modern and had more advanced technology than was the case in the US where there was no urgency in renovating or replacing aging facilities or production lines. The war thus inadvertently played a key role in modernizing Japan's factories.

High levels of literacy among the Japanese and a good educational system helped make this possible. The rapid pace of change and dissemination of new technologies in factories necessitated constant job training and upgrading of skills, a task made easier by the fact that Japan's blue-collar workers were relatively well-educated with a good foundation in math and science. It also helped that workers came to enjoy relatively secure employment and did not feel threatened by the introduction of new technologies. The spread of an implicit lifetime employment system after World War II facilitated worker acceptance of labor-saving technologies that were resisted and became a focal point of unrest in other industrialized nations.

Japan also benefited from having new frontiers at home and abroad. Rebuilding the economy and developing the hinterland of Japan proved a powerful stimulus, as did the massive migration of young Japanese from those hinterlands to urban areas. This migration sparked demand for housing, transportation and consumer goods. Overseas, suddenly, by the 1960s, Japanese consumer electronics began to take world markets by storm. These markets represented a new frontier that Japanese exporters, most notably in autos and electronics, have been successfully tapping ever since.

Corporate Japan also benefited from the high savings rate of the Japanese people. In the mid-1950s the savings rate of families was about 13 percent. As incomes rose over the course of the miracle so did their savings, averaging 25 percent of disposable income by 1974, more than quadruple the American rate (Allinson, 1997: 101). People saved because there was no social security system, meaning that people had to salt away money in good times in preparation for lean times. This inclination is strong in a nation prone to natural disasters and inured to hardship. In addition, land and housing is relatively expensive and in pursuit of the ubiquitous 'My Home Dream' (owning one's own house) there is a strong tendency to save. There are other reasons why Japanese tend to have a high savings rate, but the consequence is a large pool of capital that is almost all saved in bank or postal savings accounts. Even in the late 1990s, less than 10 percent of Japanese owned stocks or bonds. Government policy kept interest rates on bank accounts low, meaning that corporate borrowers could also borrow at low rates. Thus, the high savings rate and a government decision to favor producers over consumers by keeping interest rates low gave Japanese firms a competitive edge in terms of the cost of capital. In expanding and modernizing production facilities and adopting new technologies, this proved an important factor in the success of Japan, Inc.

The so-called three jewels of the Japanese employment system – lifetime employment, seniority wages and enterprise unions – are often cited as important factors in propelling economic growth. Lifetime employment and the *nenko* (seniority) wage system worked to the mutual advantage of workers and employers. Workers gained job security and steady wage increases while employers cultivated the loyalty, commitment and skills of their workers. Firms anticipated that workers would spend their entire career at the same firm, meaning that there would be ample opportunity to recoup the substantial investment in time and money spent on training workers. In-house training programs only made economic sense if firms could count on keeping their skilled employees, and in this regard the lifetime employment system succeeded. Job security also facilitated the introduction of new labor-saving, productivity-enhancing technologies because unions and workers did not feel threatened by innovation. They knew that the company would take care of its workers and not discard them for short-term, bottom-line considerations.

The seniority wage system also was based on economic logic. Under this system young workers are paid relatively little in exchange for the promise that once they reach a certain level of seniority they will be rewarded for their loyalty with relatively high wages. Thus, initial wages are usually pegged below worker productivity, but eventually rise to exceed worker productivity. This system is also seen to suit the life-cycle income needs of workers, boosting wages when they reach their forties at a time when various family-related expenses usually rise. For employers, this system made sense because in the aftermath of war, when capital was scarce, the prevalence of new workers meant that wage outlays were kept low. This conferred a competitive advantage on Japanese firms, at least until the age pyramid of the workforce in the late 1980s shifted towards older, more expensive and less productive workers who were also relatively less adept with the proliferating new technologies.

Enterprise unions helped ensure a minimum of labor turmoil. In the late 1940s and early 1950s Japan experienced a period of intense labor conflict that is difficult to reconcile with perceptions that harmony is a traditional characteristic of employment relations in Japan. Radical unions frequently engaged in work stoppages, strikes and factory takeovers while employers struck back with the normal array of union-busting measures, often with the complicity of government officials and the help of gangsters (Hein, 1990; Whiting, 1999). In the end, the firms prevailed, weeding out activists and taming the labor movement by basing unions within each establishment. Thus, instead of having a union of all automotive workers like the United Auto Workers (UAW) in the US, each company sponsored and kept tabs on its own union. This created a forum for dialogue, compromise, input, information sharing and confidence-building measures that helped forge close bonds between workers and managers. The gap between management and workers is much smaller in Japan than in other industrialized nations in terms of wage differences and treatment of employees. The relative absence of bitter labor disputes and the cooperative spirit engendered in the workplace have contributed to Japan's economic success.

It is also clear that low spending on social security and defense favored recovery because there was little diversion of scarce funds into such programs. The government relied on the US to provide military security and on companies to offer job security. Low military spending freed up money for more productive allocation and investments. There was an inclination to place the burden of social security on the family, tapping into Confucian values of filial piety and traditions that placed great importance on the family unit. The needs of the retired, aged and infirm were considered the duty of the family with minimal government assistance. It was only in the late 1970s that Japan initiated extensive social welfare policies.

Japan was also fortunate in enjoying favorable external economic conditions. The price of oil remained extremely low until 1973, an important consideration for a resource-dependent nation like Japan. This meant that the burgeoning energy requirements of Japanese industry did not have much of an impact on the costs of production. In addition, the world economy in general experienced relatively robust growth in the 1950s and 1960s, creating good markets for Japanese exports. It was important that Japan enjoyed free access to the US market and that there was an improving global trading environment in which levels of protectionism were declining significantly and extensively under the auspices of the General Agreement on Trades and Tariffs (GATT) which was launched in 1948. With US support, Japan gained membership in GATT in 1955.

ADVERSARIAL TRADE

Some commentators also argue that as Japan tapped into export markets, it kept its own market tightly protected. This unreciprocal pattern of trade did not become an international issue immediately, mostly because the US chose to ignore or dismiss such problems (Lincoln, 1990; Prestowitz, 1990). It was not until the late 1970s that Japan first began to run significant trade surpluses with the US; before that the American government was inclined to sacrifice what many considered negligible commercial interests in Japan for the sake of the security alliance (Forsberg, 2000). In addition to maintaining cordial bilateral relations, the US sought to further its Cold War-inspired objective of transforming Japan into the bulwark of the 'Free world' in Asia (Schaller, 1985). Initially through tariffs and the strict control of the foreign exchange that was needed to purchase imports (in the 1950s and 1960s the yen was not accepted for settlement of international transactions), the government was able to reserve the domestic market for domestic producers. Foreign producers were given limited access until domestic producers could produce competitive substitutes. Industrial cartels and price fixing were condoned by the government, creating markets closed to foreign enterprise. Cozy procurement relationships among the businesses grouped together in the large industrial conglomerates – *keiretsu* – and by the government also served to limit foreign penetration. As Japan bowed to

international pressures to lower tariff barriers, critics argue that it fell back
on non-tariff barriers that had the same stifling impact on imports. These
predatory trading practices proved successful in protecting the domestic
market and spurring exports (Prestowitz, 1990). Japanese exporters could
subsidize exports from profits generated in the domestic market where
prices were generally higher than those charged overseas. The home market
thus became an export platform subsidized by Japanese consumers.

Protectionism benefited corporate Japan at the expense of consumers
who faced high prices. This is thought by some observers to be represent-
ative of a larger pattern in which producers have been systematically
favored over consumers in Japan. In terms of various regulations, low
interest rates (savers receive small returns, corporations borrow cheaply),
price fixing, cartels, product liability, land use, infrastructure development,
etc., it is argued that the government has routinely sided with Japan, Inc.
Thus, one could argue that one of the factors favoring Japan's rapid
postwar growth is the tolerance of the Japanese people for such practices.
In return for the benefits bestowed on corporate Japan, Japanese workers
received job security, a steadily improving standard of living and a shared
sense of national success.

A DUAL ECONOMY

It is also suggested that Japan's economic success has been uneven. One of
the great achievements of rapid economic growth in Japan has been in
limiting income disparities. However, disparities do exist, particularly in
terms of the employment conditions, job security and wages offered by
small and medium-sized businesses and subcontractors. Japan's world-
beating corporations, such as Sony, Honda, Toyota and Toshiba, represent
the most modern and advanced firms. The system of implicit lifetime
employment and the other perquisites of full-time employment are generally
limited to such modern, large corporations and cover less than 30 percent
of the workforce. The majority of Japanese workers are not employed at
these corporations and do not enjoy the same level of security and wages as
their counterparts in the dominant corporations. During business down-
turns, small and medium-sized firms, many of which are subcontractors of
globally renowned firms, lay off workers, cut back on overtime, trim
bonuses (which can reach some five months of annual salary) and make
other such adjustments. When assessing the success of large companies like
Toyota, it is important to bear in mind that the parts-producing subcontractors are dependent and vulnerable. They are often asked to shoulder
many of the cutbacks and costs necessitated by slack business, in effect
insulating the core workforce from the vicissitudes of the business cycle.

SHOCK ABSORBERS

Women workers also have contributed considerably to Japan's economic success, although their role has not been fully recognized nor well-compensated. This subject will be treated at greater length in Chapter Seven, but suffice to say here that women have served as shock absorbers for the Japanese economy in a way similar to subcontractors. Women workers remain on the disadvantageous periphery of the Japanese employment system, often working as unpaid workers in family businesses or as permanent part-time or as low-level, full-time office and blue-collar workers. Their relatively low wages and limited benefits make them an attractive source of cheap labor and in this sense they help subsidize the favored core workforce of full-time, male workers. When hours or workers are cut to cope with the business cycle, women bear a disproportionate share of the burdens of adjustment (Brinton, 1993). Women workers have thus helped make possible the job security and benefits that firms have bestowed on male employees in the core workforce.

GROWTH AS IDEOLOGY

The income doubling plan announced by Prime Minister Ikeda in 1960 symbolizes the commitment of the government to growth at all costs [*Doc. 5*]. This ideology of GNPism became the mobilizing and unifying ideology of the dominant LDP. It was an enormously popular program that generated a unified vision and was made possible by sustained government intervention. The stimulus of massive public works associated with the 1964 Tokyo Olympic Games spurred growth beyond ambitious targets while the success of those Games was taken as confirmation that Japan had recovered from the war and reentered the community of nations. However, as discussed in Chapter Nine, the heady years of double-digit growth brought Japan both the benefits and costs of a mature economy, providing a reminder that the sun also sets.

THE SETTING SUN

During the 1970s the fortunes of the Japanese economy dimmed for a variety of reasons. The ideology of growth was no longer as compelling and the environmental costs of the 'miracle' stirred a popular backlash against unfettered development. More importantly, Japan was rocked by the rapid surge in oil prices orchestrated by OPEC (the Organization of Petroleum Exporting Countries) in 1973. The oil-price rise fueled inflation, raised production costs, sparked industrial cutbacks and caused recession in the economies of Japan's trading partners. This jolt to the Japanese economy was preceded by the decision of the US to abandon the 1944 Bretton-Woods system of fixed exchange rates in 1971 that led to an appreciation in the value of the yen. The yen had been pegged at 360 to the US dollar since the Occupation and this relatively low value helped stimulate demand for Japan's exports. As a result of the US decision, the value of the yen rose to 310 to the dollar in 1971 and since then there has been an extended rise in the value of the yen. For Japan, the results were mixed. Imported natural resources became cheaper in yen terms, thus helping firms lower production costs and therefore export prices. However, the yen's appreciation dampened foreign demand for Japanese products.

As a consequence of rapid growth in the 1950s and 1960s, Japan in the 1970s had become a mature economy. It had already tapped into the dynamism of the domestic and overseas 'new frontiers' mentioned earlier in this Chapter and in the absence of fresh frontiers was unable to sustain such high levels of growth. In addition to confronting the limits of growth, Japan was experiencing heightened competition in export markets for heavy industrial products such as steel and shipbuilding. Regional rivals such as Korea and Taiwan had an edge on labor costs and were quickly climbing the technological ladder, closing the gap with Japan. Japan's labor unions had successfully negotiated wage increases and job security, limiting employer options when confronted with the twin challenges of stiffer competition and recession. The government sponsored a political solution to this economic problem by switching from a policy of picking winners to a policy favoring recession cartels with subsidies and tax breaks for 'sunset' industries. This approach protected jobs and won votes, but postponed the restructuring of the economy. Protecting domestic producers of a variety of industrial products made Japan a high-cost economy, forcing domestic producers of exports to rely on relatively expensive domestic inputs. This meant that Japan's leading companies carried its lagging companies. In the wake of the sharp appreciation of the yen in 1985, this situation became even less viable, forcing exporting companies to lower production costs by relocating production facilities offshore. In 1989, amid the hubris of the bubble economy, when the Japanese economic juggernaut seemed unstoppable and commentators spoke of a Pax Nipponica, Bill Emmott's *The Sun Also Sets: Why Japan Will Not Be Number One* (1989) seemed poorly timed. Since then, his analysis has proved prescient about the woes, discussed in Chapters Nine and Ten, that have beleaguered Japan in the 1990s.

CHAPTER FIVE

JAPAN AND ASIA: PAST AND PRESENT

A LINGERING LEGACY

Many Japanese people and their government have not yet come to terms with the consequences of the Imperial Army's fifteen-year rampage and occupation of Asia between 1931 and 1945 when over 15 million Asians perished due to Japan's expansionist policies. The government has encouraged a collective amnesia regarding Japan's shared past with Asia through its powers of textbook censorship and centralized education policies (Hein and Seldon, 2000). Many Japanese regard themselves as victims of World War II and few recall the sustained victimization of neighboring countries that claimed so many victims and left such deep scars in these nations. Within Japan, debate over the war continues and there are many Japanese who defend their nation's actions, arguing that the excesses have been invented or exaggerated and that Japan's actions in Asia at that time were justified. Political leaders have sent mixed messages over the years, generating uncertainty in the region about whether Japan has taken responsibility for its past actions and is sincerely contrite about the devastating consequences of its aggression. As a result, generally good relations between Japan and other Asian nations remain troubled by the ghosts of the past (Wakamiya, 1999).

The past resonates powerfully in contemporary Japan, especially regarding the unresolved and controversial legacy of its wartime actions. Many Japanese politicians continue to argue that Japan was motivated by a desire to liberate Asian nations from Western colonialism. They point out that following the Pacific War, the process of decolonization brought freedom and independence to former colonies in Asia, suggesting that Japan deserves credit for promoting this process by challenging the colonial powers and nurturing Asian nationalist movements. Prime Minister Ryutaro Hashimoto (1996–98) is perhaps the best-known exponent of this view and he enjoys strong support for his position among other conservative politicians and citizens' groups such as the War Bereaved Families of Veterans' Association. In 1995, the Diet conducted considerable debate over a resolution marking the fiftieth anniversary since the end of the war. What began as an effort to put the past behind Japan by issuing an unambiguous apology became the focus of intense political debate. Finally the Diet passed a compromise resolution that did little to convince other Asians that Japan was apologizing or taking responsibility for its past conduct [*Doc. 6*]. The final wording watered down the apology and tried to justify Japan's actions in the context of world history. Prime Minister Tomoiichi Murayama (1994–96) later added his own less ambiguous apology on the anniversary of Japan's surrender [*Doc. 7*].

What is it that other Asian nations want Japan to take responsibility for? Wherever the Japanese military operated in Asia it committed serious and extensive war crimes. Massacres of civilians, gruesome medical experiments on prisoners of war (POWs), mistreatment of POWs, random rape, systematic rape of tens of thousands of young women forced into sexual slavery, looting, famines, ethnic cleansing, forced labor, etc., claimed countless victims (Tanaka, 1998). The arrogant and often cruelly violent behavior of the Japanese troops made a mockery of the Pan-Asian ideology espoused by the government at that time, leaving a lasting impression (Chang, 1997; Honda, 1999; Sato, 1997; Toer, 1999). While claiming to be engaged in building an Asia run by and for Asians, Japan was merely seeking to replace the Western colonial powers as the regional hegemon. Japan's invasion of Southeast Asia from 1941 was motivated by the search for the natural resources needed to continue its ongoing war in China, which began with its take-over of Manchuria in 1931 and escalated significantly after 1937 (Barnhardt, 1988; Goto, 1997; Marshall, 1995). The impending threat of an economic boycott by the US in protest against Japanese aggression in China left two choices: withdrawal and negotiations over the future of China or expansion of the war so that Japan would not be vulnerable to such economic pressures. For a variety of reasons, the Japanese government opted to widen the war, spreading the catastrophe it started in China to the rest of the region. As Goto (1997) argues, the ideology of Pan-Asianism and the liberation of Asia that was used to justify invasion was merely a cover for Japan's self-interests and desire to feed its war machine with the abundant raw materials available in the region.

The liberation argument also has a China-sized hole. There was a consensus in Japan that in order for it to catch up with the Western powers it also needed to engage in imperialism, especially since it was poorly endowed with the natural resources needed for its industrial development. Due to geographical propinquity, rich reserves of natural resources and a potentially huge market, China was the obvious target for Japan to realize its ambitions. China was an independent nation in 1931 when Japan invaded and took over the Chinese province of Manchuria, and in 1937 when it escalated the conflict and sought to subjugate all of China. Since the end of

World War I, Japan had become the leading imperial power in China and had the largest economic stake in the country. The rising tide of Chinese nationalism, however, threatened Japan's substantial continental interests and the consequent political turmoil undermined its economic ambitions in China. The decision to subjugate China, still a sovereign nation at the time, was aimed at safeguarding Japan's interests and helping it achieve its ambitions. Thus, where Japanese military actions were concentrated and most destructive it is hard to sustain the thesis that Japan came as a liberator looking out for the interests of fellow Asians.

Pan-Asianism also fails to explain Japanese colonialism in Korea or Taiwan. Resentment against Japan remains most vibrant in Korea because there the depredations of Japanese rule were experienced longest and Koreans remain very bitter and emotional about Japan's perceived failure to admit and take responsibility for what happened during the colonial era (1910–45). Japanese colonialism did facilitate significant economic development, but the Japanese made the same mistakes as colonial rulers elsewhere around the world. Colonial rule was based on racism, inequality and violence, provoking a nationalistic backlash that remains surprisingly powerful today. In addition, the Korean minority is the largest non-Japanese ethnic group resident in Japan and still suffers from discriminatory treatment. This treatment helps fuel contemporary Korean anger towards Japan.

ATONEMENT AND WAR GUILT

The Japanese government maintains that all claims arising from the war have already been settled in the San Francisco Peace Treaty. Thus, suits by groups of Asians who press various claims against the Japanese government are routinely rejected because they are seen to have no legal foundation. International jurists have criticized this stance, arguing that the treaty only dealt with state-to-state claims and did not prejudice the claims of individuals, but this argument has not been accepted by the Japanese government. Thus, colonial subjects who fought with or otherwise assisted the Imperial forces (but were later denied pensions because they lost Japanese citizenship), women who served their sexual needs, people forcibly brought to Japan as workers and POWs have had their claims rejected in the Japanese court system. Favorable rulings in lower courts have been overturned or vitiated on appeal. The official line is that these issues have been resolved even though the steady stream of court cases suggests that these lingering grievances continue to fester. However, since most of the victims are aging, time may bring a sort of resolution. On the other hand, Nobel Prize winner Kenzaburo Oe has argued that coming to terms with the past is a precondition for improved relations with Asia, a sentiment that has earned him the ire of right-wing activists who regularly harass him [*Doc. 8*].

Inevitably, the manner in which Germany and Japan, allies during the war, have coped with the burdens of history invites comparison (Buruma, 1994). As McCormack argues:

> In the scales of the twentieth century, the misery, suffering, destruction, and dislocation caused by Japanese expansion and war in mid-century was of a magnitude comparable to the German, and the contrast between the two countries in terms of how they face their own history at century's end is striking. The contrast between Japan and Germany in respect to the payment of war compensation is stark. In reparations, compensation, and pensions, by 1991, the German government had paid out the sum of 86.4 billion marks (6.9 trillion yen), and the German Treasury estimated that payments of a further 33.6 billion marks (2.7 trillion yen) would continue until the year 2030, for a total of around 10 trillion yen (roughly one hundred billion dollars). ... By comparison, Japan had paid out a paltry 250 billion yen, forty times less, and less than is paid in a single year in pensions and benefits to Japanese veterans and their families. (McCormack, 1996: 245)

In addition, unlike in Japan, neither the government nor prominent politicians in Germany deny or try to justify their nation's actions during World War II and German companies have acknowledged and compensated wartime slave labor.

Japan has been unable to lift the incubus of its shared history with Asia because the official version of this history is deeply flawed, and government leaders have failed to convey a sense of sincere remorse or contrition remotely comparable to that displayed by postwar Germany. Carefully calibrated gestures and hedged admissions of wrongdoing have instead generated perceptions of a nation eager to bury the past before taking its measure. As McCormack, an Australian historian, suggests:

> The consistent Japanese focus on its war experience as victim (Hiroshima and Nagasaki), rather than as aggressor (Nanking, Singapore and count-less other cities), contrasts with Germany's public penitent stance. The continuing efforts to sanitize the history that is taught to the country's youth, and especially to deny the massacre at Nanking and the atrocities of Unit 731 at Harbin and elsewhere, and the countless atrocities against women, evoke distrust and suspicion on the part of Japan's neighbors. (McCormack, 1996: 245)

Hein and Selden (2000) argue that this is because the Japanese do not believe that the rewards justify the costs, unlike the Germans who desperately want to be accepted by other Europeans as part of Europe.

TEXTBOOKS AND MASOCHISTIC HISTORY

Some historians in 1990s Japan argue that Japan has been excessively self-critical in appraising its wartime conduct. They assert that the 'victor's history' generated at the Tokyo War Crimes Tribunal is biased and unfairly critical of Japan's actions. In their view, in order for Japanese to regain pride in their nation they need to develop a more sympathetic under-standing of Japan's war record. The decision of the government to permit revisions to secondary school textbooks as of 1996 that take a more critical view of this record has been harshly opposed by this group, other ultra-nationalist organizations and conservative politicians.

In contrast, critics of Japanese textbooks both in Japan and abroad assert that for too long the government has whitewashed the national record in Asia. The government has censored textbooks and downplayed incidents, employing circumlocutions and euphemisms that tend to minimize the negative consequences and shift responsibility away from the Imperial forces. In the view of these critics, the slight revisions approved in 1996 are a belated and small step towards a full reassessment of the past. Rather than masochistic history, they argue that Japan has embraced a government-sponsored, self-serving collective amnesia that fails to impart to students a balanced understanding of what Japan did in the region and why this continues to complicate contemporary relations with Asia.

Since 1982, the governments in China and Korea have made Japanese textbooks an issue in their foreign relations by denouncing the watered-down history taught to Japanese students. In response to pressure from these governments and in recognition of the weight of historical research affirming that tragic excesses were committed by the Imperial Army, by the mid-1990s the Japanese government began to permit more leeway in how the past is characterized.

The case of Ienaga Saburo, a prominent Japanese historian, illustrates how the government has constructed an evasive version of history [*Doc. 9*]. Censorship by the government of the history textbook he wrote for high school students has been the focus of several lawsuits since 1965. The government argued that his views on Japan's actions in Asia were too negative and would not approve them for use in the school system without significant revisions. The government required him to delete certain sections regarding the medical experiments of Unit 731 and widespread rape, arguing that the facts had not been fully researched (see Gold, 1996 for a summary of what is known about the activities of Unit 731). His description of Japan's invasion of China as 'aggression' was deemed too negative. The Ministry of Education favored substituting 'aggression' with the phrase 'military advance' because, 'In the education of the citizens of the next generation it is not desirable to use a term with such negative implications to describe the acts of our own country'. (Buruma, 1994: 196). In other cases the government has toned down descriptions of the massacre known as the Rape of Nanking, settling on vague references to the number of casualties and enigmatically suggesting that they died in the chaos. Eyewitness accounts of massacres, news reports and the field diaries of soldiers describing the carnage they perpetrated have still not been officially sanctioned as accurate and thus high school students could graduate thinking that 'chaos' was the real culprit in Nanking.

Time and good research have vindicated Ienaga as all of the disputed interpretations and facts censored by the government have been proven by younger Japanese historians. In 1993 the Tokyo High Court ruled that the government exceeded its powers in censoring the textbooks he had written, but even now the debate over how the past should be taught is bitterly contested. Right-wing historians argue that young Japanese need to develop more pride in their nation while proponents of a full accounting of the past see more honor in forthright apology and improved future relations with Asia.

COMFORT WOMEN

Perhaps no single issue is as emotive and bitterly disputed as is the case of the comfort women. There is considerable proof that an estimated 140,000 young women, mostly teenagers from Korea, were forced into serving as sex slaves for the Japanese troops between 1932 and 1945. These are the so-called comfort women. Responsibility for this sordid system, and even its very existence, was denied by the Japanese government until a Japanese researcher found archival documents in 1992 that indicated official complicity at the highest levels in the military and bureaucracy (International Public Hearing Report, 1993). Subsequent research and the testimony of comfort women and former soldiers have verified the reliance on coercion in recruiting these girls to staff what are euphemistically known as 'comfort stations' supervised by military officials. These girls report that they were raped and beaten at the outset before having to serve as many as thirty soldiers a day (Hicks, 1995).

Comfort women were a priority because the military authorities wanted to minimize sexually transmitted diseases by closely monitoring their health. For this reason, recruiters sought out virgins. Military leaders believed that the provision of sex slaves was preferable to soldiers roaming the countryside and ravishing local women; in China such actions had stoked anti-Japanese resistance. It is a measure of how important the comfort women were considered that they would frequently arrive at newly conquered territories or battlefronts along with provisions and ammunition.

The Japanese government's manner of dealing with this sordid story of sexual slavery is revealing. Despite persistent rumors and allegations, the government denied that such a system even existed. Confronted with damning archival evidence, the government then denied that it was involved, shifting responsibility on to private entrepreneurs. When this was shown also to be untrue, the government then argued that the comfort women were not coerced into service. Finally, under the weight of mounting evidence and widespread denunciations of its position of grudging and qualified admission of wrongdoing and responsibility, in August 1992 the government accepted responsibility and issued an apology. Subsequently, the government sponsored a non-governmental organization, the Asia Women's Fund (AWF), to provide 'sympathy money' to former sex slaves in order to evade official compensation. Only a handful of women have accepted offers of compensation, belying accusations by some Japanese that they have only come forward in order to extort money from Japan now that it has become a wealthy nation. Most former comfort women have refused offers from the AWF because they argue that this organization was set up only for the purpose of allowing the Japanese government to evade accepting direct responsibility. They are still waiting for direct compensation and letters of apology from the government, but since the government maintains that all issues of compensation have been settled, the situation appears to be at an impasse. Agencies within the United Nations and various human rights organizations in Japan and abroad continue to campaign for direct compensation and more research into some of the missing pieces in the comfort women puzzle.

Right-wing historians have sought to deny, minimize and mitigate this grim chapter in Japan's history. They argue that the women willingly signed up and that the government bears no responsibility because private entrepreneurs ran the comfort stations. They argue that the numbers of women involved have been vastly inflated. In addition, they argue that since the women were paid it is a simple case of prostitution and in this regard the story of the comfort women is essentially similar to that of other women everywhere war has been waged. This perspective is increasingly difficult to defend as more evidence and eyewitness accounts emerge that contradict the conservative version. There also appears to be no evidence of other instances in history of a government-sanctioned, military-operated, institutionalized system of sexual slavery involving tens of thousands of teenage girls.

THE NANKING MASSACRE

Did the 1937 Nanking Massacre [*Doc. 10*] really happen? This might seem like an absurd question, but Shintaro Ishihara, elected governor of Tokyo in 1999, is on record as having denied that the looting, rape and assembly-line murder reported by eyewitnesses ever took place. Iris Chang, the author of *The Rape of Nanking* (1997), has been the target of vitriolic attacks by the Atarashii Rekishi Kyokasho o Tsukuru Kai (The Japanese Society for New History Education) and other ultra-nationalist groups. Even the Japanese Ambassador to the US took the unprecedented action of publicly denouncing her book. Chang's scholarship was careless regarding certain details, but her basic points are similar to those of many Japanese writers who have published works concerning what happened in Nanking, based on their careful research and solid documentation. Their reports about the atrocities committed in the name of the Emperor have been backed up by soldiers who participated in the rampage and by the testimony of Chinese eyewitnesses (see Honda, 1999). Yet, prominent conservative historians continue to dispute that the Japanese forces committed atrocities against Chinese civilians and even go so far as to blame Chinese irregular forces for the killings. They dismiss the testimony of Japanese soldiers, saying they were brainwashed by the Chinese fifty years ago when they were imprisoned after the war. As in other areas of history concerning Japanese wartime excesses, they argue that research is inconclusive and thus it is not appropriate to discuss these issues in textbooks.

This would not be important except for the fact that in *fin-de-siècle* Japan, the conservative historians are enormously popular and very influential. Nobukatsu Fujioka's books on Japan are bestsellers, conveying a message that critical views of Japan's conduct are unjustified and unfair. His positive interpretations of Japan's wartime conduct have struck a chord in the public and his views are given prominence in the mass media. Yoshinori Kobayashi, also a member of the Japanese Society for New History Education, is a popular cartoonist who espouses similar views. His *manga* are serialized in a popular weekly magazine and he is also a prominent figure in the mass media.

Why are so many Japanese eager to accept these fanciful and extremely self-serving renderings of Japanese history? The right-wing efforts to turn back the hands of the clock to a time when history was less embarrassing and the dark spots more obscure has an obvious appeal. Clearly there is also a nationalistic backlash and a desire to shake off the burdens of the past. A nation that has focused its energy on building a better tomorrow has little inclination to dwell on the shame of the past. Perhaps the public mood in the 1990s has been affected by the prolonged recession and the battering the national pysche has sustained during this troubling decade. In addition, suppression of the shameful incidents of history for so long meant that an unprepared public was faced with a deluge of critical commentary at home and abroad during the 1990s. It is not surprising people found it difficult to reconcile such criticism with what they had learned at school. Accepting the new revelations about the dark past meant putting the older generation on trial and taking on the thankless task of atoning for the sins of past generations. Many Japanese are also concerned that accepting the emerging critical view of history would prove costly in terms of compensation claims at a time when Japan was experiencing considerable economic difficulties. It is also the case that many of the young do not feel they are obliged to answer for the past and find it irritating that others should expect them to remain mired in the dark past when the future beckons.

A respected journalist for the *Asahi Newspaper*, Katsuichi Honda, counters such views by arguing that the past cannot be denied and that the orchestrated amnesia adds to Japan's shame. In his view, Japan,

> ...unlike Germany and Italy, has not followed up on the war crimes of its own people. By not acknowledging these crimes, we fail to grasp the complete picture of our own national character. Lacking this understanding, we keep appealing to the world, talking about Hiroshima and Nagasaki and the nuclear situation. We, therefore, gain a reputation for emphasizing our role as a victim without ever reflecting upon our own violent aspect. (Honda, 1999: 139)

CONTEMPORARY TIES

It would be misleading to suggest that contemporary ties between Japan and Asia are dominated by arguments over history. Economic ties are strong and generally mutually beneficial. Japan is the world's leading donor of foreign aid and approximately two-thirds of its Official Development Assistance (ODA) is funneled to Asian recipients [*Doc. 11*]. Overall, Japan provides about one-half of all ODA received in the region. In addition, the Japanese government lends substantial sums of money at concessionary rates to Asian governments, mostly for large infrastructure projects. Some observers view the concentration of ODA and concessionary lending in Asia as a form of war reparations, especially in the case of China. It also makes sense to focus on Asia since it represents a significant market for Japanese producers and increasingly is a platform for offshore production by Japanese producers driven from the high costs in Japan (Hatch and Yamamura, 1996; Katz, 1998; see also Chapter Ten). Thus, it is in Japan's self-interest to stimulate development and nurture stability in a dynamic region that is closely tied to Japan's future economic prospects. Japan's private sector has invested in and lent heavily to Asia and has thus also played a constructive role in promoting regional development.

However, Japan has been less successful in accommodating the consequences of its success in nurturing development in Asia. One of the sources of tension between Asian economies and Japan is the widespread perception that the Japanese market is closed. There is no secret that these nations would prefer trade to aid and look on the Japanese market as a natural export market for the various products Japan has helped them to produce. In certain areas there has been some success in selling to Japan, but the natural engine for regional development has spluttered due to protectionist practices.

Japan's relations in Asia have steadily improved since 1974 when Prime Minister Tanaka was greeted in the region by anti-Japanese riots protesting against Japanese economic dominance. In response to this unexpected outbreak of anti-Japanese sentiments, the government reevaluated its regional profile and crafted a policy aimed at winning the hearts and minds of its fellow Asians. In 1977 Prime Minister Fukuda committed Japan to assist ASEAN (the Association of Southeast Asian Nations) in large-scale industrialization projects; ODA was increased and he toured the region without incident. Japan also renounced military intentions and worked hard to broker a resolution to the post-Vietnam War problems engulfing Indochina. Morrison argues that Japan's assumption of a political role in helping to nurture stability and integration in Southeast Asia during the late 1970s marked a watershed in Japan's post-World War II foreign policy (Curtis, 1994: 146). The continued emphasis on forging political, economic and cultural relations in Asia has worked to mutual advantage.

In *Asia in Japan's Embrace* (1996), Hatch and Yamamura point out that Japan is the leading investor in the region and thus plays a dominant role in influencing the scope and nature of regional industrialization. They argue that after the steep appreciation of the yen in 1985, Japanese *keiretsu* (corporate conglomerates) flocked to Asia and built up regional production networks. The construction of offshore production facilities has had a generally positive impact on the Japanese political economy, but they raise concerns about the dependent development promoted in the region by corporate Japan with large dollops of government assistance. In essence, Japan plays a key role in determining which industrial sectors are promoted in which countries and uses its technology and capital in ways that undermine national sovereignty and enhance Japan's bargaining position. They also raise the concern that the exclusionary business practices of the *keiretsu* in Japan are being replicated in Asia, creating the possibility that it will become a zone characterized by the closed practices that have kept foreign economic penetration limited in Japan.

In 1997, a chain of events, initially linked to foreign currency speculation, led to a region-wide severe economic crisis that had consequences eerily reminiscent of Japan's burst bubble (Ries, 2000). Asset prices and currency values tumbled, scores of banks and other firms went bankrupt, huge sums of money evaporated and the human misery index sky-rocketed. Since then the impetus for the rise of the Asian bubble and its subsequent bursting have been traced to Japanese banks. Unable to make money in the depressed Japanese economy, they aggressively sought business in Asia, making the same mistakes there that they had made at home – lending without careful credit assessment and not monitoring how the borrowed funds were used. Speculative investments in stock and land deals, fueled largely by Japanese capital, pumped up the asset bubble during the 1990s. In 1997, when Japanese banks refused to roll over loans and retreated from further lending, the resulting credit crunch led to an economic débâcle of immense proportions. In response to the crisis, however, Japan mounted a generous financial bailout and earned considerable goodwill for doing so [*Doc. 12*].

MULTILATERAL PARTICIPATION

Japan's political and security roles in the region are focused on multilateral organizations. The most important of these is ASEAN (the Association of Southeast Asian Nations) which has ten members from Southeast Asia. Japan is a dialogue partner with ASEAN and participates in annual summits with leaders from around the region. Cambodia served as the site of Japan's first major postwar diplomatic initiative. In 1993, with the cooperation of ASEAN, Japan sponsored and led UNTAC (United Nations Transitional Authority in Cambodia) to facilitate democratic elections and deliver that nation from the trauma of prolonged violence. This was the first time that Japanese troops had returned to Asia in the postwar era and the experience has gone a long way in reassuring Asian neighbors that they do not need to fear a resurgence of Japanese militarism. Thus, this humanitarian endeavor enabled Japan to make considerable progress in burying the ghosts of its shared past with Asian nations. The non-confrontational, consensus-building approach to diplomacy of ASEAN is shared by Japan and provides it with an opportunity to broaden and deepen its regional posture in a non-threatening manner.

Since 1994, the ASEAN Regional Forum (ARF) has served as the focus of regional security dialogue, involving the ASEAN 10 and other nations in the region, such as China, Russia and the US. In the post-Cold War era, Asia is a region with many sources of friction and a number of smoldering conflicts. In this context, the relative paucity of regional fora and webs of organizational relationships is considered a major vulnerability. Japan is credited with urging ASEAN to create the ARF as a way of coping with perceived threats and of recognizing the need for a forum to exchange views and information while engaging in confidence-building measures. Japan views North Korea and China as the major threats to continued regional peace. Asian Pacific Economic Cooperation (APEC), established in 1989, is the leading Pan-Pacific economic organization with twenty-one members, including Japan, and has taken the lead in promoting free trade, investment and economic cooperation. As with ASEAN and ARF, Japan values the multilateral, consultative approach in APEC and welcomes the opportunity to broaden dialogue on economic issues outside the context of its close bilateral ties with the US.

THE FUTURE

The ongoing and lively public debate over the past is revealing about society. Japan is certainly not the only nation in the world with skeletons rattling around its historical closet. There is a powerful temptation to close the door on that past, but it is hard to bury the past and keep it buried; history is always a battleground in the present and the terms of debate and interpretation are not easily controlled. In the 1990s the French and the Swiss have also had to face newly discovered inconvenient truths about the conduct of older generations during World War II, while Americans have begun to disinter atrocities committed during the Korean War. Following the death of Emperor Hirohito in 1989, there has been an outpouring of troubling revelations in Japan. Until he died, many people held back out of respect for what he symbolized. And, as Dower argues, since he was never held accountable for his conduct during the war, nor ever accepted responsibility for the devastation his nation unleashed in Asia, many Japanese felt that there was no point in their doing so (Dower, 1999). Perhaps his death released them from their silence and inspired a reckoning of accounts. What is clear is that diaries were suddenly 'discovered', archives yielded their secrets, memories sharpened and the past that had been hastily buried suddenly returned with a vengeance. There is much to digest and much of the new information is not appetizing. However, as in other countries, some Japanese will learn to cope with their checkered past and carry their burdens with dignity while others will choose not to.

What a difference twenty-five years makes. Anti-Japanese riots in 1974 have given way in 1999 to an infatuation with Japanese pop culture throughout the region. Young Asians are avid consumers of Japanese fashion, music, cartoons, television programs, fads, food, etc. In much of Asia, and especially among the young generation, the wartime and colonial past with Japan is not a major issue. Japan is widely admired and the Japanese are emulated and viewed as 'cool'. In Korea and China, the past is fading more slowly and resentments linger more prominently than in the rest of Asia, but in these nations too there is a mania over Japanese pop culture.

Throughout Asia, Japan is more a source of inspiration than suspicion and worries about a revival of Japanese militarism are shared by few. Japan accounts for approximately two-thirds of the regional economy and is seen as a powerful engine of growth and development. As good as the situation appears at century's end, however, it is hard to assess the potential damage to intra-Asian relations that might be caused if any one of the numerous sources of regional conflict erupts. The relative peace and stability that prevails in Asia at the turn of the century may not last and serious conflicts could quickly erode many of the advances Japan has made in nurturing good relations. From Japan's perspective, the most threatening uncertainties emanate from North Korea and China, while Southeast Asia appears to be a cornerstone of its regional diplomacy. The prospects of reunification on the Korean peninsula improved in 2000, forcing the Japanese government to reconsider its regional policies.

CHAPTER SIX

JAPANESE SECURITY

THE US–JAPAN ALLIANCE

The close alliance between the US and Japan remains the centerpiece of Japan's foreign policy and the foundation of its security. During the nearly seven-year Occupation (1945–52), the US government was able to impose, nurture and develop relationships that have kept the nations bound together despite the inevitable bilateral strains. As a result of the Cold War bargain between the US and Japan, hammered out in the waning days of the Occupation, the US gained rights to base its troops in Japan and in exchange agreed to provide security for Japan. The US sought to have forward-based troops mostly as a deterrent against Soviet adventurism in Asia, although the communist 'menace' became more broadly defined to include China, North Korea and later, North Vietnam. The original 1951 Security Treaty was modified in 1960 amid considerable public criticism [*Doc. 15*]. From the beginning it has been a lop-sided arrangement in that the US is obliged to defend Japan, but not vice versa. It is also lop-sided in that the Japanese government has, in reality, little influence over what the US military does on the bases, nor does it have control over the overseas deployment of troops based in Japan. Revelations that the US regularly ignored Japanese prohibitions on the presence of nuclear weapons in its territory between 1956 and 1972, apparently with the government's acquiescence, highlight the fundamental imbalance in the alliance [*Doc. 13*]. The presence of 47,000 foreign troops in Japan coexists uneasily with the pacifist Constitution and has been a critical issue in domestic political debate throughout the Cold War era (1947–89) and since [*Docs 1 and 3*].

The US–Japan Security Treaty has been a source of both friction and strength in the overall bilateral relationship [*Doc. 14*]. The bases are often an irritant for the Japanese who live in the surrounding areas because of the noise and dangers of training missions and the criminal activities of soldiers. The concentration of the bases in Okinawa has meant that this island prefecture has suffered more than its fair share of the burden (Johnson, 1999). It was not until 1972, in response to strong Japanese pressure, that the US agreed to return Okinawa to full Japanese sovereignty. Prior to that the US had made this island group a *de facto* US militarized territory. Okinawans harbor resentments towards both the Japanese and US governments since they have not been consulted over bilateral defense agreements that affect them. Okinawans still hold the Japanese responsible for the destructive and bloody battle of Okinawa in June 1945, and many do not consider themselves to be ethnic Japanese (an opinion many mainland Japanese share). Due to lingering anti-Japanese sentiments, it was the only prefecture in Japan that Emperor Hirohito never visited.

The brutal rape of a twelve-year-old girl in 1995 by US marines brought anti-base resentments to a head and since then the US and Japan have accelerated negotiations over reducing and relocating US bases (Johnson, 1999). About 75 percent of the land allocated for US bases in Japan is in Okinawa and more than 60 percent of the 47,000 troops are stationed there. Friction is also linked to the substantial money Japan pays to support US bases and troops, an estimated $2.5 billion in direct budget outlays in 2000*, covering almost 80 percent of related costs. This host nation support, known in Japan as the *omoiyari yosan* ('sympathy budget'), began in 1978 and has grown rapidly. In a time of tight budgets in recession-hit Japan during the 1990s, the escalating costs of maintaining the US troop presence has become a politically sensitive topic.

On the other hand, the US security presence is unobtrusive to most Japanese and appreciated by many who oppose a remilitarization of Japan. Many Japanese remain haunted by the ghosts of militarism and see the US military presence as a safeguard against a return to the past. In addition, the bilateral alliance reassures Japan's neighbors in Asia, easing concerns that still linger about Japanese militarism and signaling that the US will remain engaged in the region. Other Japanese across the political spectrum worry, however, that the US security presence might involve Japan in some conflict against its wishes and that it symbolizes a diminution of Japanese sovereignty.

Japan's reliance on the US for its defense and the benefits of close economic relations have meant that Japan in practice has a foreign policy that more often than not is subservient to the US foreign policy agenda. As the relationship has matured over the decades, the Occupation-era mentality on both sides of the Pacific has faded only slowly; thus the patterns of interaction sometimes appear frozen in time and at others demonstrate a great deal of change. To some degree, Japan has been successful in asserting its own agenda and in emerging from the shadow of the bilateral alliance. Troubled as the relationship may seem at times, it remains, as former US

---

*Official Japanese sources give the figure as 260 billion yen, roughly $2.5 billion, although Johnson (2000) cites a figure of $5 billion but gives no source for this figure.

Ambassador Mike Mansfield (1977–88) was fond of saying, the most important bilateral relationship in the world bar none.

THE REACTIVE STATE

Japan has often been criticized for having a weak and vacillating foreign policy. Michael Blaker characterizes Japanese diplomacy as reactive and minimalist (Curtis, 1993). Rather than taking the initiative or articulating a strategic vision, he sees Japan merely coping with issues and problems as they crop up. In doing so the government has not met its own expectations nor those of its neighbors and partners. In addition, Japan has left its future in the hands of others, a situation that breeds dissatisfaction. Blaker defines minimalism as the practice of grudgingly making the least possible concessions required to avoid provoking a crisis, usually in US–Japan relations. More often than not these concessions are related to persistent bilateral trade frictions and involve opening Japan's market. However, in relying on the US (or other nations) to engage in *gaiatsu* (foreign pressure) to do what is in Japan's own interests, as a means of overcoming domestic pressure groups opposed to reforms that will actually benefit Japan, the government is poisoning the bilateral relationship (Schoppa, 1997). Orchestrated foreign bullying may be effective but it is a poor substitute for domestic political leadership and provokes a lingering nationalistic backlash.

Japan's defensive diplomacy is costly in that other nations do not fully appreciate what Japan is contributing and it breeds resentments in Japan because its efforts and sacrifices are overlooked and minimized. In the absence of bolder actions and sweeping gestures made in a decisive and timely fashion, Japan often appears selfish, parochial and cipher-like on the international stage. It has not wielded political and diplomatic clout commensurate with its economic strength. Despite aspirations to join the UN Security Council, many critics argue that the absence of demonstrated leadership and global vision preclude such a role. Supporters point out that within the confines of its bilateral alliance and the constraints of multilateralism, Japan has exercised leadership and tried to promote an alternative global vision. During the 1997 Asian currency crisis Japan advocated a stabilization fund, but this was initially opposed by the US. Since then, Japan's criticisms of IMF orthodoxy and its proposal for a stabilization fund have quietly drawn support. Such examples suggest that an inclination for a low-profile, behind-the-scenes role has denied Japan the credit it deserves in resolving international problems and advocating an alternative vision to that propounded by the US.

TRANSFORMING JAPAN'S SECURITY POSTURE IN THE 1990s

In 1999, the Diet approved a new set of defense guidelines that clarify the cooperation and support that US forces can expect from the Self-Defense Forces (SDF) under a variety of different contingencies [*Doc. 16*]. The new guidelines commit the SDF to provide logistical support and to conduct search-and-rescue operations in rear-areas during emergencies in unspecified areas surrounding Japan. These provisions sound mild and quite limited, but in the context of Article Nine and the longstanding taboo on deployment of Japanese forces for collective defense, they represent a controversial expansion and clarification of what Japan will do in an emergency. Former Prime Minister Morihiro Hosokawa (1993–94) has led a muted chorus of domestic criticism, asserting that the new guidelines amount to a *de facto* security treaty revision [*Doc. 17*].

The revised guidelines were a response to the ambiguities in what the SDF could and could not do in the event of hostilities breaking out in the region. They were also a response to the perception of the new threats to regional peace and stability that emerged in the post-Cold War era. Many Japanese political leaders have reservations about the Constitutional constraints on Japan's military forces in the context of rising security threats. In addition, the US government has called on Japan to become more active in collective self-defense in the region. Under the new guidelines, Japan has stretched the envelope of its security posture within the confines of the Constitution. Commentators note that the assumption of enhanced and wider security responsibilities marks a significant change from the marked reluctance to do so that characterized Japan's defense policies in much of the post-World War II era. There have been growing concerns that if American forces were drawn into conflict in Asia and did not receive even limited Japanese support, the security alliance and bilateral relations would suffer irreparable damage.

Providing security for a nation that ran a massive trade surplus of $79 billion with the US in 1999 has not yet become a significant political issue in Washington, but lop-sided trade is a recurring concern for policy-makers in both governments. This is especially true at times when economic frictions are allowed to overshadow the mutual benefits in the overall bilateral relationship. The perception that Japan is getting a free ride on defense does not hold up under scrutiny, but such accusations are dusted off during periods of turbulence in bilateral relations.

Ironically, the US imposed the constitutional constraints on the Japanese military but seems to have been regretting it ever since [*Doc. 18*]. Beginning with General MacArthur in 1951, the author of Article Nine, the US has continually pressured Japan to beef up its military forces and assume more responsibility for regional defense. MacArthur's demands that Japan establish military forces for its own defense were parried by Prime Minister Yoshida, who was worried that Japan might be called into a combat role on the Korean peninsula. At this time Japan did create a small, armed force that evolved into the SDF, but did so in a minimalist way, reflecting strong national reservations about remilitarization. Japan steadfastly refused to participate in collective defense, maintaining that the Constitution only permitted the right of self-defense. President Nixon renewed US pressure in 1969 when he requested Japan to assume a greater role in ensuring the stability of East Asia.

In 1978 the US and Japan agreed for the first time on guidelines on defense cooperation and it is at this time that Japan agreed to pay for hosting US troops. However, the security relationship remained a sensitive political issue in Japan. In 1981, for example, Prime Minister Zenko Suzuki had to renounce a recently signed communiqué with President Ronald Reagan, reaffirming the importance of the 'alliance', because the media hounded him for using a term considered too militaristic. In contrast, his successor, Prime Minister Yasuhiro Nakasone, took a more hawkish stand towards the Soviet threat, similar to that of President Reagan. In 1983 he declared to the *Washington Post* that he intended to turn Japan into 'an unsinkable aircraft carrier', and agreed to extend the scope of Japanese navy patrols in surrounding sea lanes. It was also under his leadership that Japan openly breached the informal limit on defense spending of less than 1 percent of GDP that had existed since 1976. His willingness to tread on taboo topics and sensitivities offended many, but also widened the security debate in Japan and encouraged pragmatic thinking about how Japan could best secure its defense and broader interests.

To some extent, in the 1990s the move to strengthen the bilateral security alliance with the US challenged the momentum generated by the initial post-Cold War euphoria and sentiments in Japan that favored enhanced reliance on multilateral arrangements and organizations. It soon became apparent, however, that the end of the Cold War did not mean the end of security problems in Asia. Moreover, given the serious, smoldering issues, it was soon apparent that multilateral approaches in the absence of a multilateral security architecture in Asia would not suffice. Asia at the turn of the century has no shortage of frictions over islands, reefs, energy resources, fisheries, etc., that impinge on Japan's security. In addition, the neighborhood has grown riskier with the missile tests by North Korea and a status quo-challenging China. In this atmosphere, President Clinton and Prime Minister Hashimoto agreed in 1996 to reaffirm the security alliance and explore ways to enhance its effectiveness in coping with perceived threats to stability in the Asia-Pacific region. The 1999 guidelines are the tangible, if not limited, fruit of that intensified dialogue on collective security. In a process that began with Prime Minister Nakasone, the domestic taboos that governed security issues since 1945 have all but faded away, like many other verities in late twentieth-century Japan.

The change in Japan's security posture has been driven by the experience of the Gulf War (1990–91), modernization of the Chinese armed forces and the development of missile technology and nuclear capabilities in North Korea. In addition, the US has steadily kept pressure on the Japanese leadership to take on a greater share of the burden of Asian security, commensurate with its own interests and capabilities.

A NORMAL NATION

The 1991 Gulf War proved to be a humiliating experience for the Japanese government. Never has a nation contributed so much, some $13 billion in financial support, for so little reward. Japan found itself subjected to criticism for what amounted to checkbook diplomacy. Japan's unwillingness to place its troops in harm's way while close allies did so became a source of criticism and rebuke. In a war that clearly involved Japan's vital strategic interests – unimpeded access to oil – this passive, risk-free approach to security and shifting of the dirty work to other nations made a mockery of Japan's ambitions to join the UN Security Council. In the wake of this costly embarrassment, a leading conservative politician, Ichiro Ozawa, stirred debate by calling for Japan to become a 'normal' nation. In Ozawa's view, Japan had failed the test of leadership and had not assumed the responsibilities commensurate with its global power and influence. For Ozawa, normal meant that Japan had to reassess the constitutional constraints on its security posture in a manner that would enable it to respond effectively to military crises and threats. In the context of Japan's determination to secure a seat on the UN Security Council, Ozawa argued that Japan could not merely look on while other nations took on the burden of security and peace-keeping [*Doc. 19*].

Ozawa's views represent a significant extension of those expressed in the 1980s by former Prime Minister Yasuhiro Nakasone (1982–87). He too has challenged the taboos and criticized what he viewed as the self-serving pacifism that had anchored Japan's postwar security policies. He played a key role in passing legislation in 1993 that enabled Japan to participate in overseas peace-keeping operations (PKOs) and to support UNTAC (United Nations Transitional Authority in Cambodia). The participation of Japanese troops in various PKOs, albeit under tight restrictions mandated in the Diet, showed the world a different Japan. The rehabilitation of Japan's international reputation gained momentum with its generous and crucial $3 billion financial support for UNTAC. This effort was headed by a Japanese national, Yoji Akashi, and featured extensive Japanese involvement in preparing for and monitoring democratic elections in Cambodia.

While Cambodia's problems have not been solved as a result of UNTAC, Japan gained international kudos for its efforts. It also marked the first return of Japanese troops to Asia since the war, helping to assuage bitter memories that linger in the region, and in that sense normalizing relations with Asian neighbors.

The passage of the new defense guidelines in 1999 with barely a murmur of public debate was a far cry from the street protests that rocked Tokyo in 1960 when the Security Treaty was revised and renewed. However, by the mid-1990s the opposition Socialist Party was a spent political force, partially because it abandoned its longstanding opposition to the security alliance and had lost its ideological *raison d'être*. Clearly the public mood has changed considerably on security issues, but there is still a lingering ambivalence about revising the Constitution.

NORTH KOREA (DPRK)

Developments on the Korean Peninsula explain why Japan has shed its reticence on security matters. Reports concerning North Korea's program for developing nuclear weapons first surfaced in 1994. Subsequently, North Korea conducted shorter-range missile tests and in 1998 it fired a missile over northern Japan, raising the alarm in Tokyo. Given the legacy of hatred generated by Japanese colonialism in Korea, longstanding bilateral hostility and a severe economic crisis in North Korea during the 1990s, the mere possibility that North Korea (DPRK) could strike Japan with nuclear weapons drastically altered the strategic landscape in Northeast Asia.

The missile tests took the Japanese public and government by surprise. Suddenly North Korea became a major factor in Japan's foreign policy deliberations and its reassessment of its defense posture. In the wake of the missile tests, the Japanese government warmed to the idea of joining with the US in developing a system for Theater Missile Defense (TMD). 'Theater' is a reference to the vaguely defined area covered by the system, an ambiguity that enables the Japanese government to play down the significance of TMD regarding Taiwan, a serious point of contention with China. However, it is widely assumed that TMD does encompass Taiwan and South Korea since otherwise it would not make much sense. The political inhibitions that have served as a powerful constraint on Japan's military spending and security initiatives have melted away, widening the scope for actions that would have been deemed irresponsible and unconstitutional prior to the tests. The Japanese had previously been reluctant to join this initiative which is aimed at developing and deploying technologies to counter the threat of ballistic missiles. China has clearly expressed its opposition to TMD, calling it a provocation and threat to regional peace. However, faced with the nuclear threat from North Korea, the Japanese government has rebuffed Chinese complaints, committed itself to TMD and agreed to US requests to clarify and expand its posture on collective security.

PEOPLE'S REPUBLIC OF CHINA

The modernization of the Chinese military forces gained momentum in the 1990s and this has also fanned concerns in Japan and increased its awareness of its own vulnerabilities. China's estimated military budget recorded double-digit annual growth throughout the 1990s, a trend that has drawn extensive media coverage in Japan and has given credence to those who claim that the Middle Kingdom harbors hegemonic ambitions in Asia.

The legacy of war remains a significant factor in bilateral relations. When Premier Zhang visited Japan in 1998, he made it clear that all is not forgotten or forgiven, pressing his hosts at every turn to come clean about the past and atone for the various atrocities inflicted on the Chinese people between 1931 and 1945. Japan and China also have been at odds over Taiwan and the US–Japan Security Treaty. The new defense guidelines have been condemned in Beijing and it accuses Japan of supporting what it refers to as Washington's containment strategy towards China. China fears that the new guidelines mean that Japan would support the US against China in the event of conflict between the mainland and Taiwan and asserts that Japan's stance threatens eventual reunification with Taiwan. China also points to the presence of US troops and forward-basing facilities for the US Seventh Fleet as destabilizing factors in the region. Japan's decision in 1999 to participate in research on anti-ballistic defense has equally drawn the ire of the Chinese government because it might neutralize China's current strategic advantage. The two nations have also been at odds over the sovereignty of what Japan calls the Senkaku Islands (Daiyotai in Chinese), rocky outcrops that lie between Taiwan and the Okinawan islands.

LINGERING TABOOS – ARTICLE NINE AND THE THREE NON-NUCLEAR PRINCIPLES

Article Nine of the Constitution bans the development of military forces and eliminates Japan's sovereign right to wage war. This article is unique in the world and is the reason the Japanese Constitution is often referred to as the Peace Constitution. As the only nation to have experienced the devastation of atomic bombs, Japan has assumed a unique role in global efforts to halt nuclear proliferation and eliminate nuclear weapons. It has embraced three principles that have served as the basis of its nuclear policy: (1) no development of nuclear weapons; (2) no possession of nuclear weapons; and (3) no introduction of nuclear weapons on Japanese soil.

Article Nine and the three non-nuclear principles have established the parameters of Japan's debate over defense, but these parameters have been challenged for some time (McCormack, 1996). Japan has the third-largest defense budget in the world and maintains a navy larger than Great Britain. It boasts a modern airforce and has total military forces numbering 235,000 troops. Since 1976 Japan had an informal policy of limiting defense spending to less than 1 percent of GDP, but since the mid-1980s this informal barrier has been broached. In 1995, for example, the official defense budget was approximately $50 billion, just over 1 percent of GDP, but if defense spending is calculated as it is in Britain, the figure rises to $70 billion and 1.6 percent of GDP. In addition, the gap between rhetoric and reality is highlighted by recent research that indicates that the Japanese government permitted the US to maintain nuclear weapons in Japan between 1956 and 1972, including an extensive nuclear infrastructure [*Doc. 13*]. It also appears that Prime Minister Eisaku Sato (1964–72), who won the Nobel Prize for embracing the non-nuclear principles as government policy, confided to US diplomats in 1969 that he thought they were 'nonsense'.

Public opinion has been strongly against the development of nuclear weapons throughout the postwar era, but this may be changing. In 1999, Shingo Nishimura, the parliamentary Vice Minister for Defense, publicly suggested that Japan reconsider its ban on developing nuclear weapons and was sacked for his remarks. He went on to suggest that Japan needed a nuclear deterrent to make sure that neighboring nations would be deterred from attacking or using their nuclear arsenal. However embarrassing his remarks may have been for the government, it is apparent that his views on nuclear weapons are no longer limited to an extreme fringe. Certainly Japan has both the technological capabilities and sufficient weapons grade plutonium to develop nuclear devices in short order, and with the threat from North Korea it has the motivation.

It is increasingly difficult to reconcile the existence of a large military force and large defense budget with the words and spirit of the Constitution. The Japanese courts, however, have ruled that the SDF is constitutional because the military forces are solely for defensive purposes and Japan cannot project its military power because it lacks aircraft carriers, bombers or long-range missiles [*Doc. 20*]. However, regardless of the wisdom of maintaining military forces, the Constitution seems fairly clear on the unconstitutionality of the SDF, especially if one looks back at the parliamentary debates about Article Nine that preceded ratification of the Constitution. Certainly there was no doubt in the minds of the Americans who wrote the Constitution, or of Japanese lawmakers who ratified it, that there were no loopholes that would accommodate the present SDF.

The debate over defense thus moves in tandem with the debate over the Constitution. The calls for constitutional revision have grown more strident in the 1990s in no small part because of the gap between the pacifist ideals of the Constitution, and the prevailing realities in contemporary Japan. In 2000, the government established a constitutional review council in the Diet. Ardent nationalists would like to rid Japan of what they view as an alien imposition and see rising support for a more pragmatic approach to security as a chance to advance their agenda. Other conservatives generally support preserving the Constitution with some minor amendments. The dwindling numbers of progressive and liberal voters also favor retaining the Constitution and are proud of its idealism and protection of civil rights. They fear that rewriting the Constitution would, at the extreme, facilitate a revival of militarism, and at a minimum vitiate the protections of human and political rights guaranteed by the current Constitution (Dore, 1997). In the context of revising the Constitution, the nostalgic nationalism expressed by Prime Minister Yoshiro Mori that Japan is a divine nation centered on the Emperor generated heated controversy. His remarks, during a speech in May 2000, not long after taking over from the critically ill Prime Minister Keizo Obuchi (1998–2000), were widely condemned as reminiscent of wartime Shinto-based, ultra-nationalism and for ignoring the constitutionally mandated separation of the state and religion. Commentators depicted the outpouring of criticism directed against Prime Minister Mori's remarks as a good sign that his views do not reflect public sentiments.

CHAPTER SEVEN

WOMEN IN JAPAN

Assessing the position, status and role of women in Japan is controversial and difficult because most assumptions on which one bases one's judgements are culturally rooted and the debate hinges on issues of satisfaction. In Japan, it is frequently argued that women enjoy high status and a privileged position in society and that the perspectives of Western feminists are not appropriate because the social and cultural context is different. Proponents of this view focus on the powerful role of women in the family as proof that women are seeking and finding fulfillment within the context of traditional roles. Women often control family finances, doling out an allowance to their husbands and allocating remaining resources, while also playing a central role in feeding, nurturing and making educational decisions affecting their children (Iwai, 1993). While there is some truth to this perspective and some women do find fulfillment within traditional roles, it is evident that a growing number of women are choosing to break the mold.

The popular stereotype of meek, submissive Japanese women has long obscured the reality of their lives, status, experiences and perspectives, and, by the end of the twentieth century, is no more than a condescending caricature at odds with contemporary reality. Opinion polls of women in the 1990s indicate that they are not terribly fulfilled, nor feel that they are treated as equals in society or within the family. Most agree that their lives are much better than those of their mothers and grandmothers and there is scant sentiment to return to the darker days when young brides were at the mercy of the men and older women in the family. More importantly, more and more women are carving out roles in the economy and society that are not consistent with traditional ideals.

The consequent tension between lingering attitudes and the changing reality of women in Japan animates the debate on gender. It is important to bear in mind, however, that what constitutes emancipation in the eyes of the West is not necessarily the desired ideal in Japan. Women are encountering many of the same problems arising from discrimination and sexist attitudes, but do not necessarily respond or cope in the same manner. Like anywhere, women do desire equal treatment, respect, freedom from harassment, assault and discrimination. They also desire a society free from constraints based on their gender and one that provides support for their multiple responsibilities as wives, mothers, workers and caretakers for the elderly. Women remain the fulcrum of the family and, despite the tremendous transformation experienced in Japan, they have helped maintain a degree of family stability that is the envy of other industrialized nations. Divorce rates remain low by Western standards, but have risen from 0.73 per 1,000 people in 1963 to 1.94 in 1998, a nearly threefold increase. The greater economic independence of women means that they no longer have to stay married and the social stigma attached to divorce has attenuated over the years. Nonetheless, single-parent families are rare in Japan and few babies are born out of wedlock, fostering a stability that has ebbed away in other industrialized nations trying to cope with the myriad problems generated by volatile and fragile family situations.

To understand women in Japan one has to grasp the magnitude of change that has occurred in the postwar era and resistance to the consequences of those changes. This friction between the way life has been and the way it is becoming constitutes an important social dynamic. Japan has been transformed by economic development, urbanization, improved transportation and communications, etc., in ways that have had a ripple effect on the family and traditional roles for both men and women. However, the currents of transformation are offset by a degree of inertia and an inclination towards limited and incremental change. Rural Japan has been the bastion of conservative traditions and the patriarchal *ie* system that relegated women to an inferior position in society and gave the head of household enormous legal power over all other family members. This *ie* system was formally brought to an end with the new American-sponsored Constitution, but the attitudes and inclinations of patriarchy remain strong and widespread. Vestiges of this patriarchal system remain, such as the Civil Code requirement that a married couple adopt one family name and register under one *koseki* (family register maintained by the government), in most cases (97.2 percent) meaning that the wife is obliged to take her husband's name and join his family *koseki*. Even as Japan has become increasingly urbanized – about 60 percent of Japanese live in cities with populations over 100,000 – traditions and conservative tendencies still reverberate powerfully through society.

WOMEN AND WORK

As noted in Chapter Two, the Japanese Constitution is quite progressive regarding women's rights, but progress in realizing these rights in society has been dilatory. There has been a series of legislative initiatives in the late 1980s and 1990s aimed at improving women's position in the economy, but these have not yet produced the desired results. It is telling that the overall labor force participation rate of women has remained at about 40 percent between 1960 and 2000. There is growing recognition that women have trouble balancing the competing demands for their time and energy at home and in the workplace. Government legislation aims to make it easier for women to balance the various roles they are expected to assume, but this goal remains elusive. Despite the ratification of the UN Convention for the Eradication of All Forms of Discrimination Against Women in 1985, the enactment of the Equal Employment Opportunity Law in 1986, the 1991 Childcare Leave Law and the 1998 Elderly Care Law, women remain far behind men in the workplace in terms of job status and pay. In addition, partly as a consequence of inadequate government policies relevant to working women, birth rates are dropping and the family faces unprecedented strains because of the need to provide care for the aged. These various laws reflect the fact that there is a growing number of women who are taking on multiple roles, but they face significant difficulties in assuming these varied responsibilities in the absence of necessary support mechanisms. Husbands have not yet begun to share many of the burdens of family care and household work, making it difficult for women to take care of these tasks and pursue careers. As Brinton points out, 'Thus, just at the point when legislation propounds equal opportunity for men and women, social conditions are promoting strongly unequal time obligations to the family' (Brinton, 1993: 236). She expresses pessimism about the prospects for improvement in this regard since social attitudes about family roles change very slowly.

In most families in Japan, both the wife and husband work outside the home as paid workers. Since the 1980s, more married women have entered the paid labor force and currently less than 40 percent of families depend only on the husband's earnings. However, the assumption that most women are full-time housewives lingers despite this changing reality. Wives' earnings are critical to family finances and thus not working is not a viable option for most married women. This is an important phenomenon that has accelerated since the 1980s, but social attitudes and government policies that assume women will give priority to the family, mean that they have little help with day care, elderly care and household work. The gap is narrowing, but working women often find themselves confronting frustrations and difficulties in balancing their various roles because of the lag between their everyday reality and the social context within which they function.

THE LABOR FORCE PERIPHERY

As there is a strong assumption in society and within families that women should place a priority on household and family responsibilities, married women who work often require flexible work arrangements that enable them to juggle these various demands. In general, however, full-time workers are expected to place a priority on their work duties and there are few concessions to working women. Women who need to work but also need flexible schedules that leave time for household duties are forced to seek part-time employment opportunities since flexitime, work sharing and similar innovations are somewhat rare in Japan. This means that women often take on less challenging jobs with fewer responsibilities, lower wages, limited benefits and negligible prospects for promotion and wage increases. As of 1997, 62 percent of working women were employed on a full-time basis compared to about 75 percent in the US.

Aside from the need for a flexible work schedule, the tax system is also credited with nudging women into *arubaito* (part-time work). This is because if a man's wife earns over a certain amount of money, both of their incomes are taxed at a higher rate. In addition, in many firms the family would be subject to losing some important benefits, such as a housing subsidy or dependents' allowance when other family members work full-time. Thus, in considering why women seek part-time work, it is important to bear in mind the tax penalty for working full-time, the potential loss of a husband's benefits, the cost of private day care for young children and the inadequacy of elderly care that forces many women to play the main role in taking care of aging relatives.

This tendency in women's labor supply behavior is matched by labor demand conditions. Employers are eager to cut outlays on wages and social benefits and thus seek women to work as part-timers or as temporary/dispatched workers. These non-standard employees have proliferated because they are relatively cheap, wages rise slowly, promotions are rare, benefits are negligible and there is no need to contribute to government social insurance programs. In 1999 the government moved to address this issue by banning the employment by client firms of temporary agency workers for more than one year on non-standard worker conditions, but opinion is divided over whether this ban will have a significant impact. Critics point out that there is no requirement for firms to hire temporary workers on a full-time basis after the one-year period and that the government has lifted most restrictions on which categories of work firms are allowed to employ temporary workers. It is important to bear in mind that in Japan, part-time workers often work a virtually full-time 40-hour week, but are designated as part-timers purely as a means for the firm to save money on benefits, bonuses and wages. Recent court cases suggest that women workers are having some success in seeking judicial remedies for such blatant abuses, but they remain widespread.

Women workers are also shunted into dead-end jobs because corporate personnel officers expect that women will marry before they turn thirty years of age and leave the workforce to rear children and thereafter return as part-time workers. Thus, from the perspective of the firm, heavy investments in training women workers will not pay off. The logic of the lifetime employment system and continuous on-the-job training does not translate well in terms of the life-cycle needs of women workers. Firms have opened up positions for women in the managerial training track, but as Lam notes, few women apply and retention rates are low. Lam argues that this is partially due to the desire of women workers to emphasize marriage and family responsibilities (Lam, 1992). The failure to modify the employment system to accommodate the life-cycle needs and responsibilities of women workers often makes it an unviable option. Employment policies designed for men and based on the dated assumption that a wife will take care of family and household duties make it especially difficult for young women to pursue managerial careers. In this context, it is easy to understand why women account for less than 1 percent of managers in corporate Japan.

The heavy household burdens shouldered by women and attitudes of firms towards women workers explain why relatively few women pursue high-status careers in Japan. Nearly 40 percent of working women work as part-time, non-standard workers on the periphery of the employment system where they do not enjoy the job security of the core labor force. It is often argued that women workers serve as the shock absorbers of the Japanese economy, helping firms cope with business cycle fluctuations. Employment adjustments such as layoffs or redundancies have generally been concentrated among non-standard employees, most of whom are women.

During the prolonged recession of the 1990s, the 'flexible rigidities' of the Japanese employment system described by Ronald Dore have looked more rigid and costly while the flexibility has been largely at the expense of women workers (Dore, 1973). Layoffs, reduction of hours and other cutbacks are concentrated among these employees while the largely male core labor force has, at least until the late 1990s, not been affected. In this sense, it is argued that such 'flexibilities' imposed on mostly female, non-standard workers help subsidize the expensive 'rigidities' (lifetime employment, seniority wage increases, bonuses and various benefits) accorded to the mostly male core labor force.

THE WAGE GAP

It is telling that among all of the industrialized nations, the wage gap between men and women is largest in Japan and it is the only country in the OECD in which this wage gap is widening. Significantly, women earn only slightly more than half what men earn and the prospects for narrowing this gap appear limited because of the high proportion of women employed under non-standard arrangements as part-time, temporary or dispatched workers. The labor force participation pattern of women remains M-shaped, meaning that most working women withdraw from the labor force for child rearing and then return once these duties decline, usually involving a sustained career hiatus. It is indicative that only 28 percent of women with children under the age of three are working in 1998. Upon returning to the labor market, few women return to their previous job and most take on positions with less responsibilities and pay. It is also significant that the greatest growth in jobs during the 1990s has been in non-standard work involving part-time, temporary and dispatched workers. This growth in non-standard work arrangements is a response by corporate Japan to the need to trim labor costs, but the consequences for women's career prospects have been largely negative.

Some women prefer to have the flexibility and relative freedom that comes with non-standard working conditions and are not eager to settle into better paid, full-time positions in the core labor force. Many OLs ('office ladies' engaged in secretarial, information technology and administrative work) work on a dispatched-worker basis and live at home with their parents and postpone marriage and having a family. They are welcome in designer boutiques all over the world as they are famous for their overseas shopping sprees and high disposable income. This is because the heavy demands and responsibilities of full-time work, often unattractive working environments, low initial pay and the unraveling of the lifetime employment system make increasing numbers of young workers, both men and women, leery of joining the core labor force. This represents a significant shift in attitudes from the 1960s when few questioned the merits of sacrificing everything for the company because they got security and rising standards of living in exchange.

EDUCATION

The structure of work opportunities means that the returns on education remain lower for women than men. Tachibanaki argues that discrimination explains why investment in women's education produces lower returns in terms of employment opportunities and career earnings (Tachibanaki, 1996). Brinton suggests that because families know that the return on the education of daughters is lower than for sons, families are more inclined to spend more on their sons' education. In addition, Japan is the only industrialized nation, including Korea, in which there is a yawning gap between the expressed educational aspirations of mothers for sons and daughters (Brinton, 1993: 204–5). Brinton argues that the educational system and labor market have developed in ways that systematically disadvantage women. For example, the training system in firms that leads to promotion is tied to uninterrupted tenure, something that women with husbands and children can rarely manage. In university, women tend to be concentrated in humanities rather than departments with stronger career orientations. Since these institutions have evolved in ways that limit the development of women's human capital, and society pressurizes women into investing heavily in the human capital of males to whom they are attached, it is not surprising that the consequences are evident in career and wage outcomes. Regarding the gender gap, Brinton argues:

> The relative insignificance of education in predicting women's employment patterns is mirrored by the absence of marked change in the behaviors of young women in the mid 1980s compared to their counterparts nearly two decades earlier. Although the younger women are better educated, employment discrimination against highly educated women and the force of strong marriage norms have perpetuated gender stratification. (Brinton, 1993: 187)

Although about one half of women, as of 1998, attend post-secondary educational institutions (slightly higher than the figure for men), more men attend four-year university courses. Of course this is a major change from 1960 when only 10 percent of women continued their education after high school. However, many women go to two-year junior colleges or vocational schools rather than four-year universities. This greater investment in the human capital of sons rather than daughters has become more pronounced in the 1990s' recession, leading to speculation that continued differences in educational attainment will ensure that women's progress in the workplace will be limited. On the other hand, more families only have one child, meaning that daughters' educational desires do not have to be sacrificed for their brothers. It is also possible that the impending labor shortage in Japan, due to shrinking family size, will eventually facilitate women's career advancement because there will not be enough male workers.

RECRUITMENT

Women also continue to suffer discrimination in job recruitment. Only in 1999 did newspapers end the practice of posting job openings in separate sections by gender. Most students gather job information and receive invitations for job interviews at job fairs arranged at their university or school, or at larger events sponsored by job information agencies. Others find job information in readily available job information publications and by attending company recruiting sessions. As was widely reported in the media during the 1990s, many young women have not been able even to get interviews and have been discouraged from applying for jobs by corporate personnel representatives. The Ministry of Labor has warned against such practices, but women contend that they remain commonplace. In the tight job market of recession-hit Japan, companies favor young men, partly because they know that retention rates are higher and partly out of a sense that men have a responsibility to provide for their families and thus deserve a priority in applying for any openings. Women also report that they are frequently asked inappropriate questions at interviews that would not be asked of male candidates, regarding their dating habits, marriage plans, living arrangements and other personal matters.

LOW BIRTH RATE

The burdens of multiple roles carry important consequences for women and society. Most social scientists ascribe the low birth rate in Japan (1.34 children per woman in 1999) to the expense and difficulty of raising children. The consequences of this low birth rate are further discussed in Chapter Eight. The support mechanisms common in other advanced industrialized societies that encourage women to have children are judged inadequate in Japan. For example, women recently gained the right to take maternity leave and to go back to their original job, but this legislation does not cover the smaller companies where many women work. Moreover, during the maternity leave, only women working full-time receive 40 percent of their pay from social insurance as of 2000, while those working as non-standard workers receive nothing, making it extremely difficult for many families to make ends meet. Since rearing children in Japan is costly in terms of child-specific costs, derailed careers for women and frequently the loss of considerable income to have a child, the birth rate has declined well below the rate needed to maintain current population levels.

Moreover, public day care centers frequently have rigid rules about when children have to be dropped off and picked up, making it difficult for working mothers to avail themselves of these facilities. As a result, many working women opt for more expensive private care, but this is not an option for many women and is a constraint even on those who are better off. Elderly care is an additional onerous burden that is largely assumed by married women. Facilities and home assistance for the aged are limited and, as a consequence, many women find that caring for aged relatives is a full-time responsibility that leaves little room for work outside the home. Families face stark choices between often depressing public facilities, expensive private facilities or caring for aging parents at home. This latter alternative is common, but makes it extremely difficult for women to continue with their careers. In 2000, the introduction of the Nursing Care insurance program promises partially to alleviate this burden through the provision of expanded elderly care services (see Chapter Eight for further discussion of this program).

THE BIRTH CONTROL PILL

In 1999 the Ministry of Health and Welfare approved use of the birth control pill for women, bringing an end to a more than three-decade campaign by women's rights organizations. The government had withheld approval of the pill since the 1960s out of concerns that its usage might promote promiscuity and lead to an erosion of traditional feminine roles. The medical community also opposed use of the pill, citing concerns about the effect on women's health and inconclusive data on its safety. In addition, critics argue that many doctors derived substantial unreported income from performing abortions and thus opposed approval of the pill. Since condoms and the rhythm method have been the most widely used forms of contraception in Japan, there have been many unplanned pregnancies. As a result, Japan has had one of the highest abortion rates in the world, with estimates running to over 1 million per annum in the late 1950s and remaining by some estimates in the hundreds of thousands through the 1990s (Jolivet, 1997).

The government had been planning to approve the pill earlier, but then the rising threat of AIDS and other sexually transmitted diseases (STDs) led to the cancellation of approval out of a concern that it would lead to a rise in unsafe sex. Feminists and other critics argue that the ban on the pill reflected male domination of politics and society. Some argue that concerns about Japan's declining birth rate also made bureaucrats reluctant to give women more control over their fertility. The government's decision to approve the pill is widely linked to the unprecedented, speedy approval for the anti-impotence drug Viagra in 1999. In this case, the government decided that foreign drug trial studies were sufficient and reliable. This undermined its position on the pill, which was based on the presumed need for further research and the unreliability of foreign research findings. The fast-track approval for Viagra made the government's stance on the pill increasingly untenable, opening it to a barrage of criticism for having a double standard on sexuality and reproductive health.

Few experts think that the pill will become widely used because of publicity concerning the side-effects, but the pro-pill lobby argues that the main point is to give families and women the right to make decisions free of government and patriarchal interference. Francis Fukuyama, a conservative intellectual, has asserted that the introduction of the pill will have a devastating impact on Japanese society, facilitating the emergence of a host of social ills that exist in Western, industrialized societies that he controversially ascribes to the use of the pill [*Doc. 21*].

SEXPLOITATION

The sex industry is estimated to account for nearly 1 percent of GDP in Japan, a figure equivalent to the defense budget. Pornographic magazines, videos and *manga* (comic books) are widely available in shops and from vending machines. Tens of thousands of foreign women, mostly from Southeast Asia, are issued visas as entertainers, but most of these women work in the welter of 'soaplands' and massage parlors (where many Japanese women also work) that are found in cities and towns all over Japan (Bornoff, 1991). Since the mid-1990s, sexual material has become more explicit and even mainstream magazines regularly feature what is called *heyanudo* ('hair nudes' – photos revealing pubic hair).

Women's groups in Japan credit the enormous pornography industry with shaping and reinforcing demeaning attitudes and abusive actions among men towards women [*Doc. 22*]. The Prime Minister's Office in 1999 reported that one in three women in Japan is subject to physical assault and one in five has been subject to some form of sexual assault. There has been arising awareness of *sekuhara* (sexual harassment) and many companies have instituted employee-sensitivity programs. Lawsuits against Japanese companies in the US during the 1980s and the tremendous financial liabilities associated with sexual harassment cases focused the attention of corporate Japan on the need to get serious about such workplace abuses. In addition, the old practice of *katatataki* ('tapping on the shoulder'), by which managers would pressure women in their late twenties to quit, is no longer so blatantly practiced. However, it is noteworthy that even in the 1990s, saleswomen in car showrooms wear badges identifying them as a 'sales pretty', suggesting that their primary qualification for work is their youth and looks.

In cooperation with the police, subway and train companies have cracked down on the numerous *chikan* (molesters and exhibitionists) who frequent public transportation networks and neighborhood groups post anti-*chikan* signs to warn young women to be careful. It may not be that the situation has grown measurably worse, but rather that society has become more open in recognizing that these problems exist and more forceful in trying to stem such social ills. Cases of wife and child abuse are certainly reported with far greater frequency in the media than previously, perhaps indicating that attitudes are becoming less tolerant of such behavior towards women. In the 1990s, Interpol indicated that Japan was the largest source of internet child pornography. After considerable lobbying by various citizens' groups, the distribution of such materials was made illegal in 1999 (Mercier, 1999). Less encouraging is the phenomenon of entrepreneurs opening *sekuhara* (sexual harassment) bars where clients pay to act out their fantasies on hostesses dressed up as secretaries, schoolgirls, etc. There are dubious cultural arguments suggesting that Japan is more tolerant about deviant sexuality, but Japanese women's groups argue that pornography, juvenile prostitution, harassment and degradation of women is about power, not sexuality.

Perhaps the tide turned in 1999 with the passage of new legislation banning sexual harassment and a major court ruling against the ex-Governor of Osaka, 'Knock' Yokoyama, a former comedian. The once popular Governor was hit with a large fine for assaulting one of his female campaign workers and public disapproval of his conduct forced him to resign from office. Until the 1990s, prominent figures could expect to weather such controversies, but public expectations have risen. The implications of the Yokoyama case are expected to be far-reaching, sending a strong signal that the courts and public opinion will no longer accept the 'wink and nod' approach to dealing with abuses of women's rights. This may encourage more women to speak out against such behavior.

CHAPTER EIGHT

DEMOGRAPHIC TIME-BOMB

As Japan shuffled into the new century, it did so as the most rapidly aging nation on earth. As of 1999, there were 21 million Japanese over the age of 65 out of a population of 126 million, making Japan second only to Italy among advanced industrialized nations in terms of highest average age. It is predicted that by 2015, about 25 percent of Japanese will be over age 65, compared to almost 17 percent in 1999, and by 2025 Japan will become the oldest society in the world. Japanese society is rapidly graying due to the drop in fertility, extended life expectancy and the aging of the baby boomers born soon after World War II. The birth rate has fallen from 4.54 children per woman in 1947 to 2.1 children in the 1960s to 1.34 children in 1999. This decline is explained by the rising number of single women (the government estimates that one out of seven women born in 1980 will never marry) and the preference for smaller families. Smaller family size is related to the higher average length of education for women and rising levels of labor force participation by them. In 1975 the number of women working outside the home was approximately 12 million, rising to 20 million by 1993 (Yamamoto, 1997). Aging in Japan has also accelerated due to the sharp rise in life expectancy. Average life expectancy for men increased from 50 years in 1947 to 77 years by 1995, while that for women rose from 54 to 83 years over the same period. As a consequence of this increased longevity, by 2025 it is estimated that 4.3 percent of the population will be over 85 years old, a fivefold increase from 1965. One implication is that those suffering from senile dementia will rise from an estimated 1 million in 1990 to a projected 2.62 million by 2015 (Yamamoto, 1997).

Most experts agree that society is not yet ready to cope with the burdens and needs of a large elderly population. It is generally agreed that the aging crisis is one of the most serious challenges facing Japan in the twenty-first century as it struggles to balance the needs and interests of the young and old. More Japanese commentators are raising the alarm that the future of Japan will be bleak and its influence will decline as a result of this aging crisis. It is expected that economic growth will slow as the labor force shrinks, savings will drop and the level of business investments and residential construction will fall because of a shrinking population. The government also faces a fiscal crisis, and citizens face higher taxes because of the costs associated with pensions and care for the aged. Given the extent of these problems, how is society coping [*Doc. 23*]?

FAMILY-BASED ELDERLY CARE

The near absence of welfare services for the elderly is based on the implicit assumption that families will take care of their aging relatives. This assumption is based on the Confucian principle of filial piety and the deep respect accorded to the elderly. This respect is expressed at many levels, including an employment system in which status, power and wages are closely tied to seniority. Japan is a society where considerable deference is shown to elderly people and their experience is highly valued. Within the family, where patriarchal patterns remain strong, older males are accorded a position of dominance in their household. Given the practical and ideological importance of the family in Japanese society, it is not surprising that the government sees the family as the natural and desirable provider of care for the elderly. This inclination of the government to integrate the family into its social welfare policy is not only cultural; in general the government has refrained from the generous cradle-to-grave approach to social services and benefits that is common in Europe. Firms are expected to provide employment security and families are expected to take care of their own, meaning that until the 1990s the government mostly played a limited role in providing the range of social welfare services and benefits common in other advanced industrialized societies.

It is important to bear in mind, however, that the ideals and values of society serve as an inspiration that may not always be realized in practice. Respect and deference to the aged is pervasive, but so is neglect, irreverence and frustration. The film *Ballad of Narayama* (Dir: Imamura, 1983) is set in a rural region of Japan in the late nineteenth century. The family and village dynamics reveal a deep ambivalence about the elderly. They are valued for their wisdom, experience and special skills, but also looked upon as a family burden. The film depicts the practice of *ubasteyama* (legend suggests that in some areas families abandoned their elderly on a mountain to die) as a practical response to the constraints on family size created by limited food resources. In order for younger males to marry and bring a wife (and future babies) into the family, the elderly had to be sacrificed. Throughout the film there are mixed images of the elderly and frequent scenes of the young demonstrating irreverence and hostility towards them. Certainly the film was made with an eye to contemporary concerns, and the practice of *ubasteyama* has been compared to the placing of old people in *rojin* homes (old age homes). There is a degree of discomfort with this practice and a sense that families are abnegating their responsibilities, even if the facilities are good and the condition of the patient requires professional nursing care – there is still a strong value placed on dealing with family problems at home.

Ever since the publication of Sawako Ariyoshi's 1972 novel, *The Twilight Years*, commentators have lamented the inadequacy of the elderly care system in Japan. The novel portrays a working woman at her wit's end trying to balance the competing demands on her time from office and home, including a senile but very active father-in-law, and how this difficult situation is complicated by the husband's failure to shoulder a share of the burden at home and the absence of adequate professional/community support. Since then, more and more women are working and facing a similarly impossible situation. A researcher at Tokyo University, Noriko Yamamoto, is critical of the family-centered approach to elderly care, arguing that it is out of touch with ongoing changes in the family and among women. Her research focuses on

> ...Japanese caregivers' strong internalization of the societal norms regarding filial caregiving and how this value is structurally maintained within Japanese society. The norm also has caused the social policy regarding the care of the elderly in Japan to remain heavily dependent on family caregivers, especially females. However, the high value assigned to caregiving also means that caregivers are tolerating enormous difficulties. Therefore, services to help these caregivers should be expanded in Japan. ... The cultural norm of filial responsibility seen in Asian countries including Japan should not be used as a reason for policies that are unduly restrictive to the lifestyle choices of those individuals whose elderly parents happen to be afflicted by physical or cognitive impairments. (Yamamoto, 1997: 174)

Government policies and societal norms, however, continue to place the burden of elderly care on the shoulders of women. Women, already busy as wives, mothers and workers, are also expected to become nurses for the aged. It is estimated that 85 percent of the elderly receiving care at home are cared for by female relatives (Harris and Long, 1999). This gender-based division of labor is indicative of patterns among the older generation in Japan and serves to make the care of the elderly an issue that strongly influences women's careers and their families.

To a degree, some women are willing to take on this task, internalizing the societal norm because of a feeling of *on* (social debt or obligation). Lebra defines *on* as 'a relational concept combining a benefit or benevolence given with a debt or obligation thus incurred' (Lebra, 1976: 91). In the context of the family, parents have bestowed much upon their offspring and thus reciprocating their accumulated kindness is considered natural and a way of assuming the responsibilities that *on* places on one. Some wives live up to social norms by caring for their husband's parents out of the same sense of *on* – the obligations assumed by the husband are internalized by the wife since they are jointly responsible for all that accrues to the family unit. Ultimately, they have little choice since there are very few options.

It has become increasingly apparent to the Japanese that this situation is not ideal and puts far too much pressure on families. Moreover, these traditional expectations are out of sync with transformations in the family. In 1980 nearly 70 percent of the population over the age of 65 lived with their families, but by the late 1990s this figure had dropped to about 50 percent. In some rural regions that have suffered depopulation because of the migration of young people to job opportunities in urban areas, the percentage of elderly people living with their children is even lower. Moreover, many urban Japanese live in cramped apartments and are unable also to accommodate an elderly relative. Despite the value society places on grandparents living with their children and grandchildren, the number of households including three generations has declined from 19.2 percent in 1970 to 12.5 percent in 1995 (Yamamoto, 1997). This significant change in the configuration of the Japanese family will affect the policy of basing elderly care initiatives on the family [*Doc. 24*].

Opinion polls are only indicative, but a *Asahi Newspaper* poll in 1994 found that 68 percent of women in their thirties and forties did not want to take care of their parents when they became frail and unhealthy. Also in 1994, *Time* magazine conducted a poll that found that a greater percentage of Americans (63 percent) than Japanese (23 percent) indicated that they would take care of their parents at any cost, a finding that shook stereotypes and raised eyebrows. The domestic media has also reported that many young women are reluctant to marry because they do not want to assume the onerous obligation of caring for their husband's parents, a trend that reportedly is making marriage more difficult for eldest or only sons whose wives are expected to take on this obligation.

PUBLIC POLICY

What has been viewed as a family problem best dealt with at the family level has become a major public policy issue, exposing deep fissures in society. (For a detailed discussion of policy-making concerning the elderly, see Campbell, 1992.) The emphasis on home care versus institutional care means that there have not been enough nursing homes for the elderly who really do need institutional care. In the 1990s the government has belatedly developed policy responses to the shortage of elderly care facilities and began training home health care workers. The guiding principle of these new plans is to emphasize home and community-based systems that encourage older people to live with a minimum of dislocation and a maximum of independence for as long as possible. Not only is this approach economically more viable, but it is also in accordance with the emphasis on the family as the foundation of the elderly care system. In addition, there is recognition that too many reasonably healthy, aged people are placed in geriatric hospitals where the level of care is more than necessary and too expensive. Thus, the government plans call for the construction of more modern, subsidized nursing home facilities that provide an assisted living environment. Progress towards meeting the ambitious targets of the central government's plans vary by region because local authorities are expected to assume responsibility for implementing the directives. Given the state of town and prefectural finances, in some areas national goals and standards will not be met unless there are generous subsidies. Critics also suggest that initial estimates for the costs of caring for the elderly are based on optimistic assumptions about containing medical costs and wage outlays for service workers. Under the current national health system, it has been difficult to institute a division between case evaluation and service provision, creating an economic incentive for doctors to prescribe more expensive medical treatment and care.

NURSING CARE INSURANCE

The difficulties of instituting reform result from the volatile mix of a family-centered ideology, prolonged recession, a bureaucracy inclined to create a sound fiscal foundation for any reform proposal, and politics. From the mid-1980s until the mid-1990s, efforts to impose a sales tax to fund social welfare programs, at the insistence of the Finance Ministry, proved the undoing of Prime Ministers Nakasone and Takeshita while Prime Minister Hashimoto fell partially as a result of increasing the consumption tax in 1997. Tax increases are never popular, especially in a scandal-ridden era when public confidence in the government and political leadership has been at an all-time low. For public relations purposes the consumption tax has been touted as the solution to looming insolvency of the national health and pension schemes, and it is always rationalized in terms of supporting social services, but the government has stopped short of making this a binding legal commitment. The public has not been as enthusiastic about funding bail-outs of various well-connected banks, agricultural cooperatives and other financial institutions and there are doubts that the new taxes will actually go to the promised social services.

The most important new government policy aimed at addressing the needs of the aged is a compulsory nursing care insurance scheme. It aims at providing needed funds for elderly care while also giving taxpayers a sense that there would be direct benefits of paying into the fund. In April 2000, in response to the anticipated costs of elderly care, the government introduced the nursing care insurance scheme for those over the age of 40. Those enrolled in this scheme pay 2,500 yen a month plus additional payments levied by local governments. However, implementation of this scheme has been complicated by the politics of elderly care. It took a long time in the 1990s to develop a consensus among government policy-makers, politicians, local authorities and those involved in delivering elderly care services that an institutional response was needed, let alone what it should be. Under the public care system, local municipalities will dispatch nurses to care for the elderly at home and will set up facilities around the country to provide other care services. It is estimated that 2 million elderly people are enrolled in the plan as of 2000.

However, at the end of 1999, just as preparations were proceeding to implement the insurance plan, the new Minister of Health and Welfare, Shizuka Kamei, forced a postponement in collection of the insurance premiums. In his view, the new policy would destroy Japan's long tradition of children taking care of their parents. He has lobbied for the payment of cash allowances to families who look after the elderly themselves without help from public services. He and his supporters in the Liberal Party also argue that all social services for the elderly should be paid for by the consumption tax.

It is argued that the new insurance scheme will encounter the same problems that plague the national health insurance system, namely that one-third of the people covered are not paying their premiums. Critics argue that it will not be possible to raise the consumption tax sufficiently to cover the anticipated costs and thus there will be insufficient revenues to cover the program. Certainly his position has drawn some support, but not from the families who have become exhausted from caring for physically weak or incapacitated parents. The media have drawn attention to this 'nursing hell' and thus there is public support for the government to play a more decisive role in helping families cope since almost all Japanese are or will be affected.

Given that women are the primary care givers, the new public care system is seen as addressing their growing desperation in balancing the competing demands on their time and the stress this causes in their families. Since a growing number of families depend on the income of working women, the absence of public care services for the elderly has kept women at home or working on limited schedules, harming family finances, inter-rupting women's careers and generating friction within the family.

By 2004, the government projects that 3.1 million elderly people, 12.9 percent of those aged 65 or over, will require nursing care. About 2.3 million are expected to receive the services at home and the remainder will receive care at elderly facilities. The system will also be strained by the provision that people between the ages of 40 and 64 who suffer from age-related ailments will also be eligible for the service. Given the magnitude of the projected demand for nursing services, there are concerns that many municipalities will be unable to deliver the level of services outlined in the nursing care legislation and will require more central government assistance and more private sector participation than originally planned.

PENSION AND MEDICAL CARE SOLVENCY

Coping with the challenges of the most rapidly aging society, in which the number of aged needing care will double between 1997 and 2020, reaching a total of 5.2 million, is rightly described as 'mission impossible'. Japan's demographic time-bomb poses enormous challenges to society and is expected to strain both the medical care and pension systems. Clearly, taxes will have to rise dramatically and benefits will have to be trimmed or con-strained in some fashion in order for society to accommodate the needs and interests of the elderly without sacrificing those of younger generations.

Is the pension system viable? As of 1997, there were 4.4 workers per retired person, but by the year 2020 it is estimated there will be only two workers per retired person. In Japan's 'pay-as-you-go' system, this means that if benefits are not trimmed and eligibility for pensions remains unchanged, the pension contributions of two workers will have to be as high as the total for 4.4 workers, a taxing prospect for younger generations. In 1997, workers contributed 17.5 percent of their paychecks towards the national pension scheme but this will have to rise to an estimated 34 percent of basic earnings by 2025 to maintain the current benefit structure. Clearly, this is an undesirably high burden on the economically active population and will impinge on their quality of life.

The government's budget woes are worsened by rising medical costs. After the age of 70, elderly Japanese pay almost nothing for health care and spending on them now constitutes one-third of the entire national health budget. And, as pension outlays rise more rapidly in Japan than anywhere else in the OECD, by 2020 they could reach some 14 percent of Japan's GDP, nearly triple the average among the English-speaking countries of the OECD and even surpassing the level in some of the continental European nations. Combined pension and medical outlays could rise from 36 percent of GDP in 1997 to 44 percent in 2025, close to the projected OECD average at that time.

The ripple effects in society of a rapidly aging population are diverse and complex. Since the mid-1980s, researchers have found a widening of income disparities in a society where equality is cherished and more than 90 percent of the population routinely identify themselves in annual surveys as part of the middle class. The Japan Institute of Labor has published research indicating that the aging of society is the main factor behind widening income disparities in Japan (Ohtake, 1999). Ohtake finds that the degree of inequality within an age cohort increases with age due to the fuller realization of the rewards of human capital investments such as education and to what he calls the chance factors that affect individuals. He estimates that about one-half of the increase in inequality evident in Japan is due to an aging population in which these factors are becoming increasingly influential. The cohort with the largest income disparities is growing fastest and thus the trend is towards greater inequality. As Japan rapidly ages, it will inevitably face the social strains and challenges of widening disparities.

REFORM

In 2000, the government enacted a pension overhaul plan that will cut some benefits by 5 percent and increase the age of eligibility to 65 by 2013 from 60 years of age. By 2025, this reform is projected to save the government more than $100 billion per annum. Few analysts expect this to be the final word on pension reform and further cuts in benefits and limits on eligibility are expected. Tax increases are also likely. Raising the investment returns on pension funds would also help lessen the need for increases in contributions. Other options involve cutting benefits and rationing health care. It is also likely that the elderly will be asked to pay more for the nursing and medical services they receive.

Clearly, the sudden worsening of the dependency ratio will force society to make some hard choices in balancing the needs and interests of different generations. It is estimated that pensions and health costs will claim about one-quarter of national income by the year 2020 and will continue to rise. As the longevity of the Japanese rises, this means that government benefits are being paid out over a longer period of time to an aging population with expanding needs for medical care.

With the baby-boom generation (born between 1946 and 1955; fertility peaked in 1947 with an average of 4.54 babies per woman compared to 1.34 in 1999) retiring and the inexorable rise in the number of retirees per employed person, the financial circumstances of the elderly will generate considerable debate. Until the twenty-first century, taking care of the aged has been considered good and affordable. However, as the dependency ratio increases, political confrontation over the level of benefits and who qualifies for government programs has intensified. In the absence of means testing (determining who is eligible for benefits based on the economic situation of a given recipient), the benefit structure is regressive because it does not favor relatively needy elderly, while those who are well-established financially usually receive higher benefits because of longer coverage and better pay. Since the well-off elderly tend to be asset-rich but cash-poor, mobilizing income from such assets is often suggested. However, since most assets are held in the form of a home, the sense of insecurity related to mortgaging it as a way of raising retirement income constitutes a considerable obstacle.

Instituting reform has been a difficult process and will not get any easier as older voters will wield considerable power at the polls and can be expected to resist wholesale rollbacks (Campbell, 1992). But given the pressing need of raising revenues and trimming costs, more decisive and unpopular actions are expected. Policy analysts point out that there is a nexus between labor supply, government reforms and employer decisions. Raising the age of eligibility represents a real threat to the economics of the aged in the absence of initiatives aimed at providing job opportunities for this labor pool. If the age of retirement is maintained at 60, postponement of access to pensions lengthens the time that retirees must live off their own resources. In this context, some form of post-retirement employment may be necessary and tax incentives for firms that employ elderly workers are probable.

Even with reforms, the impact of high taxes on younger workers will be severe. By taxing the young heavily to pay pensions for the old, the government will be overseeing a massive intergenerational transfer of wealth from the relatively poor to the relatively rich. This situation will be untenable as poorly paid workers living in cramped rental housing cannot be expected happily to pay for the pensions of retirees living in their own homes. Nor will they be content to pay higher pension premiums for lower benefits. The government estimates that a 30-year-old worker at a private company can now expect to pay 61 million yen into the pension system, but will only receive 50 million yen in benefits.

The paltry returns of the government pension plan and the prospects of paying more for less are some of the reasons why the government backed the 'Big Bang' (actually a gradual process stretching from 1997 to 2001) leading to the deregulation of financial services and foreign entry into what had been a relatively closed sector. It is expected that pension fund managers will perform better in a climate of competition in which they are judged by their performance and will have free access to a broader range of financial products and services.

THE LABOR SHORTAGE

The dearth of babies and the rapid aging of society also threatens Japan with a labor shortage. By the year 2010, the government estimates that two workers will retire for every new worker entering the workforce. It is of course hard to project what the shape of the future labor force will be like, but there is growing concern that this labor shortage will make Japan the land of the setting sun. Technological advances could suddenly change this bleak outlook and there is also considerable room for the more effective tapping of the vast pool of underemployed and unemployed women in Japan. Japan has in many respects squandered this significant reserve of human capital. However, in order to integrate women more fully into the labor force, attitudes must change, the employment paradigm must be modified to accommodate the life-cycle needs of women and public policies must be enhanced to lessen the obstacles to their labor force participation (see Chapter Seven). This is a daunting agenda, but the alternative is a greater reliance on foreign workers.

There is a marked reluctance in Japan to accept greater numbers of foreigners in a society that thinks of itself as homogeneous and prizes an imagined ethnic purity. In 1993 the resident foreign population in Japan reached 1 percent of the entire population of 125 million, a landmark that was not greeted with unalloyed joy. Like everywhere else, Japan suffers from racism and discrimination against foreigners (see Chapter Ten). There is little likelihood in the near future that there will be significant support for accepting a larger permanent foreign population. In April 2000, Governor Shintaro Ishihara of Tokyo stirred controversy in admonishing the Self-Defense Forces to be vigilant about *sangokujin* (third-country nationals – a seldom-used discriminatory and inflammatory reference to Koreans and Chinese resident in Japan) in the event of an earthquake. This remark was reminiscent of *senjin gari* ('Korean hunting' – massacres) conducted by vigilante groups in Tokyo and Yokohama in the wake of the 1923 Kanto earthquake.

The current situation allows the government to keep immigrant labor in legal limbo, thus preventing the emergence of a permanent community of immigrants (for a critical assessment of this situation, see Shimada, 1994). Japan does have immigrant workers but the current situation allows the government considerable discretion in deciding to accept and deport foreign workers, depending on business conditions in the construction and sex industries where most immigrants find work. However, there will be a continuing demand for foreign workers because someone will have to work the *san-k* jobs (*kitanai, kiken* and *kitsui*, i.e., the dirty, dangerous and difficult jobs) not filled by Japanese. Foreign workers also may be needed to provide services to the elderly and to support the pensions of retirees. Moreover, the shortage of skilled workers in the IT sector also increases the attraction of permitting expanded immigration of skilled workers and has led the government to make it easier for such workers to receive long-term visas. Changes in immigration laws in 2000 and relaxed visa procedures offer some prospect for an improvement in the legal status of foreign workers in Japan. It seems unlikely that the government will follow the suggestions of a recent UN report to accept 600,000 immigrants per annum, or a total of 17 million by 2050, to cope with its demographic time-bomb, but it is clear that there are good reasons to permit a larger influx of foreign workers. How to accommodate these workers and respect their human rights remains a significant challenge.

CHAPTER NINE

PARADIGM SHIFT IN THE 1990s

Mired in recession during the 1990s, Japan is facing the consequences of prolonged economic malaise. It enters the twenty-first century as the world's leading debtor nation, with total public debt amounting to 123 percent of GDP, a result of massive counter-cyclical government-spending packages aimed at stimulating recovery and rescuing the financial sector from insolvency. From a nation that enjoyed double-digit growth and minimal unemployment throughout the miracle years discussed in Chapter Four, growth has become anaemic and unemployment has sky-rocketed. The twin pressures of recession and economic deregulation have generated a powerful riptide with considerable consequences for the employment system. This system seems to be unraveling as companies discover that measures which saw them through past slumps are exhausted. Corporate Japan can no longer afford the rigidities and high costs of lifetime employment and seniority-based wage scales (*nenko*). The social contract between employers and employees based on security and loyalty is a likely casualty as firms gradually pursue more aggressive restructuring. What went wrong [*Doc. 25*]?

A SYSTEM THAT SOURED

Katz argues that the system that propelled Japan to economic success in the 1950s and 1960s has soured (Katz, 1998). In his view, the policies, priorities, regulations, institutions, protectionism and practices that generated the economic miracle were appropriate for the recovery and catch-up phase of development, but were less relevant as the Japanese economy matured. He argues that the Japanese government shifted from industrial policies aimed at picking winners and encouraging success in certain promising sectors to protecting sunset industries and postponing the adjustments and restructuring needed as a consequence of Japan's economic transformation. In its attempts to facilitate a soft landing for troubled sectors in heavy industry, the government saved jobs but also saddled Japan with a high-cost economy. Systematic protectionism irked trading partners and also harmed some of the more successful sectors of the economy that depended on Japanese-made inputs. The restrictions on competition generated by recession cartels (industry associations that divided market share and colluded to set prices with the acquiescence of the government) and protectionist practices that prevented, limited or marginalized foreign participation had a negative effect on productivity and innovation.

Since the 1970s, the success of Japan's leading firms obscured the backwardness prevailing in other sectors. In the wake of the oil shocks in the 1970s, the more dynamic firms carried the economy, but this situation proved untenable over time. A sclerotic system continued to funnel investments and workers into moribund sectors, even after they lost their international competitive advantage to newer rivals, making it ever more politically difficult to institute overdue reforms and a transition towards policies and practices that made more sense in a mature economy. Some sectors, such as financial services, never faced real competition and developed sloppy, lax practices that severely damaged the economy. As a result, the problems of the sunset industries festered and the transition needed to ensure Japan's continued competitiveness was delayed. In response to these self-inflicted wounds, Japan's world-beating producers of cars and electronics have shifted a significant proportion of their production overseas, where quality inputs are available at competitive prices. They have retreated from an economy distorted by cartels and anti-competitive policies because intensified global competition has forced them to rationalize production and respond to market incentives and penalties. Belatedly, industry and government are pursuing an agenda of restructuring and deregulation aimed at renovating the economy and making Japan more broadly competitive.

The Bubble economy of the late 1980s, a time when the juggernaut of Japan Inc. appeared ready to dominate global markets, proved to be the last gasp of the system (see Chapter Ten for a further discussion of the bubble). The subsequent decade-long recession is the worst in the postwar era and has exposed the weaknesses that resulted from prolonging policies, institutions and practices suited to the era of rapid growth. As Japan slowly emerges from the recession at century's end, overdue restructuring and transformation are being set in motion. The official unemployment rate nudged 5 percent in the summer of 1999, an unusually high level by Japanese standards, but unofficial estimates peg the jobless rate at between 8 and 10 percent. The dawn of the new century was welcomed by at least 3 million jobless Japanese, many of whom will join the ranks of the long-term unemployed because of a tight labor market and limited prospects for older, more expensive workers lacking appropriate skills.

After the intense labor–management battles of the immediate postwar years, firms developed a system of benefits and human resource practices that constitute corporate welfare. A low jobless rate has been assumed to be intrinsic to the Japanese system due to this tradition of corporate welfare. Companies have been reluctant to let staff go because they have viewed protecting jobs as a social responsibility. However, the media and public opinion leaders in business and government have shifted from berating restructuring as an inappropriate Western business practice to describing it as an imperative for survival. Clearly the rules of the game have been rapidly changing, but at what cost?

THE CHANGING EMPLOYMENT PARADIGM

Corporate welfare in Japan has significantly minimized the social dislocations that accompanied recession in other advanced industrialized economies. The commitment to lifetime employment through good and bad times has been a form of welfare provided at the expense of the private sector. Unlike firms in the US and Europe, Japanese employers have resisted laying off large numbers of workers. Japan Inc., however, is not immune to market forces. As the barriers to international trade recede and deregulation stimulates competition, pressure on companies to restructure has accelerated. Firms have tinkered with existing features of the employment paradigm to buy time. Reducing overtime and bonuses, pay cuts, transfers, recruiting freezes, outsourcing, forced early retirement and heavier reliance on part-time and temporary employees have helped rein in high labor costs and permitted a 'soft' restructuring. However, in the absence of high growth, the economic rationale of the existing employment paradigm is less compelling. What made sense in the 1950s does not necessarily make sense in the twenty-first century. It is telling that at the end of the 1990s there has been a reduction in full-time jobs and most new job creation has been concentrated in part-time and temporary employment. Employers are not hiring full-time workers because they do not want to assume the risks and burdens of employing workers for their entire careers. Liberalization of government regulations on temporary work in 1999 heralded the advent of a more flexible, less secure and performance-based employment system and a retreat from the rigid, secure and costly employment system that has characterized Japan since World War II. The so-called three jewels of the Japanese employment system – lifetime employment, seniority wages and enterprise unions – are all gradually fading in importance.

In the 1950s there was a scarcity of skilled labor and capital. In these circumstances, lifetime employment and a seniority-based wage system made sense. The firms invested heavily in training their employees and thus wanted to keep them as long as possible in order to recoup the costs and enjoy the fruits of these costly in-house programs. Lifetime employment was aimed at inculcating loyalty and served the interests of employers and employees. The seniority and tenure-based wage system was predicated on paying workers below their productivity for a number of years and above it thereafter. The seniority wage system made sense because new employees' wages were quite low and they had an incentive to stay with the firm. Thus labor costs in the 1950s and 1960s were kept low by the bias towards relatively new and cheap workers. As these workers' tenure increased, however, so did their wages. By the late 1980s and 1990s, firms were top-heavy with these more expensive workers just as the nation plunged into the prolonged recession. Workers were now collecting on their loyalty just as firms faced difficulties in keeping up their end of the bargain [*Doc. 26*].

The aging of the workforce has saddled Japanese firms with a rising proportion of well-paid, less productive senior employees. The percentage of employees older than the age of 45 has jumped from 34.8 percent in 1976 to 48 percent in 1997, swelling wage outlays at a time when cost cutting has become the new management mantra. This is why the fastest growth in unemployment has been among men aged 45–54, employees who are being forced into retirement before they can collect on their seniority. They are usually the most expensive employees and least adept at the new technologies proliferating in the office, rendering them a target of restructuring. The media in the late 1990s carried many stories about firms bullying senior employees into retirement by threatening to reduce pension and severance payments, by assignment of menial tasks, denial of per-quisites and other forms of harassment. The sense of betrayal among workers and the sundering of the social contract by corporations constitutes one of the bitter legacies of restructuring in Japan, eroding the trust that had been nurtured between employers and employees during much of the postwar era.

RESTRUCTURING

Corporate welfare in Japan has meant that the government has relied on companies to provide job security and thus did not need to develop an adequate safety net. Workers in Japan do not have access to a generous unemployment compensation scheme and programs for retraining or job placement are considered inadequate, especially compared to those in continental Europe. For this reason, the retreat of Japanese firms from offering full-time, lifetime employment carries enormous consequences. Through attrition and hiring freezes, more than one million full-time jobs were eliminated between 1998 and 1999. Only about one-third of the labor force of some 65 million had been covered by the security of lifetime employment, but that percentage is shrinking as firms begin shedding the practices of the past that no longer make sense and are no longer afford-able. Japan's employment paradigm depended on steady growth and thus the hard times of the 1990s and the advent of greater international competition within Japan has forced a reassessment.

The Economist (20 November 1999: 75–6) predicts that the 'great purge' of Japan Inc. is only just getting underway, a belated response that has caused existing problems to fester and worsen. The steady stream of announcements in 1999 by all the leading corporations about massive job cuts indicates that corporate Japan is serious about restructuring and that it has become an accepted, mainstream idea. The greater inclination of firms to outsource various services previously handled in-house, such as training, procurement, recruitment and information technology, is generating pressures for even greater trimming of staff levels. This continuing erosion of an employment paradigm in which security has been given in return for loyalty carries significant consequences for the economy. Not all observers agree that this erosion is taking place and blame media hype for overstating the extent of transformation. They point out that the mass firing of workers has still not happened in Japan and probably will not (Fingelton, 1995). However, even if the existing core labor force at the large firms has predominantly escaped unscathed, it does seem clear that this core is shrinking and that the favorable employment conditions associated with it apply to ever fewer numbers of workers. The transition will be slow, but the trend towards more flexible employment arrangements is driven by the new logic of the Japanese economy.

The impending labor shortage in Japan will accelerate pressures for reform of the employment system. From 2000, the working population began to shrink and is projected to reach an annual rate of decline of at least 1.5 percent by 2014. The headaches of high unemployment at the end of the twentieth century will give way to the problems of recruiting and retaining young workers. Younger workers have already demonstrated a relatively high level of job hopping; it is estimated that about one in three university graduates changes jobs in their first year of working. Now that the social contract implicit in the employment system has been broken, it will be increasingly difficult for firms to cultivate the loyalty of young workers skeptical about the promised rewards of a seniority wage and promotion system. Given the inverse correlation between age and ability to master the rapidly changing skills of information technologies, younger workers will command a premium and will not be as patient as their predecessors in waiting for promotions, power and responsibilities. In order to attract more young recruits and to induce more women to remain in the workforce while raising families, self-interest will drive firms to shift towards merit-based promotion and pay, more flexible work arrangements, better child-care options, paid maternity leave and less sexual discrimination. Given the ethic of equality that still powerfully resonates in Japan, how will firms maintain morale in the face of growing income disparities among employees?

TRANSFORMATION, DEREGULATION AND *GAIATSU*

Gaiatsu is used to refer to the pressure that the US and other trading partners periodically put on Japan to 'mend its ways', transform the structure of its economy and reduce trade deficits by stimulating domestic demand. Trade disputes have marred the bilateral Japan–US relationship since the Nixon administration sparred with Prime Minister Eisaku Sato over textiles in 1969. Since then, the economic relationship became politically charged and successive administrations sought to deal with the Japan 'problem' (ballooning trade deficits) by forcing Japan to change. In 1986, at a time when the 'Ron and Yasu' (President Reagan and Prime Minister Nakasone) relationship was helping to heal the rift caused by economic frictions, the Maekawa Report was issued. The findings supported stimulation of domestic demand as a way of lessening corporate dependence on export promotion and thus reducing frictions with trading partners. This recommendation marked a watershed in government thinking about the economy in that domestic consumption had been limited by high prices connected with a job-intensive, byzantine distribution network that served to keep prices high. In addition, interest rates on savings were set at low levels, credit cards were very rare and housing was extremely expensive, factors that worked to depress domestic consumption. In general, producers had been favored over consumers, but in order to implement the recommendations of the Maekawa Report, this bias had to shift in favor of consumption.

This gradual reorientation of the economy has been greeted by Japanese with enthusiasm even if implementation has been somewhat dilatory. *Kakaku hakkai* (price destruction) has led to significant reductions in prices for a range of consumer goods since the mid-1990s. Prices still remain high by international standards, but have declined remarkably. Shopping malls, superstores, credit cards, sales and imported goods have proliferated. Overseas retailers such as Toys 'R' Us and The Gap have rapidly expanded operations with great success. This opening of the Japanese market and abandonment of practices, policies and institutions that served artificially to limit demand have helped improve living standards of many Japanese and have generated a variety of responses and changes that are slowly transforming society. Expectations and aspirations among the young are affected, for better and worse, by the rise of consumerism. It is common to hear laments about this rising tide of materialism and the decline of spiritual values. However, on the positive side, there is more room for self-expression, greater tolerance and in myriad ways the government and business have been forced to become more responsive to a more demanding public that is becoming accustomed to getting its way.

The days of *kanson mimpi* (bureaucratic arrogance based on the assumption that people exist to serve the government) are numbered and the relations between the state and its citizens are changing perceptibly. Certainly this is not just a result of catering to the interests and convenience of consumer-citizens, but the consequences of creating such an atmosphere are partially responsible for the enhanced empowerment of the people and their demands for greater accountability and transparency. The practice of lavish wining and dining at the taxpayers' expense may not have ended for top officials, but there has been a marked decline in such excesses now that these expenses are open to public scrutiny and are published in news reports. Similarly, *dango* (public works bid-rigging), *amakudari* (literally 'descent from heaven', a reference to bureaucrats who receive cushy, well-paid post-retirement positions with firms in sectors they formerly monitored) and other collusive practices are slowly fading as the public demands greater transparency. In this sense, ongoing economic transformation is having unintended consequences that bode well for the polity.

The transition to a new employment paradigm is being driven by internal pressures for change, but to some extent the sharp increase in foreign direct investment (FDI) in Japan is reinforcing this trend. Until 1998, foreign direct investment in Japan remained negligible and Japan has the lowest level of FDI as a percentage of GNP among the OECD nations. In the early postwar years the government actively discouraged FDI by imposing restrictions on foreign exchange, affecting the repatriation of profits and making land ownership by foreigners difficult. In those days, there was also a sense that economic opportunities in Japan were limited. Japan dismantled formal barriers to investment inflows in the 1960s, but informal barriers, red tape and exclusive procurement practices in the government and business community continued to limit foreign penetration and depress investment inflows. By the 1980s, Japan had become a high-cost production base where the cost, time and effort of trying to break into the market was deemed excessive. From the Japanese perspective, foreigners were not trying hard enough and merely making excuses for their poor performance.

In the wake of the 1980s bubble, however, trillions of yen evaporated in record time, creating a devastating recession. This implosion of the economy and a flood of revelations about corrupt practices, incompetence, low productivity and lagging diffusion of information technology under-mined national self-confidence and forced a reassessment of the virtues of accommodating increased foreign participation in the Japanese economy. As the recession persisted, ideas that once seemed anathema, such as restructuring and deregulation, suddenly seemed compelling. The nose-dive of the financial sector put significant pressure on the bank-centered *keiretsu* (large industrial groups) and the cozy, indulgent relationships that existed among member companies. Massive debts and losses began to unravel business relationships, and practices that had permitted low returns, low profitability and ill-considered investments could no longer be accommodated. *Keiretsu* banks lent on the basis of group solidarity more than careful risk assessment and have paid the price. Firms could borrow at negative real interest rates and without any effective market signals, and many squandered vast sums of capital on projects or expansion based on spurious business plans. As Japanese leaders sought to integrate Japan into the world economy more fully and reciprocally, the prospects of heightened international competition in the midst of this meltdown of Japan Inc. generated considerable anxiety. In this context, the success of the US in rebounding from its economic problems of the 1980s became, in some respects, an inspiration and a model for solving Japan's myriad problems.

In the late 1990s, deregulation and restructuring became the catchwords for recovery. By trimming the stifling power of the bureaucrats and by forcing businesses to focus on profitability and performance, many hoped that Japan could restore its economy to health. Whether in fact there has been significant progress on either front is still a matter of debate, especially since the government has wiped away old regulations only to add new ones. In addition, recovery towards the end of the century has been propelled by vast sums of government spending, including huge public works supplemental budgets. However, the financial 'Big Bang' (actually a gradual process implemented between 1997 and 2001) and a more favorable business operating environment have worked to attract a sudden increase in FDI [*Doc. 27*].

In 1998, FDI totaled some $13 billion, double the figure for 1997. In the first quarter of 1999 alone, FDI nearly equaled the record 1998 tally, indicating surging foreign interest. Asset prices were depressed and companies were more desperate because of tight credit conditions and a stagnant market. While FDI at these levels is small compared to other countries, this sudden escalation of FDI marks a watershed in Japan. Large financial firms have made major deals in the sector hit hardest by the slump and affected most by deregulation measures. The government has encouraged an expanded foreign presence as a means of enhancing competitiveness. It is widely acknowledged that Japan lags behind in financial services and IT and thus foreign expertise is desired. Even so, Japan is relatively closed since FDI remains about 0.25 percent of GDP. Its population and GNP are about one-half the level of the US, but FDI is thirty times greater in the US. However, the upward trend seems destined to continue out of necessity. Foreign participation has saved companies and jobs. In addition, especially in financial services, internationalization is raising levels of customer service, performance and productivity. Moreover, as more foreigners invest in Japanese firms, either directly or through share ownership, management will be judged more than before on performance and will need to respond accordingly. Eventually, it is expected that greater corporate accountability and transparency will have a dynamic impact throughout the economy, but in the short term these changes are also forcing a process of transition for which some firms are not well prepared. The pressures for change coming from overseas are also matched by gathering internal pressures (Nikkeiren, 2000).

THE UNRAVELING NEXUS

The nexus of power in Japan has been described as an Iron Triangle between big business, the bureaucracy and LDP politicians. The collusive and cooperative relations that prevailed among these groups defined and drove Japan Inc. This Iron Triangle may better be described as a loose coalition of interest groups that worked together when common interests dictated. These groups can claim credit for overseeing the economic miracle, but they are now considered responsible for the malaise that hangs over the archipelago.

It appears that the close ties that characterized this nexus of power are unraveling, as are the cohesion and power of the component groups. For example, as a result of the burst bubble, the cozy system of corporate cross-shareholding is eroding and thus is the relative passivity of shareholders. Until the mid-1990s, corporations arranged to have large blocks of their shares held by other corporations, a mutual arrangement that was designed to insulate the market from volatility and corporate boards from demanding shareholders. However, firms have begun unraveling these cross-share-holding arrangements in order to make more efficient use of their capital. Formerly passive shareholders, especially in the giant life insurance sector, have lobbied for better performance and higher dividends as they also face pressures to make their capital work more profitably. The government has also moved to ban the activities of the *sokaiya* (corporate extortionists connected with the *yakuza* gangsters) who demand large sums of money in exchange for not raising embarrassing questions at shareholder meetings. The *sokaiya* sometimes also intimidate others from being too critical of management and thus deny shareholders an important forum for holding management accountable for its performance. Up until the 1990s this was a common business practice involving billions of yen in payoffs and unsecured 'loans'. The police have cracked down on both the extortionists and those who authorized payments, leading to some high-profile convictions that have shed light on the murky connections between corporate Japan, the government and the underworld (Whiting, 1999). Popular dissatisfaction with government and business owes much to the disclosure of these practices.

A COMPELLING NEW LOGIC

There are a variety of reasons why the logic of the Japanese economy is changing. It will take some time for the consequences to take root, but change is inexorable as aspects of the system become increasingly less appropriate and less sustainable. There are strong external and internal forces promoting changes and forcing innovations that are slowly undermining the foundations of the Japanese economic system. The *keiretsu* that have occupied the commanding heights of the postwar Japanese economy are being transformed both by external and internal forces that are slowly changing the way business is organized, performed and judged.

The external forces consist of intensified market competition, stimulated by globalization, IT and sustained pressures on Japan by its trading partners to deregulate and liberalize its economy. Japanese exporters can no longer afford to subsidize high-cost sectors in the domestic economy because the discipline of market forces in the form of intense competition is forcing cost-cutting measures across the board. As the domestic economy becomes more open to foreign competition, firms no longer have the profitable local market to themselves and thus can no longer pass on the costs of subsidizing the high-cost producers in Japan. The price gap between prices charged overseas (lower) and those charged at home (higher) for similar products is shrinking because Japanese consumers have more choices and are benefiting from the increased competition unleashed by market liberalization. In addition, Japanese consumers have been educated by their increased travels abroad and by media exposés about this price gap, generating pressures towards parity. In sectors where Japan is a large producer, the import ratio remains low but is gradually rising, indicating that over time even the most uncompetitive and cosseted sectors are being exposed, by degrees, to the same discipline of market forces. This will heighten pressures on these companies to restructure and reinvent themselves for survival.

Just as intensified global competition both overseas and in the domestic market is driving the reconsideration of the virtues of the old paradigm, there are growing internal forces promoting change. The concatenation of forces dubbed the Iron Triangle is unraveling. Leading business organizations such as Keidanren and Nikkeiren are at the forefront in pushing for change. Business leaders scarcely conceal their impatience with what many regard as a Third World political system and a second-rate bureaucracy. In recent years both organizations have produced a barrage of reports and mounted an unrelenting media campaign that aim directly at the dismantling of the old paradigm. They seek to overhaul the employment system and roll back the influence of the government and politicians in the economy. By degrees, they are having success in recasting the terms of debate, defying the mandarins and rewriting the rules of the game. For the leaders of Japan's leading corporations it is a question of survival in the unforgiving and impatient world of commerce.

In addition, the increasingly high-profile and ubiquitous presence of foreign competition in the form of joint ventures and foreign takeovers is introducing new standards of accountability and transparency. Foreign companies have taken over three of Japan's auto companies, the venerable Long Term Credit Bank and countless other firms in virtually all sectors of the economy. This is a tectonic shift in the Japanese economy and something unimaginable until the mid-1990s. In the days when the market was relatively closed, there was a broad consensus on the rules of the game and everyone more or less followed them. The opening of the market has led to an erosion of this consensus and as fewer firms adhere to the old rules, the old system is gradually being transformed. International standards and rules are replacing the old ways and thereby further undermining the foundations of the prevailing paradigm.

The cracks and seams of this paradigm are all the more visible as the implications of the demographic time-bomb become more apparent. The rapid aging of society and the impending labor shortage are rendering the existing system less appropriate and sustainable. Clearly, Japan needs to integrate women more fully into the economy and tap this largely squandered pool of human capital. This implies, *inter alia*, that an employment system designed with married men in mind, men who could depend on their wives to look after all matters related to family and home, needs to be overhauled (see Chapter Seven). Working mothers, caring for children and nursing aged parents, need a more flexible employment system that is sensitive to their life-cycles and enables them to reconcile the competing demands of home and work more effectively. The current company-centered system has intruded on the private and family lives of male workers, putting work first. However, this system was based on the assumption of their having a full-time housewife. As more and more married women work in order for the family to make ends meet, many women are no longer in a position, nor inclined, to underwrite the patriarchal employment model. Society can also ill afford the relatively low returns on women's educational investment; most of Japan's highly educated women are usually employed as poorly paid part-time workers in dead-end, low-responsibility jobs with scant benefits. A more female-friendly, flexible and secure form of long-term employment would enable Japan's most talented women to pursue careers commensurate with their abilities and allow corporate Japan to employ them more productively.

Aside from the internal forces for change generated by business leaders and the demographic time-bomb, the IT revolution is introducing a new economy and transforming how the old economy does business. The internet and e-commerce are only just beginning to make inroads, but it is apparent that many of the old rules no longer apply in this dynamic sector of the economy. Seniority and security are not key features of this world and the new mentality, values and aspirations of mostly young workers in this sector are forcing changes in how they are recruited, remunerated, promoted and retained. Old-economy businesses are also more aggressively exploring how the IT revolution can improve productivity, cut costs and provide an entrée into new ventures, suggesting that technological innovation will have pervasive consequences. Business to business e-commerce is estimated to be roughly 70 trillion yen in 2003 compared to 9 trillion yen in 1998. In 2000, for the first time the number of mobile phone users (55 million+) exceeded those using fixed lines, and more than 10 million of those are using their phones to connect to the internet.

The surge in IT business means that job training needs to focus on the need for specialists and move away from the generalist training rotation that has been common in large corporations. Workers are also coping with the decline in lifetime employment in a single firm by upgrading their own skills in order to enhance their own lifetime employability in different firms. To cope with the mismatch between supply and demand for IT workers, firms are also modifying their recruitment practices and creating portable pensions that are facilitating mid-career job mobility.

In spite of all these external and internal forces of change, the status-quo paradigm still dominates, but time does not seem to be on its side. Skeptics point out that deregulation and the liberalization of the economy is in the hands of the bureaucrats and that thus it is unlikely that they will permit wholesale changes that will weaken their power and narrow their remit (Murphy, 1996, 2000). At best, Murphy argues, there may be a vitiation of their influence and a small reduction of state intervention in the economy, but a deep-seated suspicion of market forces and a belief that corporations have social responsibilities that outweigh profits and shareholder interests means that the architects of the old system will work to reinvent the old system rather than allow wholesale transformation. Defenders of the status quo point to the limited fallout from the prolonged recession and a good record on equitably distributing the fruits of growth in the postwar era as a reason for retaining the existing paradigm, but as unsettling as change may be, how long can Japan afford to ignore the signs and logic of change? Paradoxically, the success of the postwar model has also been the cause of its undoing, creating a mature economy that is functioning within a system designed on the basis of high growth, muted market forces and decisive government intervention, features that appear less relevant and evident with the advent of the twenty-first century.

Perhaps the most devastating indictment of the postwar system has been the Bubble, its collapse and the weak response that has served to prolong the crisis. The flaws of the old system have been exposed dramatically. The collusive, corrupt and opaque practices intrinsic to this system are identified as the culprits in what went wrong. The public has learned about the dubious land deals, *tobashi* (a way of favoring wealthy stock customers), and the pervasive corruption among politicians and bureaucrats that were part of the business culture that prevailed in the postwar era. A lack of accountability and transparency permitted incompetence and negligence on a grand scale. By posing as architect and guarantor of this system, the government is implicated in orchestrating the débâcle and for having fostered systemic moral hazard. This means that there was a pervasive belief that ultimately there was no risk because of the government's implicit role as guarantor and thus people acted accordingly with predictable results.

More devastating to the credibility of the system and its stewards has been the policy paralysis that has gripped Japan in the 1990s. During this lost decade the government postponed dealing with the huge insolvency problems caused by the collapse in asset prices, allowing them to fester and put the entire financial system at risk. By the mid-1990s the risk was so apparent that when banks borrowed money overseas they were forced to pay what was known as the Japan premium.

The response of the government has also been instructive about the flaws of the patterns and practices associated with the old system. The economy has been put on a life-support system consisting of massive supplemental public works spending and low interest rates. Most analysts and many citizens fault this *dokken kokka* approach for mortgaging the future, burdening future generations with massive debts of dubious value and not addressing what ails the economy. Many Japanese openly question whether more bridges, dams and roads to nowhere are the answer. This response is further criticized for lining the pockets of the vested interests without facilitating the changes in policies and practices needed to transform the Japanese economy. By resorting to the practices of the past in this crisis, the bureaucrats and politicians are criticized for displaying a troubling bankruptcy of ideas that discredit them and the system they represent.

The lost decade of the 1990s has impressed on many Japanese that the mandarins and the politicians who stand to lose most from deregulation are part of the problem and greatly responsible for the prolonged recession. The powers of suasion exercised by the government to enforce its writ are declining in correlation with declining confidence and trust in their stewardship. Moreover, the forces of globalization that are changing the way businesses are run and exposing them to greater accountability and transparency are also affecting how bureaucrats and politicians function. Certainly, the vested interests of the old paradigm are skillfully defending their privileges and working to limit the scope of change and reform. Thus, it seems probable that in this time of transition old ways and new ways will coexist for some time and only slowly will the practices of the past recede in favor of the new logic driving the economy.

A NEW FRONTIER

In the postwar era, Japan's economy has been transformed and has grown because of its success in tapping the dynamism of two new frontiers. During the 'miracle' years the huge migration from the countryside to the cities stimulated consumption, innovation, productivity and transformed the structure of the economy. Since the 1960s, Japan has tapped the frontier of export markets in ways that have generated wealth for the country, eased and postponed structural adjustments, and forced the pace of innovation and productivity at home.

Where is Japan's new frontier? Where are the new sources of growth, innovation and dynamism? The new paradigm will be shaped powerfully by the aging of society, the need to integrate women more fully, and to some extent foreign workers, into the labor market and the ongoing IT revolution. The logic of the prevailing paradigm cannot accommodate or impede these forces, but it is too soon to speculate on the outcome they imply. What is clear is that Japan's future depends on how resolutely Japan can shed the practices and patterns of the past that handicap the economy and have made it difficult to translate Japan's enormous wealth into shared public prosperity.

CHAPTER TEN

JAPAN AT THE CENTURY'S END

THE LOST DECADE

Crisis and turmoil have a way of defining a people and their society. Japan has experienced prolonged and pervasive adversity in the recession-plagued 1990s, shaking beliefs, inclinations, relationships and patterns of behavior. As Japan enters the twenty-first century, it is emerging from a decade of profound change, driven in no small part by the wave of developments in the tumultuous 1990s that have acted as a curtain call for the postwar era. The verities of postwar Japan are fading rapidly or have disappeared altogether, signaling what some commentators refer to as the third great transformation in modern Japan. Perhaps one of the most profound changes has occurred in the way that citizens view their government as a series of scandals and exposés of negligence, incompetence and mismanagement which have undermined the edifice of power and status of those who rule.

The rhetoric of deregulation and reform also owes its popular appeal to widespread skepticism about the wisdom and skills of those who make and enforce the regulations and wield power. The reforms and dynamics unleashed in the 1990s are considered on a par with the changes instituted after the Meiji restoration (1868) and during the American Occupation (1945–52). It is too soon to comprehend the shape, breadth and pace of change in this emerging era of transformation, but limning the depths of the final decade of the twentieth century sheds light on why more and more people believe that the ways of the past are discredited and part of the problem, and thus why there is a growing consensus that reform, perhaps incremental at first but inexorably far-reaching in coming decades, is imperative [*Doc. 28*].

THE EMPEROR'S DEATH

In 1989 Emperor Hirohito died, bringing an end to the Showa Era (1926–89). His reign witnessed Japan's descent into military expansionism, the devastation of World War II and the incredible postwar recovery. The Japan he left behind was unimaginably different from the Japan he inherited from his father and yet despite extensive transformation there are also elements of continuity. Given the hardships inflicted and suffered under his name during the war, it is worth pointing out how well respected he remains among the Japanese who lived longest under his reign. The contradictions of society were perhaps best exposed during the funeral ceremonies, attended by foreign dignitaries from around the globe, whose presence indicated just how far Japan had been rehabilitated in the eyes of the world community. A god-king once likened to Hitler by the Allies, subjected to the disapprobation of the Allies during World War II was now, in death, accepted as the respected symbol of a renovated nation boasting a super-charged economy and a degree of peace and prosperity scarcely imaginable to those who surveyed the rubble that was Japan in 1945. The contradictions and ambivalence of the Japanese people were also on display. There was a public outpouring of grief throughout the archipelago, with mourners thronging the streets of Tokyo and visiting the Imperial Palace in their hundreds of thousands to offer condolences, while older Japanese tearfully shared reminiscences and the nation fell into a somber mood. This public evocation of loss was matched by record business in video rental shops as many Japanese switched off the extensive TV coverage of the traditional rites and retreated into their private spheres and interests. Soon after his death the economy also swooned, marking the beginning of the end of the miracle economy.

THE BURST BUBBLE

The bubble is a retrospective term that refers to the steep appreciation in asset prices that occurred in Japan during the late 1980s. Bubbles and subsequent crashes have occurred throughout history and are usually described as irrational, involving a collective mania spurred on by contagious optimism that what is bought today can be sold tomorrow for a higher price. At some point the crowd realizes that prices cannot be sustained at stratospheric levels, resulting in panic selling, an implosion in prices and economic crisis. Stock and urban land prices soared to unpre-cedented heights in Japan, with the stock average doubling between 1987 and 1989 and land prices in central Tokyo rising even more furiously. Just as suddenly as asset prices rose, however, they plummeted in 1990 and have remained depressed throughout the 1990s. This correction in asset prices is known as the bursting of the bubble. At the turn of the century the Nikkei stock average remains less than half the level it reached at the peak and urban land prices remain down by a similar proportion.

Why did the asset bubble occur? There are a variety of theories and many factors are seen to have contributed to the dizzying spiral in asset prices. Like speculative spirals throughout history, price increases were fed by greed and a herd mentality, and were made possible by excessive liquidity and easy credit. In addition, a continuing escalation in prices for both stocks and land became a matter of faith and investors remained confident, even as prices plummeted, that there was still untapped upward momentum if they remained invested and patient. A decade later, in the midst of a prolonged recession, it is hard to credit the leap of faith made by speculators and investors at that time. There was a powerful group psychology that encouraged people to suspend their judgement and worry more about being left out of the boom. As more punters poured more and more money into land and stocks, prices escalated out of control.

The bubble was not merely a result of this speculative frenzy. It is argued that Japan's current account surpluses and government restrictions on overseas investment by individuals and institutions during the late 1980s created a huge pool of excess money sloshing around Japan. The decision to allow a steep appreciation in the value of the yen in the Plaza Accords of 1985, aimed at reining in Japan's rising trade surpluses, is also thought to have contributed to the conditions that produced excess liquidity. In the absence of alternative investment vehicles, and with extremely low interest rates on bank deposits and government bonds, this surplus capital was funneled into stocks and land, driving an appreciation in asset prices and wildly optimistic speculation. At one point, the land in Tokyo alone was supposedly more valuable than all of the land in the US. The average price/earnings ratio on the Nikkei exceeded 65, more than quadruple the historic price/earnings ratio of the Dow Jones stock index in the US.

The government interest rate policy also contributed to the speculation by making it very cheap to borrow money, injecting huge sums of money into a system already awash in capital. The government was promoting expansion with cheap money and managed to spur growth averaging 5 percent between 1986 and 1989, at a time when other leading economies languished in recession. With interest rates at low levels, bankers had to lend more money to turn a profit and thus they aggressively expanded lending without careful credit assessment. Nor did they or government banking authorities monitor how the money was used. With what seemed like a green light from bankers and government officials, companies borrowed vast sums of money to expand production facilities and also engaged in *zaitech* – asset speculation designed to boost company balance sheets. Double trading – borrowing money for speculation – also became a common practice. With the government running a loose money policy and bankers eager to lend money, risks were thought to be minimal and mega-projects were launched without concern for returns or worst-case scenarios.

Lavish spending, speculation, over-investment and an absence of risk assessment made for a volatile combination. The government popped the bubble by raising interest rates five times in 1989 as a way of trying to prevent asset inflation from spilling over into the rest of the economy. The Central Bank's efforts to contain inflation burst the bubble, but the house of cards built by speculative fever was fragile anyway and it was only a matter of time before a shock sent it crashing down. The government may have hoped for a soft landing, but instead Japan was mired in recession during the 1990s. In the wake of the bubble, Finance Ministry bureaucrats have been blamed for mismanaging economic policy, causing the crash and failing to pursue policies that would effectively address the problems that had accumulated during the bubble era. Bankers have been accused of lax lending policies and incompetent credit risk assessment while the *yakuza* (gangsters) stand accused of manipulating bankers and bureaucrats to secure huge loans for speculative and illegal activities. Whiting argues that many of the *jusen* (bank-related real estate lending institutions) had *yakuza* ties known to both the bankers and government overseers (Whiting, 1999). Much of the loan default problem can be traced back to these *jusen*, suggesting that the bubble was a giant con game that enriched the mob at public expense.

The collapse of land and stock prices sent shock-waves throughout the Japanese archipelago and brought the financial sector to its knees. Suddenly the land that served as collateral for almost all of the bank loans was worth less than the original loans. Those who had borrowed money for stock speculation were also unable to repay their loans. Until the end of the 1990s the government tried to keep the lid on how bad the problem of loan defaults was, mostly out of concern that revelations would spark a panic and further worsen already severe economic conditions. There was also hope that economic conditions would improve and that with an upturn in the business cycle, bankers and lenders would be able to work their way out of the mess. However, business conditions in the 1990s remain depressed and the bad-loan problems festered to the point of intractability. The government could no longer stand by while the nation's entire financial system teetered on the edge of insolvency.

Taxpayer-funded bailouts of the banks and related financial institutions have restored stability to a wobbly financial system, but at the expense of public confidence in the credibility of government leaders and bankers. In addition, there is a lingering sense that public explanations just don't add up and the bailouts are unfair programs for the benefit of vested interests. Official estimates of the total bad debt run as high as $600 billion, about the same as the US Savings and Loan Bank crisis of the 1980s in an economy half the size. Unofficial estimates peg the bad debt at closer to $1 trillion.

THE BINGE

The shortlived bubble era, 1986–91, was a time of ostentatious and conspicuous consumption. Corporate entertainment money flowed in record levels and the *narikin* (newly rich individuals) vied to outdo each other in exuberant, if not tasteless, excess. Restaurants sold noodles topped with gold flakes, imported designer goods sold at grossly inflated prices, flashy sedans became common sights in the entertainment areas and a society that placed great value on restraint and understatement went on a collective binge. Art was purchased at astronomical prices, with Van Gogh's *Sunflowers* fetching some $40 million. Marketers even advised foreign companies to sell their products at high prices in Japan because Japanese consumers associated high prices with quality and would thus shun bargains.

The real estate market overheated, pricing affordable housing out of the reach of the average salaryman. An apartment of 75 square meters within ninety minutes from the office in central Tokyo cost 8.5 times the average annual salary of a salaryman, more than double the housing cost to salary ratio in other advanced industrialized nations. 'Reasonably' priced apartments in Tokyo's 23 wards cost 1 million yen per square meter. A million US dollars in Tokyo would buy a relatively small, shoddily-built house with virtually no garden. But there was a pervasive faith that land prices only rose and indeed that had been the case in the postwar era. So even when prices seemed astronomical, families mortgaged their futures to the hilt, confident that twenty years down the road their investment would be considered a shrewd coup.

The wealthy collected golf club memberships and they too became a field for speculation and incredible valuations. Second home and resort communities sprouted up around the country, bringing the influence of the bubble to some rural areas. It seemed as if the cult of mammon had suddenly spread a mass hysteria among a people not inclined to crass materialism.

The bubble gave rise to immense wealth for the lucky individuals who had bought land or stocks at the right time, suddenly creating significant socio-economic differences among people who all viewed themselves as 'middle class'. Japan had been enormously successful in evenly spreading the fruits of the economic miracle, but this achievement and the social cohesion it generated was tested by the sudden and sharp disparities fueled by the asset bubble. Society suddenly faced the challenges generated by the emergence of 'haves' and 'have nots' and the tensions caused by evident differences in means and lifestyle in a nation that values conformity and uniformity.

HANGOVER

The bubble-induced hangover lasted a decade and the consequences will be felt well into the twenty-first century. The human toll has been enormous.

Observers remark that the post-bubble experience in Japan has been relatively benign compared to the restructuring that swept through corporate America following the 1987 stock market crash. It is true that layoffs and unemployment have been very limited, but the misery index can be measured by other means. Many families had assumed massive, multi-generation mortgages to acquire housing, only to see the value of their property plummet below the level of their outstanding loan. This phenomenon of negative equity has helped depress consumption in Japan as families spend as little as possible to compensate for the folly of bubble-era purchases. Some landowners who had pledged their land as collateral for loans lost their land. Many families lost everything in the crash, not having hedged their heavily leveraged bets, and the media carried reports of debtors disappearing, presumably to escape creditors and assume new identities. Families suffered a rising divorce rate and children were yanked out of university because tuition had become an unaffordable expense. The media focused on the rising number of heads of households committing suicide so that their families could collect money from life insurance policies. In 1999, the number of suicides hit an all-time high of 33,000 and 20 percent of those deaths are attributed to debts or job loss, nearly double the corresponding figure for 1998. The growing cardboard-box communities of homeless men gathered in train station areas bore testimony to the hardship not captured in the rosier official statistics on unemployment. So too did the shift of many young female university graduates into the sex industry and the rise in juvenile delinquency.

The crash also affected corporate Japan, but weighed more heavily on small- and medium-sized businesses. Larger corporations still enjoyed favored access to credit, especially if they were connected to a *keiretsu* group. Smaller firms suddenly found it difficult and expensive to borrow and the business downturn made it more difficult to service outstanding loans. Record numbers of corporate bankruptcies were reported throughout the 1990s, leaving ruin and dislocation in their wake.

Even the larger corporations suffered as domestic consumption also crashed. Perhaps the most significant impact involved the financial sector. The government's 'Big Bang', involving the financial sector beginning in 1997, was motivated by the moribund state of this sector and the belated realization that the absence of deregulation and competition had accentuated the problems and left Japan lagging behind international competitors. Thus, on a positive note, the bursting of the bubble forced a reconsideration of prevailing practices and an embrace of reform. As discussed in Chapter Nine, the economic slump also generated changes in the institutional structure of the economy, forcing an erosion of the *keiretsu* which had controlled the commanding heights of the postwar economy. It is argued that the decline of the *keiretsu* will facilitate innovation and entrepreneurship.

The Bubble has also unleashed unprecedented criticism of Japan's corporate culture and its values of slavish conformity, personal sacrifice and reverent loyalty. The 1999 hit film, *Jubaku: Archipelago of Rotten Money*, sends a powerfully subversive message in lashing out at the basic tenets of the business world. The redeeming features of Japanese-style capitalism are depicted as the cause of the decline and as an impediment to recovery. The emerging mood of frustration, skepticism and fear is changing the way Japanese view the world and act in it. Popular author, Ryu Murakami, struck a chord with the 1999 publication of his satirical, *The Bubble: What Could That Money Have Bought*. He lampoons the taxpayer bailout of bankrupt financial institutions by listing 123 alternatives for spending the same $600 billion. Rather than pay the 'gambling debts' of profligate bankers, Murakami points out that Japan could have done something useful with this huge sum of money that would have had a lasting benefit. Such films and books are popular precisely because they question the powers that be, rare sentiments in Japan that could lead to greater transparency and accountability. It is telling that the once revered officials in the Ministry of Finance, the most powerful institution in Japan, are now mocked in the media for their once frequent attendance at *nopan shabushabu* (Japanese restaurants with mirrored floors where the waitresses wear no panties) as honored guests of bankers and others under their purview. Such behavior is neither new, nor a revelation to reporters, but is no longer tolerated, less out of prudishness than out of concern about collusion and violation of the public trust.

AUM SHINRIKYO (SUPREME TRUTH CULT)

On 20 March, 1995 members of the Aum Shinrikyo released sarin gas in Tokyo's metro, killing twelve people and making 5,500 other commuters ill. This act of terrorism was preceded by an attack against court officials in Matsumoto (Nagano Prefecture) not originally tied to Aum and was followed by a failed attempt to spread hydrogen cyanide at Tokyo's busiest commuter station, Shinjuku, on 5 May, 1995. On 16 May police arrested the guru of the cult, Shoko Asahara, and rounded up as many of his lieutenants and cult members as they could find. At the turn of the century, train stations in Japan still have large wanted posters of cult leaders alleged to be involved in planning and carrying out these terrorist acts. Cult members have been charged with the subway deaths, fifteen other killings and an assortment of other crimes.

Aum was established in 1984 in Tokyo, one of the tens of thousands of new religions that have emerged in Japan in recent decades, and was initially involved in selling quack medicines. In 1989 the government extended it recognition as a religion and the half-blind Asahara, whose real name is Chizuo Matsumoto, began to attract attention with his syncretic new religion drawing on Buddhism, Hinduism, yoga and the apocalyptic sixteenth century predictions of Nostradamus. At its peak, Aum claimed some 40,000 members, with an estimated 20,000 in Japan and other members scattered in Russia, Sri Lanka, Germany, the US and Australia.

Aum preached that the end of the world was near and that the US would ignite the apocalypse in 1997. New recruits signed over their worldly assets and lived communally in the cult's compounds where, according to critics, they were subjected to training sessions involving headgear with attached electrodes to synchronize brain waves (or erase memory), solitary confinement, food and sleep deprivation, beatings and other techniques of brainwashing. Loyal members maintain that they merely followed the teachings of their beloved leader. Sometime in 1994 Asahara is believed to have changed tack and rather than merely preparing for Armageddon, Aum began planning to initiate it. At this point Aum used its considerable assets and highly educated followers for developing weapons of mass destruction (laser, nuclear, chemical and biological).

Following the police crackdown in 1995, a majority of members left Aum and tried to return to a normal life. Four of Asahara's lieutenants were found guilty and sentenced to death in 1999 and 2000 for their role in the subway gas attacks, the murder of those who campaigned against Aum or the murder of members who tried to leave the cult. The court case against Asahara continues. In 1996 the cult was declared bankrupt in a court ruling and in 1997 the government decided not to invoke the Anti-Subversive Activities Law (1952) to ban the cult, asserting that it was, for all intents and purposes, defunct.

However, the cult has enjoyed a resurgence and membership as of 1999 is estimated at between 1,500 and 5,000. Aum also has thirty-eight compounds scattered around the country. The detention center where Asahara is held has been declared a holy site and over 100 cult members have taken up residence in surrounding buildings. Its computer business netted an estimated $57 million in 1998 and Aum representatives have purchased property around the country. In response, communities have formed vigilante groups to prevent Aum from occupying purchased premises, maintaining 24-hour vigils, and local governments, with the muted acquiescence of the central government, have refused to register Aum members as residents, thus depriving them of voting rights, health insurance and other social welfare services. The central government has responded to the reemergence of Aum by passing legislation in 1999 empowering the police to monitor and curb the activities of any group whose members are guilty of carrying out or attempting indiscriminate murder and whose leader still holds sway over the membership, effectively making Aum the only organization affected by this legislation.

In 1995, Aum became a media phenomenon comparable to the O.J. Simpson case in the US. Coverage was equally obsessive and dominated the airwaves and the printed media. Everyone wanted to know why Aum launched the worst terrorist attack ever experienced in Japan. More intriguingly, why were many of the cult's top members young graduates of Japan's best universities? Presumably, these young men and women had bright futures and had enjoyed the best educational experience that Japan could offer and yet they opted to join a peripheral cult and participated in planning the destruction of Japan. These technologically savvy recruits played a key role in producing a variety of chemical weapons and conducting experiments with various biological agents. They have also helped it establish a lucrative computer business.

It is hard to determine why Asahara decided to plan the destruction of Japan and the world. The apocalyptic predictions of Nostradamus played a key role, but much remains unknown about the guru's motivations. Various commentators have grappled with the issue of why elite students would turn their backs on good careers and plunge into an obscure new religion. It is often argued that they reacted against a strait-jacket society, the suffocation of youth and a pressure-cooker educational system; joining Aum was an extreme backlash against the conformity that is often the cost of success in Japan. Others argue that they were cajoled and flattered into joining, given enormous powers and influence at an age when they would still have relatively low-level corporate or bureaucratic positions if they continued on their 'fast track' paths in a seniority-weighted system. Still others pointed to the crass materialism and spiritual void of modern Japan as a cause for their alienation and rejection of the status quo. Yet, none of these explanations seem compelling or fully satisfying; the mystery continues to haunt the Japanese. The sense of security that the postwar Japanese came to view as a birthright and as an expression of the solidarity of the people was shattered by this cataclysmic event, forcing an uncomfortable reassessment of modern Japan and the social forces that percolate beneath the surface (Lifton, 1999; Reader, 1996).

THE KOBE EARTHQUAKE

The Great Hanshin-Awaji Earthquake struck Kobe on 17 January, 1995, leaving a path of destruction and raising questions about construction safety standards and the government's disaster relief preparations and slow response. The deadly tremor registered 7.2 on the Richter scale. The details of the damage include 6,200 deaths, 180,000 badly damaged or destroyed houses and some $100 billion in estimated damages. At the peak of the relief effort, there were nearly 1,300 shelters for more than 320,000 evacuees. About one-third of Kobe was partially or completely destroyed and more than one-half of the central district was razed by the fires feeding on ruptured gas lines and flimsy wooden housing. Most of the modern high-rise buildings fared reasonably well, but 20 percent of structures over six stories suffered significant damage. The man-made islands in the port also suffered some liquefaction and container-port facilities were devastated. Part of an urban expressway keeled over, some landmark commercial buildings were badly damaged and the urban infrastructure was clogged with debris.

The degree of the destruction and the inept response of the municipal and central governments took the nation by surprise. Some commentators at the time suggested it was an omen foreshadowing the end of Japan's heyday. High safety standards and well-planned earthquake preparedness drills offered no relief from this devastating natural disaster. Incredibly, there were no prearranged emergency relief centers and no contingency disaster plan. Offers of assistance by foreign relief agencies and NGOs were initially turned down and the Self-Defense Forces remained in nearby barracks while Kobe burned. It became apparent that some of the damage was due to shoddy construction and human error. The slow response of government authorities and the inadequate relief efforts left a lasting impression on a nation accustomed to believing that government officials knew best because they were the best and the brightest. Their incompetence and inflexibility were seen to have considerably worsened the human toll and damaged the already waning credibility of government institutions.

Beyond these profound political repercussions, the tremor hit hardest the low-income, elderly population who had inhabited the central districts. They had the least resources to fall back on and were least prepared for the costs of rebuilding. The government has tried to help with loan relief and interest rate subsidies, but many citizens have had difficulty getting back on their feet and carry burdensome mortgages for both destroyed housing and the costs of rebuilding. Recovery has taken an inordinate amount of time, partially delayed by controversies over urban redevelopment plans opposed by landowners forced to relinquish 11 percent of their land for public spaces and others who feel that their rights and voices have not been adequately represented in the process.

As late as 1999, four years after the earthquake, 5,000 out of the original 50,000 evacuated households remained in temporary housing. This is widely considered to be a man-made disaster reflecting poorly on the government authorities responsible for rebuilding the city and coping with the human tragedies that befell the community. Many earthquake survivors have returned to normal lives, shaken and impoverished, but others remained unemployed and forgotten.

By contrast, the response of young Japanese to the earthquake was widely praised as reflecting a charitable disposition not often evident among their elders. From all over the country over 1 million student volunteers poured into Kobe, offering their energy and willingness to help during the first few months following the tragedy. The enthusiasm and good intentions of these hordes of volunteers offered a stark contrast to the widely deplored sluggish and stiff bureaucratic response. As is usual in charitable endeavors in Japan, Christian groups took the lead in organizing volunteer work, but in the case of Kobe the overwhelming majority of volunteers were prodded by their own consciences and were not Christians. This has been interpreted as a welcome sign that a sense of community is alive and well in Japan. More often the media focus on signs of decay in community spirit and the rise of individualism imperiling the future of Japan.

NUCLEAR MISHAPS AND MISGIVINGS

Japan has suffered a string of nuclear accidents in the 1990s that raise serious concerns about public safety in an earthquake-prone nation with fifty-three reactors as of 2000 and ambitious plans to build thirteen more by 2010 (plans were revised in 2000, reducing the twenty projected plants by seven, constituting further fallout from the Tokaimura accident). Japan is totally dependent on imported energy and has thus invested billions of dollars since the 1950s in developing its nuclear energy program. At the end of the twentieth century, Japan derived 37 percent of its electricity from nuclear-power facilities and in response to growing power demand the government has aggressively proceeded with ambitious expansion plans.

Public concerns about the safety of nuclear power contrast sharply with official insistence that the nation's facilities are both safe and necessary. Polls consistently reveal that 70–75 percent of Japanese harbor deep misgivings about nuclear power and express fear that serious accidents will happen.

The world's most serious nuclear accident since the Chernobyl meltdown in 1986 occurred in Tokaimura in September, 1999. This small village, about 70 miles from Tokyo, is known as 'Nuclear Alley' because it is home to fifteen nuclear processing facilities. In 1999 workers at a uranium reprocessing plant accidentally triggered a runaway chain reaction that lasted for twenty hours in a facility that had no containment barriers as they were preparing fuel for an experimental fast-breeder plutonium reactor. A stunned nation learned that the accident occurred while the workers were transferring enriched uranium in stainless steel buckets and mixing the uranium by hand and then pouring it into a holding tank. The workers made a serious error in the quantities of the solution they mixed, and in order to save time and money they did not use the sophisticated processing equipment at hand that had automatic controls to prevent such an accident from occurring. Investigators found out that the workers were untrained and were actually following instructions from a company manual in illegally cutting corners and violating safety protocols. Since there would have been almost no risk of an accident if regulations were followed, there was no contingency plan for such an accident and no form of containment to protect area residents from the radiation.

Tokaimura's public authorities were slow to react and the Prime Minister's Office did not learn of the mishap for five hours. Lacking a formal request for assistance, nearby SDF troops remained at their base. The town authorities had no contingency plans and poorly informed fire-fighters arrived at the reprocessing plant during the chain reaction without protective clothing. Inexplicably, it took two days to arrange proper medical care for the three workers directly exposed to the nuclear fission. The one hospital designated for the treatment of radiation victims in every one of the emergency plans in the nation's fifteen prefectures with nuclear facilities was not, in the end, prepared to handle such cases. This exposure of official bungling and the consequences of a business more concerned about profits than safety left the public deeply skeptical about a nuclear program that has been plagued by safety flaws, radiation leaks, shutdowns, fires and cover-ups.

Prior to the criticality incident at Tokaimura, the most serious accident occurred at the Monju fast-breeder reactor in 1995. This $6 billion facility features the fast-breeder plutonium-producing technology that has been abandoned elsewhere in the world due to safety problems. Of the ten known accidents at fast-breeder plants, the Monju accident is considered the most serious. If an accident happens at a uranium-fueled reactor, the nuclear core has a meltdown while plutonium fueled reactors can explode. Since the sodium leak and fire at Monju, the plant has remained shut down. It has never performed up to expectations and has generated very little electricity. The public learned of an attempted cover-up and the destruction of evidence related to the extent of the 1995 accident when the chief investigator committed suicide and left a note implicating his superiors.

In addition to the concerns raised by the poor safety record of Japan's Power Reactor and Nuclear Fuel Development Corporation, the responsible government office, Japan's choice of plutonium-based, fast-breeder technology has given rise to suspicions that it is pursuing a civilian nuclear energy program with military implications. Plutonium does not make economic sense as a fuel because it is much more expensive than uranium. Moreover, it turns out that fast-breeder reactors are not as efficient at producing plutonium suitable for fuel as they are in producing weapons grade plutonium. Given the large amounts of plutonium in Japan, neighboring countries are wary of its intentions despite official policy barring the development of nuclear weapons.

SYMBOLS THAT DIVIDE

In 1999, while the economy languished and various social issues demanded urgent attention, the government spent a great deal of effort on legalizing the national flag and national anthem. The flag-and-anthem bill was hurriedly passed despite the misgivings of a large segment of public opinion. The Hinomaru flag, a white field with a red circle in the center, and the Kimigayo anthem have long been national symbols, but passing a bill which gives legal sanction to this status resonates powerfully in a nation still divided over its past. The sun flag is not much of an issue for most Japanese, but many consider that Kimigayo (Your Majesty's Reign) is a throwback to the era when the Emperor was an absolute monarch and, as such, is incompatible with the postwar Constitution which gives sovereignty to the citizens rather than their prewar legal status as subjects of the Emperor. Moreover, the song is a paean to the Emperor and a reminder of a painful time when Japan was waging war throughout Asia in the name of the Emperor.

To the extent that the anthem is reminiscent of Japan's militaristic past, it is rejected by progressive groups in society who feel that their nation has done too little to atone for the past. Passage of the bill in the Diet by an overwhelming majority is indicative of the dominance of conservative political forces although polls reveal greater hesitation and misgivings among the public. High school teachers express concern that the new legislation will be used to force them to raise the flag and sing the national anthem at school ceremonies. Under pressure from the Ministry of Education, more schools have done so, but there is a determined resistance to complying with such requests because many liberal educators remain distrustful of nationalism and its symbols. In other nations this might seem like much ado about nothing, but in 1999 a high school principal committed suicide to protest the growing pressure to comply. His death revealed the extent to which the national symbols are also symbols of the political fault lines that persist in society between progressive and conservative forces.

SOCIAL MORES AND DELINQUENCY

As the twentieth century drew to a close, there was palpable concern about deteriorating ethics, morals and social order. Throughout the postwar era, the young generation has been the subject of censure by their elders and they have been dubbed the *shinjinrui* (literally, 'the new species', carrying negative connotations). This inter-generational divide is common everywhere, but in Japan, where there is a strong ideology of filial piety, the repercussions are powerful for the national psyche.

A perusal of subway courtesy signs indicates just how much has changed in Japan, a nation rightly known for a generally high level of

1. Demonstration against the US–Japan Security Treaty in front of the National Diet, May 1960.

2. Prime Minister Shigeru Yoshida and Douglas MacArthur, New York, 1954.

3. Air pollution in Kawasaki, 1970.

4. Shortly before committing suicide in 1970, Yokio Mishima, noted author and founder of the right-wing Shield Society (Tatenokai), urging SDF in Tokyo to stage a coup and restore the Emperor as head of government.

5. Prime Minister Tanaka Kakuei and President Nixon meet at White House in July 1973 before separate scandals forced their resignations from office.

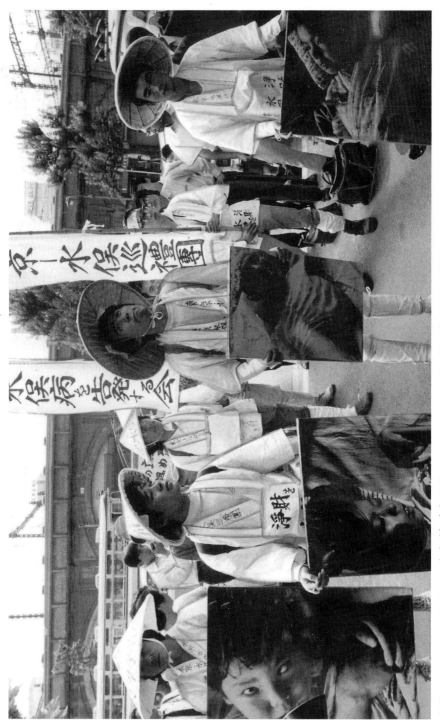

6. Protestors campaigning on behalf of the Minamata mercury poisoning victims in 1970.

7. Professor Saburo Ienaga greets supporters in front of the Tokyo high court where he filed suit against censorship of his history textbooks by the Ministry of Education.

8. Emperor Hirohito and the Empress are welcomed by pelicans on a visit to Izu in 1975.

9. Gion festival in Kyoto, 1988. Celebration of traditions remains vibrant in modern Japan.

10. Kobe earthquake, 17 January 1995. Elevated highway toppled by seismic tremors.

11. Hawaiian-born sumo grand champion Akebono performs opening ceremony at Nagano Winter Olympics, February 1998.

12. Shoko Asahara, leader of the Aum Shinrikyo cult, at a 1990 press conference.

politeness. Until the mid-1990s there were only small signs suggesting that passengers surrender certain designated seats to the elderly or pregnant. Since then, however, train companies have gone to the trouble and expense of posting signs suggesting that passengers refrain from punching train company employees, groping women, smashing ticket machines and chatting on their mobile phones, indicating the sorts of problems that seem to be occurring with greater frequency.

Ijime (bullying) is a problem that suffuses Japanese society, stretching from the classroom up to the office. Even young mothers fret about their 'park debut', the first time they visit the local park with their baby, because of the strict hierarchy of neighborhood mothers and the need to conform to the group. Wrong choices in clothes or strollers, or parenting that does not measure up, can have a devastating impact on these mothers' social life and sense of self. Bullying encompasses a variety of common social sanctions in Japan, including the tradition of *mura hachibu* (ostracization) at the village or neighborhood level. Those who do not conform to or meet local expectations are subject to a form of psychological harassment. At school, in university, on the baseball field and even in the office, bullying is intrinsic to the precise and rigid sense of hierarchy and order. It is an effective method of keeping people in their place and as such is tolerated, and indeed, to some extent, encouraged. This is not a new phenomenon, but society has become more open in discussing it. A number of student suicides and killings in the 1980s and 1990s were directly attributed to bullying at school, raising questions both about the high-pressure atmosphere of a school system that produces such behavior and a society that sanctions it as a means of social control.

Rising rates of truancy are partially attributed to bullying as targets stay away from school to avoid mistreatment. Truancy is also seen to be a rejection of the stifling conformity and rigid curriculum in a school system widely criticized in Japan for not accommodating growing diversity or stimulating creativity. In addition, truancy and the breakdown of classroom order are seen to be symptoms of a wider social problem. Compared to other societies where violent crime is far higher, Japan's problems may seem almost quaint, but they are a cause for alarm in a nation that places great value on orderly behavior. There is widespread concern that the deference to authority, willingness to accept strict discipline and *messhi hoko* (self-sacrifice) that many Japanese believe have been crucial to social order in Japan seem to be ebbing [*Doc. 29*].

In the 1990s, *enjo kosai* (compensated dating between high school or junior school girls with middle-aged men, often involving sex) has become the focus of intense public scrutiny. There is no reliable information about the extent of *enjo kosai* and participation of young women in telephone date clubs, but most guesstimates suggest that less than 5 percent of female students are involved. Stricter laws governing sexual relations between minors and adults have been enacted and teachers, monks, government officials, company executives and others with high social status have been arrested for their involvement in *enjo kosai*. Based on media reporting, it does not seem a rare phenomenon. Commentators point out that unlike most women who engage in prostitution, the girls involved in *enjo kosai* and date clubs are usually from middle-class backgrounds and not in desperate economic circumstances. It is reported that the girls are desperate for spending money so that they can purchase expensive designer clothes and accessories and pay their *keitai* (mobile phone) bills. While this materialism and exploitation of sex is lamented, few doubt that this behavior is an emulation of what is widely evident in society. For example, it was not until 1999 that Japan joined the international community in banning child pornography, and then it was mostly due to the bad publicity associated with being identified as the number one source of this seedy commodity.

The rising levels of truancy, bullying, materialism, moral laxity and delinquency among youth have spurred a national introspection, focusing on what has gone wrong. Conservatives argue that stressing ethics in school, encouraging respect for national symbols and seeking inspiration from Japan's rich traditions and culture can help alleviate the anomie and alienation that plague society. Progressives tend to focus on recasting society to permit more individuality and self-fulfillment as a means of encouraging people to identify with a community that currently seems unattractive, stifling and overly demanding of self-sacrifice for reasons that appear uncompelling to increasing numbers of Japanese.

DISCRIMINATION

Discrimination against non-Japanese and minority Japanese groups remains strong in Japan [*Doc. 30*]. Ethnic Koreans are the largest minority in Japan, numbering about 650,000. Of this total, about 150,000 are thought to be loyal to North Korea, and the political divisions on the peninsula are also evident in Japan. Most Koreans arrived in Japan during the 1930s and 1940s to work in the mines and factories to replace the Japanese males fighting in the Imperial Army. Many of the Koreans came to Japan under conditions of forced labor and endured harsh conditions. At that time, Koreans were considered subjects of the Emperor because Korea was a Japanese colony. However, after World War II, Koreans living in Japan were not granted rights as citizens and subsequent generations have remained in Japan under a permanent-resident visa status. Thus, ethnic Koreans have been raised and educated in Japan and their native language is Japanese, but they are treated as if they are foreigners. All Koreans are required to apply for residence visas and until 1998 were routinely fingerprinted, a requirement that became symbolic of Koreans' second-class status. In terms of education, jobs, housing and marriage, Koreans face pervasive discrimination, and negative stereotypes abound among Japanese. The official policy of impeding assimilation is a strain on Japanese relations with South Korea. There are no official relations with North Korea. The persistence of discrimination against several generations of Korean residents suggests that there is little inclination to address Japan's impending labor shortage by relaxing immigration restrictions.

The Ainu, an indigenous ethnic group now largely resident in Hokkaido, has been subjected to forced migration, prolonged assimilation and extensive discrimination. Like Okinawans to the south, they are often not explicitly recognized by mainland Japanese as a distinct ethnic group, but when they are recognized as such they are often the target of derogatory comments, negative stereotypes and marginalization. Okinawans, the indigenous people of the Ryukyu Islands, have endured similar treatment and see their relative poverty and hosting of a disproportionate share of US military bases as an indictment of Japanese rule.

The *burakumin* (also *eta* or *hinen*, literally 'hamlet people', – a derogatory term used to refer to the lowest caste of people) constitute a Japanese minority that has suffered discrimination since the seventeenth century. Prior to the Tokugawa era, people who engaged in activities that made them ritually impure in terms of Buddhist precepts temporarily entered into a polluted state from which they could exit once they had undergone ritual purification. However, since the Tokugawa era, this class of 'untouchables' has been hereditary and permanent. Those who worked with leather, for example, became *burakumin,* and to this day, tanning and curing of leather is dominated by them. They face discrimination in education, housing, marriage, jobs, etc., and are usually from lower economic strata. For employers and parents investigating potential marriage partners for their children, there are reportedly lists in circulation that purport to designate which districts are known to be inhabited by *burakumin*. Usually their status can be determined from the *koseki* (family registry) maintained by government offices. Since the 1970s there have been activist citizen groups advocating affirmative-action policies, social welfare programs and an end to pervasive discrimination. For the estimated 1 million Japanese who live with this stigma, greater sensitivity to their plight and supportive government programs have brought some limited relief, but they remain an underclass and a target of discrimination.

Gaijin (foreigners) from around the world encounter both the kindness and hospitality of Japanese and petty discrimination. In general, whites are treated better than other foreigners but do suffer some of the indignities and discrimination that Asians, Middle Easterners and Africans are frequently subjected to. Some real estate agencies refuse to assist foreigners. Shops, bars and restaurants still have signs barring entry for non-Japanese and other forms of harassment are regularly experienced. Many foreigners have good experiences in Japan – getting married, raising families and settling – but for too many *gaijin* significant negative experiences resulting from racism leave a lingering impression. The Ministry of Education has facilitated the arrival of large numbers of foreign students in Japan by offering scholarships in the hopes of building cultural bridges. However, government surveys indicate that for many of these foreign students the rich educational opportunities are offset by the negative images they bring home due to discriminatory treatment. In many cases this may not be a result of overt racism, but more a reflection of the closed nature of Japanese society that leaves many visitors with a feeling that they are not entirely welcome. Even *gaijin* who become fluent in Japanese and knowledgeable about Japan's history and culture often assert, and resent, that they are left on the outside.

Given the importance that the government places on *kokusaika* (internationalization) and the new demands that globalization is placing on Japanese society, the experiences of foreigners in Japan raise troubling questions about the future integration of Japan in the world community. Ivan Hall charges that Japanese insularity has fostered 'cartels of the mind' that perpetuate prejudice (Hall, 1997). Such narrow-mindedness among the elite of Japan leads to non-reciprocal and unsatisfying interactions with the rest of the world and the foreigners who come to Japan. He identifies the intellectual attitudes, institutional structures, ideological defenses and cultural hubris that drive Japanese parochialism, arguing that this undermines the interests of nations that interact with Japan. In his view, Japan benefits greatly from the opportunities available to Japanese journalists, academics, and lawyers overseas, but fails to make the same compromises and accommodations that would enable foreigners to enjoy similar benefits in Japan. Ultimately, the double standards he identifies in Japan constitute significant impediments to Japan's participation in the world community and run counter to its interests.

CHAPTER ELEVEN

IN RETROSPECT

The transformation of Japan over the last five decades of the twentieth century has been momentous, recasting the social, political, economic and cultural landscape. The pace and breadth of change has been staggering and yet some aspects of Japan seem unchanged or only slightly modified. Pockets of rural Japan remain repositories of a vanishing era while the small shops, factories and *nomiya* (bars) of *shitamachi* (downtown) remain redolent of the sounds, smells, flavors and relationships conjured up by nostalgic memories about how Japan used to be (or might have been), almost frozen in time. Time-honored traditions persist and some aspects of society still function on established patterns, but the scope of continuity has been overwhelmed by the metamorphosis of modern Japan.

Postwar Japan has experienced success in reconstructing a war-ravaged nation, raising living standards, renovating democracy, taming militarism and rejoining the community of nations. This far-reaching rehabilitation of Japan in a few decades marks an extraordinary achievement and has led to significant advances in the lives of Japan's citizens. It is stunning that despite this whirlwind of tumultuous and deracinating transformation, Japan has preserved and augmented its social capital and avoided the worst of the scourges that plague other advanced, industrialized nations. The absence of deep cleavages in society, the highly developed sense of community and success in containing the dislocation and social ills of modernization are a source of considerable strength in Japan. People are better housed, better educated, healthier, live longer and are, by virtually any yardstick, better off than their predecessors and most other people in the world. They have enjoyed political stability, economic security, low crime, good health care, decent schools, adequate housing and an extraordinary level of public politesse. Even during the prolonged adversity of the 1990s, the social fallout has been limited. Japan has not avoided the usual problems of industrialized societies, but seems to have done a better job in containing, and coping with, these problems.

The postwar model, however, has run out of steam and has lost much of its credibility [*Doc. 31*]. By century's end, the limits and constraints of this model have become ever more apparent. People do not seem particularly appreciative or buoyed by the startling success of the postwar era, and instead evince apprehension about the wide range of reforms that are currently being implemented to address the problems of a system no longer thought capable of meeting the challenges of contemporary Japan. Whether these reforms will succeed in turning the tide is unclear, but they promise more volatility and uncertainty.

There is considerable ambivalence about the rapidity of change and the erosion of tenets and verities many Japanese feel have been important to their identity as a people, their cohesion as a community and their success as a nation. This turmoil is reflected in the mix of progressive yearnings and conservative inertias that animate *fin-de-siècle* Japan. The knowledge that transformation is happening and that more is needed does not mean that the reshaping of Japan is entirely welcome. People are caught between what they see as the loss of defining values and a pragmatic assessment that it is time for modifying and discarding many of these ideals and patterns of the past which are no longer tenable in vastly altered circumstances. There is a pervasive recognition that the various quandaries facing Japan, which have been discussed in preceding chapters, are forcing change, some of which is considered overdue and necessary for improving the prospects of individuals and the nation as a whole. The vested interests of the status quo have vigilantly and successfully defended their prerogatives and interests over the decades, slowing the pace of change and diverting the impetus of reform. They continue to do so but with less success because more and more people chafe under the current system and see it as a threat to their interests.

The logic of the economic and political arrangements that have animated Japan in the latter half of the twentieth century is changing. The concatenation of common interests and agendas that bound the Iron Triangle (big business, the bureaucracy and the LDP) was never seamless and is growing less so. In conjunction with structural economic changes that are driving the 'creative destruction' of Japan Inc., there is a changing of the guard in the business world. Old-guard heavy industry is giving way to the rising companies in information technology, which espouse a different world-view and have different expectations of government. The entrepreneurial spirit that is driving Japan's IT revolution is forcing a reconsideration of educational methods, management practices and government intervention. The consequences of structural economic change will be drawn out over an extended period of time, coexisting with but incrementally subsuming the existing paradigm. This means that the private sector in the twenty-first century will gradually look less and less like the big business that has dominated the commanding heights of the economy in the postwar era. Japan will retain a strong manufacturing base, but its importance will decline relative to services and the variety of businesses linked with IT. The restructuring of corporate Japan and the changing structure of the economy suggest the possibility of significant changes in government and politics that are foreshadowed by recent moves towards deregulation, campaign finance reform and greater transparency and accountability.

Perhaps the greatest change has been in the attitudes of individual Japanese. People act less subserviently and reverently to their elected officials, civil servants, teachers, corporate titans and others who hold positions that once conferred status, power and respect. There is a sense that the edifice of power is slowly eroding, as are the foundations of that system. As a result, society is in flux and entering uncharted waters, looking for new solutions to growing social and economic problems. Uncertainty, angst and despair have inspired an incremental and hesitant social movement with no nerve center or impetus other than the rising aspirations of people and their frustrations with a sclerotic status quo. Over the decades, holding the government and corporations accountable for their actions or negligence has slowly become normal, while demands for transparency are no longer viewed as the dangerous demands of radical idealists. When faced with problems, many Japanese shrug their shoulders and seek refuge in expressions such as *shigatakanai* ('nothing can be done') and *akirameru* ('reluctant resignation'), but these inclinations are slowly fading, giving way to greater assertiveness and higher expectations among a growing number of people. This is not so much a rise of political consciousness or activism as it is a reflection of people's rising sense of entitlement and awareness of the way things are in other advanced societies around the world. Satellite television, the internet, ubiquitous telephone service, an information-churning mass media and the transformation of overseas travel from an unheard-of luxury to an item of mass consumption have had an enormous impact even in the most remote hamlets and islands. The power over disseminating information that has been a key component of the status quo is ebbing quickly in the face of a more questioning polity and a society in which the flow of information is relatively unhindered. People know more, trust less and are thus less tolerant of the opaque ways of the past. Politicians, bureaucrats and corporate leaders often may not measure up to these rising expectations and standards, but episodically and gradually they are responding. The conduct of government, business and individuals is subject to more intensified scrutiny and being assessed by a better informed and less tolerant public, creating an atmosphere conducive to improved performance, lapses notwithstanding.

Are the Japanese enjoying a more robust democracy and greater freedom, equality and justice? There is no consensus on this question. On balance, in this writer's view, there is a great deal more freedom in society, a greater accommodation and tolerance of diversity and alternative lifestyles. There are more choices and possibilities for young Japanese now than there were in the early 1950s. Although voter participation rates have grown anaemic, the disaffection of voters may not necessarily signal a decline in democracy. The media and public have become more aggressive in holding the government accountable and exposing malfeasance, negligence and incompetence. In addition, citizens' groups and non-governmental organizations have proliferated while the status-quo parties seem to have begun a wrenching and slow process of political reform in response to pressure and criticism. It is too early to assess what the impact of current reformist tendencies will be, but the information revolution is making it ever more difficult to bamboozle and muzzle the public and it is difficult to see this trend abating. In that sense, the prospects for a more robust democracy seem reasonably good.

In terms of equality, there does appear to be a widening gap in wealth and income. The current reforms sweeping through the business world have placed growing emphasis on merit and market-oriented solutions that will accentuate differences in income. Society seems inclined to accept that equal opportunity does not have to translate into equal outcomes, an attitude that reflects and supports this significant change. However, public debate over decreased social mobility and widening income disparities may yet generate a backlash against the 'winners and losers', polarizing scenario it implies.

In terms of justice, the record is mixed. Critics charge that the judiciary regularly appears reluctant to exercise its independence in cases that involve government interests. For most Japanese, however, there does not appear to be any gross sense of injustice and the law seems to be applied more or less equally to most citizens. Outrage over the favorable treatment sometimes accorded to high-ranking politicians and bureaucrats is muted. For minorities, foreigners and women, justice has proved more elusive, but recent court rulings suggest that the trend is towards more justice for those who have been burdened by more extensive experience with injustice. Some of the more onerous and egregious discriminatory requirements, regulations and abuses have abated and there is no reason to doubt the prospects for further, if only gradual, improvements.

TRANSFORMATION?

Paradoxically, as Japan enters the twenty-first century one can find signs of both an air of expectation that prevailing conditions are improving and widespread pessimism that life will be better in the future. This is a time of confusion and uncertainty as the success of transforming postwar Japan into a global economic powerhouse has given way to introspection about what went wrong. Why have the fruits of success been both so fleeting and so unsatisfying? The lost decade of the 1990s was a time when unprecedented amounts of wealth evaporated, legions of companies went bankrupt, employment security began to fade and the public's confidence in its leaders reached a nadir in response to a cascade of corruption scandals involving government bureaucrats, politicians and corporate managers. It has been a time when trust in the elite and faith in their competence has given way to widespread skepticism. The mantra of reform, deregulation and restructuring echoing throughout the archipelago – meaning different things to different people – signifies that the norms and ways of the past have been irretrievably discredited and are no longer sacrosanct. There is an acknowledgement that Japan needs renovation and transformation, even though various groups and vested interests are working to ensure that this proceeds slowly or bypasses their turf. The key is whether Japan can repeat the success it had in overcoming the odds to transform its institutions radically as it did in the mid-nineteenth century following the Meiji restoration and during the mid-twentieth century during the American Occupation. At these crucial junctures, Japan did meet the challenges of a changing world, but this does not mean that it can do so again.

The jury is still out on whether contemporary Japan is doing what it needs to do with sufficient dispatch. Will the government's zeal for managing change end up stifling and limiting the positive consequences of reform? There is evidence on both sides of this question and it will take time before anyone can answer with certainty whether or not Japan has managed yet again to turn calamity to its advantage. For those who focus on the demographic time-bomb, there is scant basis for optimism because there do not seem to be any comforting and convincing solutions to the rapid graying of society. And, even if policy changes might help alleviate some of these problems, the voting public will become increasingly aged and thus more conservative, disinclined to support radical reform measures and protective of their pensions and medical care. How can change occur in a society that will have so many elderly people who favor risk-averse policies consistent with minimal disruption to the status quo?

On the other hand, Japan has demonstrated a great capacity for change. It still has some of the most dynamic global companies, boasts the second-largest economy in the world and has an enormous store of social capital. And, many people are favorably disposed to reform and most see the need for retreating from key features of the current paradigm that are no longer seen to serve the interests of society. The ongoing proliferation and dissemination of technology is creating new frontiers and breathing dynamism into what had become a relatively moribund nation, forcing the reconsideration of what is possible and undermining confident predictions about what society will be like a few decades down the road. As it is still early on in the process of forging a new paradigm, what appear to be intractable troubles today may become manageable in ways that cannot be foreseen now. Also working in Japan's favor is the prospect of more fully tapping the potential of its women, a highly educated pool of human capital that has, in many respects, been squandered due to antediluvian attitudes and practices. The impending labor shortage is expected to open up opportunities for women and they will be given a greater chance to develop and use their skills. In this way perhaps Japan can address the overdue transition from an economy based on 'perspiration' (growth based on increasing inputs of labor and/or capital) to one that relies on 'inspiration' (growth based on innovation and rising productivity) (Krugman, 1994). It is also promising that the rising generation of workers are far more adept with IT than their predecessors, allowing Japan to tap this potential more fully. Finally, there is also reason for cautious optimism about the future because of the accumulated frustration with being a country that enjoys wealth without prosperity (McCormack, 1996). Japan can look forward to this new frontier where the economic development and wealth that has been generated in the latter half of the twentieth century becomes the basis for spreading the amenities of prosperity.

1.   THE 1947 CONSTITUTION

2.   JOHN DOWER ON THE US OCCUPATION OF JAPAN

3.   THE TREATY OF MUTUAL COOPERATION AND SECURITY BETWEEN JAPAN AND THE US, 19 JANUARY 1960

4.   CHALMERS JOHNSON ON THE JAPANESE MIRACLE

5.   THE PLAN TO DOUBLE INDIVIDUAL INCOME, 27 DECEMBER 1960

6.   THE WAR APOLOGY RESOLUTION: THE PRIME MINISTER'S ADDRESS TO THE NATIONAL DIET, 9 JUNE 1995

7.   PRIME MINISTER MURAYAMA'S APOLOGY, 15 AUGUST 1995

8.   RECOVERING THE RIGHT TO BE PART OF ASIA (KENZABURO OE)

9.   GOVERNMENT CENSORSHIP AND THE VETTING OF TEXTBOOKS

10.   THE NANKING MASSACRE

11.   THE ODA CHARTER

12.   BEYOND THE ASIAN CRISIS: SPEECH BY MR KIICHI MIYAZAWA ON THE OCCASION OF THE APEC FINANCE MINISTERS' MEETING, LANGKAWI, MALAYSIA, 15 MAY 1999

13.   JAPAN AND THE DEPLOYMENT OF NUCLEAR WEAPONS

14.   SHINTARO ISHIHARA ON JAPAN'S RELATIONSHIP WITH THE US

15.   ON THE REVISION OF THE US–JAPAN SECURITY TREATY, 1960

16.   THE GUIDELINES FOR US–JAPAN DEFENSE COOPERATION (ABRIDGED), 23 SEPTEMBER 1997

17.   MORIHIRO HOSOKAWA ON THE NEW SECURITY GUIDELINES, 5 MARCH 1999

18.   NIXON ON US RELATIONS WITH JAPAN DURING THE COLD WAR

19.   JAPAN'S ROLE IN THE INTERNATIONAL COMMUNITY

20.   THE GOVERNMENT'S POSITION ON ARTICLE NINE OF THE CONSTITUTION

21.   FRANCIS FUKUYAMA ON THE CONSEQUENCES OF THE CONTRACEPTIVE PILL

22.   THE SEXUAL EXPLOITATION OF WOMEN IN JAPAN

23.   SOCIAL POLICY FOR AN AGING POPULATION

24.   JAPAN'S DEMOGRAPHIC CRISIS: THE SOCIAL AND ECONOMIC IMPLICATIONS

25.   RICHARD KATZ ON THE RISE AND FALL OF JAPAN'S ECONOMIC MIRACLE

26.   THE DESTINY OF SALARIED WORKERS

27.   ECONOMIC LIBERALIZATION AND REFORM: JAPAN'S 'BIG BANG'

28.   JAPAN'S THIRD TRANSFORMATION: THE FIVE BRIDGES TO THE TWENTY-FIRST CENTURY

29.   MASAO MIYAMOTO ON BUREAUCRACY AND CONFORMITY IN JAPAN

30.   MULTI-ETHNICITY IN JAPAN

31.   JAPAN IN THE 1990s: ICHIRO OZAWA'S FIVE FREEDOMS

The Constitution was written in February 1946 at the orders of General MacArthur who was in charge of the Supreme Command of the Allied Powers (SCAP) that ruled Japan during the Occupation (1945–52). The earlier Japanese attempt to revise the Meiji Constitution was judged inadequate by MacArthur and his aides in correcting the problems of overly concentrated power and did not go far enough in terms of promoting civil liberties and making the government accountable to the people. The new Constitution was drafted in two weeks by a small group of Americans who lacked any formal training in constitutional law. General MacArthur has been credited with inserting Article Nine renouncing war. This Constitution was translated into Japanese and presented to the Japanese political leadership for their approval at SCAP insistence. It was promulgated with minor revisions in 1947.

Preamble,
We, the Japanese people, acting through our duly elected representatives in the National Diet, determined that we shall secure for ourselves and our posterity the fruits of peaceful cooperation with all nations and the blessings of liberty throughout this land, and resolved that never again shall we be visited with the horrors of war through the action of government, do proclaim that sovereign power resides with the people and do firmly establish this Constitution. Government is a sacred trust of the people, the authority for which is derived from the people, the powers of which are exercised by the representatives of the people, and the benefits of which are enjoyed by the people. This is a universal principle of mankind upon which this Constitution is founded. We reject and revoke all constitutions, laws, ordinances and rescripts in conflict herewith.

We, the people, desire peace for all time and are deeply conscious of the high ideals controlling human relationships, and we have determined to preserve our security and existence, trusting in the justice and faith of the peace-loving peoples of the world. We desire to occupy an honored place in an international society striving for the preservation of peace and the banishment of tyranny and slavery, oppression and intolerance for all time from the earth. We recognize that all peoples of the world have the right to live in peace, free from fear and want.

We believe that no nation is responsible to itself alone, but that laws of political morality are universal; and that obedience to such laws is incumbent upon all nations who would sustain their own sovereignty and justify their sovereign relationship with other nations.

We, the Japanese people, pledge our national honor to accomplish these high ideals and purposes with all our resources.

Chapter 1. The Emperor

Article 1. The Emperor shall be the symbol of the State and the unity of the people, deriving his position from the will of the people with whom resides sovereign power.

Article 2. The Imperial Throne shall be dynastic and succeeded to in accordance with the Imperial House Law passed by the Diet.

Article 3. The advice and approval of the Cabinet shall be required for all acts of the Emperor in matters of state, and the Cabinet shall be responsible therefore.

Article 4. The Emperor shall perform only such acts in matters of state as are provided for in this Constitution, and he shall not have power related to government. ...

Chapter 2. Renunciation of War

Article 9. Aspiring sincerely to an international peace based on justice and order, the Japanese people forever renounce war as a sovereign right of the nation and the threat or use of force as means of settling international disputes.

In order to accomplish the aim of the preceding paragraph, land, sea and air forces, as well as other war potential, will never be maintained. The right of belligerency of the state will not be recognized.

Chapter 3. Rights and Duties of the People

Article 11. The people shall not be prevented from enjoying any of the fundamental human rights.

These fundamental human rights guaranteed to the people by this constitution shall be conferred on the people of this and future generations as eternal and inviolate rights.

Article 13. All of the people shall be respected as individuals. Their rights to life, liberty, and the pursuit of happiness, to the extent that it does not interfere with the public welfare, will be the supreme consideration in legislation and other governmental affairs.

Article 14. All of the people are equal under the law, and there shall be no discrimination in political, economic, or social relations because of race, creed, sex, social status, or family origin.

Peers and peerage shall not be recognized.

No privilege shall accompany any award of honor, decoration, or any distinction, nor shall any such award be valid beyond the lifetime of the individual who now holds or hereafter may receive it.

Article 15. The people have the inalienable right to choose their public officials and to dismiss them.

All public officials are servants of the whole community and not of any group thereof.

Universal adult suffrage is guaranteed with regard to the election of public officials.

In all elections, secrecy of the ballot shall not be violated. A voter shall not be answerable, publicly or privately, for the choice he has made. ...

Article 20. Freedom of religion is guaranteed to all. No religious organization shall receive any privileges from the State nor exercise any political authority.

No person shall be compelled to take part in any religious act, celebration, rite, or practice.

The State and its organs shall refrain from religious education or any religious activity.

Article 21. Freedom of assembly and association as well as speech, press, and all other forms of expression are guaranteed.

No censorship shall be maintained, nor shall the secrecy of any communication be violated. ...

Article 24. Marriage shall be based only on the mutual consent of both sexes, and it shall be maintained through mutual cooperation with the equal rights of husband and wife as a basis.

With regard to choice of spouse, property rights, inheritance, choice of domicile, divorce and other matters pertaining to marriage and the family, laws shall be enacted from the standpoint of individual dignity and the essential equality of the sexes. ...

Article 28. The right of workers to organize and bargain and act collectively is guaranteed. ...

Article 37. In all criminal cases, the accused shall enjoy the right to a speedy and public trial by an impartial tribunal.

He shall be permitted full opportunity to examine all witnesses, and he shall have the right of compulsory process for obtaining witnesses on his behalf at public expense.

At all times the accused shall have the assistance of competent counsel who shall, if the accused is unable to secure the same by his own efforts, be assigned to his use by the State. ...

Chapter 4. The Diet

Article 41. The Diet shall be the highest organ of state power and shall be the sole lawmaking organ of the State.

Article 42. The Diet shall consist of two Houses, namely, the House of Representatives and the House of Councilors.

Article 43. Both Houses shall consist of elected members, representatives of all the people.

Article 60. The budget must first be submitted to the House of Representatives.

Upon consideration of the budget, when the House of Councilors makes a decision different from that of the House of Representatives, and when no agreement can be reached even through a joint committee of both Houses, provided for by law, or in the case of failure by the House of Councilors to take final action in thirty days, the period of recess excluded, after the receipt of the budget passed by the House of Representatives, the decision of the House of Representatives shall be the decision of the Diet.

Chapter 5. The Cabinet

Article 65. Executive power shall be vested in the Cabinet.

Article 66. The Cabinet shall consist of the Prime Minister, who shall be its head, and other Ministers of State, as provided for by law.

The Prime Minister and other Ministers of State must be civilians.

The Cabinet, in the exercise of executive power, shall be collectively responsible to the Diet. ...

Chapter 6. The Judiciary

Article 76. The whole judicial power is vested in a Supreme Court and in such inferior courts as are established by law. ...

From Gary Allenson, *The Columbia Guide to Modern Japanese History*.
New York: Columbia University Press, 1999, pp. 233–6.

DOCUMENT 2   JOHN DOWER ON THE US OCCUPATION OF JAPAN

Dower is the pre-eminent historian of the Occupation and won the National Book Award for this book, Embracing Defeat: Japan in the Wake of Defeat. *He focuses on the paradoxes and ironies of Americans imposing democracy, leading a revolution from above with minimal consultation with the people. His work is especially useful in providing details about how the Japanese people perceived and participated in the Occupation and how the Americans fell short of their ideals and principles in remaking Japan.*

... [T]he contradictions of the democratic revolution from above were clear for all to see: while the victors preached democracy, they ruled by fiat; while they espoused equality, they themselves constituted an inviolate privileged caste. Their reformist agenda rested on the assumption that, virtually without exception, Western culture and its values were superior to those of 'the Orient.' At the same time, almost every interaction between victor and vanquished was infused with intimations of white supremacism. For all its uniqueness of time, place, and circumstance – all its peculiarly 'American' iconoclasm – the occupation was in this sense but a new manifestation of the old racial paternalism that historically accompanied the global expansion of the Western powers. Like their colonialist predecessors, the victors were imbued with a sense of manifest destiny. They spoke of being engaged in the mission of civilizing their subjects. They bore the burden (in their own eyes) of their race, creed, and culture. They swaggered, and were enviously free of self-doubt.

It was inevitable that relations between the victors and the vanquished be unequal, but this inequality was compounded by authoritarian practices that were part and parcel of the American modus operandi independent of the situation in Japan. To begin with, the administrative structure that the Japanese encountered was itself organized in the most rigid hierarchical manner imaginable. MacArthur's command, after all, was a military bureaucracy, the very organizational antithesis of democratic checks and balances.

This working model of authoritarian governance was compounded by the manner in which the occupation regime implemented its directives. Contrary to the practice of direct military government adopted in defeated Germany, this occupation was conducted 'indirectly' – that is, through existing organs of government. This entailed buttressing the influence of two of the most undemocratic institutions of the presurrender regime: the bureaucracy and the throne.

From John Dower, *Embracing Defeat: Japan in the Wake of Defeat*,
New York: W.W. Norton, 1999, pp. 211–12.

DOCUMENT 3	THE TREATY OF MUTUAL COOPERATION AND SECURITY BETWEEN JAPAN AND THE US, 19 JANUARY 1960

This revision of the 1951 Security Treaty sparked riots, demonstrations and polarized politics in Japan. While it did remove the right of US forces to intervene in the event of domestic disorder, it extended the right of the US to maintain and use military bases in Japan. Critics looked upon this extensive US military presence as a continuation of the Occupation and an encroachment on Japanese sovereignty. The resulting controversy forced the resignation of Prime Minister Kishi and made the US alliance the focal point of opposition politics in the 1960s.

Japan and the United States of America,
Desiring to strengthen the bonds of peace and friendship traditionally existing between them, and to uphold the principles of democracy, individual liberty, and the rule of law,

Desiring further to encourage closer economic cooperation between them and to promote conditions of economic stability and well being in their countries,

Reaffirming their faith in the purpose and principles of the Charter of the United Nations, and their desire to live in peace with all peoples and all governments,

Recognizing that they have the inherent right of individual or collective self-defense as affirmed in the Charter of the United Nations,

Considering that they have a common concern in the maintenance of international peace and security in the Far East,

Having resolved to conclude a treaty of mutual cooperation and security,

Therefore agree as follows:

Article I

The Parties undertake, as set forth in the charter of the United Nations, to settle any international disputes in which they may be involved by peaceful means in such a manner that international peace and security and justice are not endangered and to refrain in their international relations from the threat or use of force against the territorial integrity or political independence of any state, or in any other manner inconsistent with the purposes of the United Nations.

The Parties will endeavor in concert with other peace-loving countries to strengthen the United Nations so that its mission of maintaining international peace and security may be discharged more effectively.

Article II

The Parties will contribute toward the further development of peaceful and friendly international relations by strengthening their free institutions, by bringing about a better understanding of the principles upon which these institutions are founded, and by promoting conditions of stability and well-being. They will seek to eliminate conflict in their international economic policies and will encourage economic collaboration between them.

Article III

The Parties, individually and in cooperation with each other, by means of continuous and effective self-help and mutual aid will maintain and develop, subject to their constitutional provisions, their capacities to resist armed attack.

Article IV

The Parties will consult together from time to time regarding the implementation of this Treaty, and, at the request of either Party, whenever the security of Japan or international peace and security in the Far East is threatened.

Article V

Each Party recognizes that an armed attack against their Party in the territories under the administration of Japan would be dangerous to its own peace and safety and declares that it would act to meet the common danger in accordance with its constitutional provisions and processes.

Any such armed attack and all measures taken as a result thereof shall be immediately reported to the Security Council of the United Nations in accordance with the provisions of Article 51 of the Charter. Such measures shall be terminated when the Security Council has taken the measures necessary to restore and maintain international peace and security.

Article VI

For the purpose of contributing to the security of Japan and the maintenance of international peace and security in the Far East, the United States of America is granted the use by its land, air and naval forces of facilities and areas in Japan.

The use of these facilities and areas as well as the status of United States armed forces in Japan shall be governed by a separate agreement, replacing the Administrative Agreement under Article III of the Security Treaty between Japan and the United States of America, signed at Tokyo on February 28, 1952, as amended, and by such other arrangements as may be agreed upon.

Article VII

This Treaty does not affect and shall not be interpreted as affecting in any way the rights and obligations of the Parties under the Charter of the United Nations or the responsibility of the United Nations for the maintenance of international peace and security.

Article VIII

This treaty shall be ratified by Japan and the United States of America in accordance with their respective constitutional processes and will enter into force on the date on which the instruments of ratification thereof have been exchanged by them in Tokyo.

Article IX

The Security Treaty between Japan and the United States of America signed at the city of San Francisco on September 8, 1951, shall expire upon the entering into force of this Treaty.

Article X

This Treaty shall remain in force until in the opinion of the governments of Japan and the United States of America there shall have come into force such United Nations arrangements as will satisfactorily provide for the maintenance of international peace and security in the Japan area.

However, after the Treaty has been in force for ten years, either Party may give notice to the other Party of its intention to terminate the Treaty, in which case the Treaty shall terminate one year after such notice has been given.

From US Department of State, *United States Treaties and Other Agreements,* vol. 2, pt 2, Washington DC: Government Printing Office, 1961, pp. 1633–5.

DOCUMENT 4   CHALMERS JOHNSON ON THE JAPANESE
             MIRACLE

*Johnson represents what is loosely termed the revisionist camp among
scholars and commentators specializing on Japan. He and others since have
challenged the more benign and less critical interpretations of Japan by
orthodox Japan-hands such as Edwin Reischauer, who are sometimes termed
the Chrysanthemum Club, a reference to the flower used in the Imperial crest.
This seminal work came out at a time of rising Japanese trade surpluses with
the US and gained considerable attention for its elucidation of the Japanese
government's role in guiding and nurturing the economy. His views continue
to influence public perceptions in the US and stoke concerns that the Japanese
government has orchestrated predatory and unfair trading practices harmful
to US interests.*

One clear lesson from the Japanese case is that the state needs the market
and private enterprise needs the state; once both sides recognized this,
cooperation was possible and high speed growth occurred.

Japan offers a panopoly of market-conforming methods of state intervention, including the creation of government financial institutions, whose
influence is as much indicative as it is monetary; the extensive use, narrow
targeting, and timely revision of tax incentives; the use of indicative plans to
set goals and guidelines for the entire economy; the creation of numerous,
formal, and continuously operating forums for exchanging views, reviewing
policies, obtaining feedback, and resolving differences; the assignment of
some governmental functions to various private and semiprivate associations
(JETRO, Keidanren); an extensive reliance on public corporations, particularly of the mixed public–private variety, to implement policy in high risk
or otherwise refractory areas; the creation and use by the government of an
unconsolidated 'investment budget' separate from and not funded by the
general account budget; the orientation of anti-trust policy to developmental
and international competitive goals rather than strictly to the maintenance
of domestic competition; government-conducted or government-sponsored
research and development (the computer industry); and the use of the government's licensing and approval authority to achieve developmental goals.

Perhaps the most important market-conforming method of intervention
is administrative guidance. This power, which amounts to an allocation of
discretionary and unsupervised authority to the bureaucracy, is obviously
open to abuse, and may, if used improperly, result in damage to the market.
But it is an essential power of the capitalist developmental state for one
critical reason: it is necessary to avoid overly detailed laws that, by their
very nature, are never detailed enough to cover all contingencies and yet,
because of their detail, put a strait jacket on creative administration. ... The

Japanese political economy is strikingly free of lawyers; many of the functions performed by lawyers in other societies are performed in Japan by bureaucrats using administrative guidance.

From Chalmers Johnson, *MITI and the Japanese Miracle: The Growth of Industrial Policy, 1925–1975*, Stanford, CA: Stanford University Press, 1982, pp. 318–19.

DOCUMENT 5   THE PLAN TO DOUBLE INDIVIDUAL INCOME, 27 DECEMBER 1960

Hayato Ikeda (1899–1965) became prime minister in July 1960 and introduced the Income Doubling Plan. In response to the political turmoil associated with revision of the Security Treaty, his government sought to refocus attention on economic matters. This so-called GNPism was represented by the plan for doubling individual income adopted by his cabinet in December 1960. This optimistic plan and supportive policies of the government helped Japan achieve high growth in the decade of the 1960s. Japan's GNP grew at an average annual rate of 10.6 percent in that decade, outpacing the 4.1 percent growth rate in the US. At the end of the 1960s, the manufacturing sector accounted for 30 percent of Japan's GNP, setting the stage for explosive export growth and the nation's emergence as an economic superpower.

1. Objectives of this Plan

The plan to double the individual income must have as its objectives the doubling of the gross national product, attainment of full employment through expansion of employment opportunities, and raising the living standards of our people. We must adjust differentials in living standards and income existing between farming and non-farming sectors, between large enterprises and small- and medium-size enterprises, between different regions of the country, and between different income groups. We must work toward a balanced development in our national economy and life patterns.

2. Targets to Be Attained

The plan's goal is to reach 26 trillion yen in GNP (at fiscal year 1958 prices) in the next ten years. To reach this goal, and in view of the fact that there are several factors highly favorable to economic growth existing during the first part of this plan, including the rapid development of technological changes and an abundant supply of skilled labor forces, we plan to attain an annual rate of growth of GNP at 9 percent for the coming three years. It is hoped that we shall be able to raise our GNP of 13.6 trillion yen (13 trillion yen in fiscal year 1958 prices) in fiscal year 1960 to 17.6 trillion yen (in 1960 prices) in fiscal year 1963 with the application of appropriate policies and cooperation from the private sector.

3. Points to Be Considered in Implementing the Plan and Directions to Be Followed

The plan contained in the report of the Economic Council (an advisory body to the Ministry of Trade and Industry that issued its report November 1, 1960) will be respected. However, in its implementation we must act flexibly and pay due consideration to the economic growth actually occurring and other related conditions. Any action we undertake must be consistent with the objectives described above. To do so, we shall pay special attention to the implementation of the following:

   a. Promotion of Modernization in Agriculture ...
   b. Modernization of Small- and Medium-Sized Enterprises ...
   c. Accelerated Development of Less Developed Regions
   d. Promotion of Appropriate Locations for Industries and Reexamination of Regional Distribution of Public-Sector Projects ...
   e. Active Cooperation with the Development of the World Economy ...

From Gary Allenson, *The Columbia Guide to Modern Japanese History*,
New York: Columbia University Press, 1999, 236–7.

DOCUMENT 6   THE WAR APOLOGY RESOLUTION: THE PRIME
MINISTER'S ADDRESS TO THE NATIONAL DIET,
9 JUNE 1995

The war apology resolution passed by the National Diet in June 1995 was a compromise hammered out among political parties. Progressives in Japan sought to use the 50th anniversary of the end of World War II to make an unequivocal apology to victims of Japanese aggression and thereby overcome lingering resentments and suspicions in Asia. Conservatives resisted making an unequivocal apology and accepting full responsibility for the consequences of the war. In their view, Japan's actions were justified and motivated by principled intentions and they argue that an acceptance of blame for the war would render the sacrifices of Japan's war dead and their families meaningless. The final wording of the apology resolution clouded the issue of responsibility and thus, in the eyes of many Japanese and other Asians, undermined the sincerity of the apology. The reference to 'colonial rule and acts of aggression in the modern world' has been interpreted as an attempt to mitigate Japan's actions and spread blame in a way that deflects attention away from the widespread atrocities committed by the Imperial armed forces.

PRIME MINISTER'S ADDRESS TO THE DIET, 9 JUNE 1995

1. I regard with all sincerity the fact that today the Diet has adopted this resolution, on the occasion of the 50th anniversary of the end of the war.
2. At this time, 50 years after the end of the war, the basic thinking of the Government is as I have made clear in statements and addresses to the Diet, and is consistent with the contents of this resolution. The Government will undertake to ensure that the essence of this resolution, which reaffirms the determination for peace while learning from the lessons of history, will be embodied in Japan's policies.
3. I would like to take this opportunity to express my most sincere condolences to all victims in Japan and abroad, and, based on our deep remorse for the past, to reaffirm my personal conviction that we must make every possible effort to build world peace.

RESOLUTION TO RENEW THE DETERMINATION FOR PEACE ON THE BASIS OF LESSONS LEARNED FROM HISTORY

House of Representatives, National Diet of Japan

The House of Representatives resolves as follows:

On the occasion of the 50th anniversary of the end of World War II, this House offers its sincere condolences to those who fell in action and victims of wars and similar actions all over the world.

Solemnly reflecting upon many instances of colonial rule and acts of aggression in the modern history of the world, and recognizing that Japan carried out those acts in the past, inflicting pain and suffering upon the peoples of other countries, especially in Asia, the Members of this House express a sense of deep remorse.

We must transcend the differences over historical views of the past war and learn humbly the lessons of history so as to build a peaceful international society.

This House expresses its resolve, under the banner of eternal peace enshrined in the Constitution of Japan, to join hands with other nations of the world and to pave the way to a future that allows all human beings to live together.

From the Ministry of Foreign Affairs web site: *www.mofa.go.jp*

Prime Minister Murayama, leader of the JSP coalition government with the LDP, used the 50th anniversary of Japan's surrender to articulate the progressive view of the war, to take unequivocal responsibility for the suffering inflicted on fellow Asians and to make a sincere apology for the atrocities caused by Japanese aggression. His remarks were well received in Asia and went a long way in dispelling the ill-will and negative impressions generated by the Diet's war resolution of June 1995.

The world has seen fifty years elapse since the war came to an end. Now, when I remember the many people both at home and abroad who fell victim to war, my heart is overwhelmed by a flood of emotions.

The peace and prosperity of today were built as Japan overcame great difficulty to arise from a devastated land after defeat in the war. That achievement is something of which we are proud, and let me herein express my heartfelt admiration for the wisdom and untiring effort of each and every one of our citizens. Let me also express once again my profound gratitude for the indispensable support and assistance extended to Japan by the countries of the world, beginning with the United States of America. I am also delighted that we have been able to build the friendly relations which we enjoy today with the neighboring countries of the Asia-Pacific region, the United States and the countries of Europe.

Now that Japan has come to enjoy peace and abundance, we tend to overlook the pricelessness and blessings of peace. Our task is to convey to younger generations the horrors of war, so that we never repeat the errors in our history. I believe that, as we join hands, especially with the peoples of neighboring countries, to ensure true peace in the Asia-Pacific region – indeed, in the entire world – it is necessary, more than anything else, that we foster relations with all countries based on deep understanding and trust. Guided by this conviction, the Government has launched the Peace, Friendship and Exchange Initiative, which consists of two parts, promoting: support for historical research into relations in the modern era between Japan and the neighboring countries of Asia and elsewhere; and rapid expansion of exchanges with those countries. Furthermore, I will continue in all sincerity to do my utmost in efforts being made on the issues arisen from the war, in order to further strengthen the relations of trust between Japan and those countries.

Now, upon this historic occasion of the 50th anniversary of the war's end, we should bear in mind that we must look into the past to learn from the lessons of history, and ensure that we do not stray from the path to the peace and prosperity of human society in the future.

During a certain period in the not too distant past, Japan, following a mistaken national policy, advanced along the road to war, only to ensnare the Japanese people in a fateful crisis, and, through its colonial rule and aggression, caused tremendous damage and suffering to the people of many countries, particularly to those of Asian nations. In the hope that no such mistake be made in the future, I regard, in a spirit of humility, these irrefutable facts of history, and express here once again my feelings of deep remorse and state my heartfelt apology. Allow me also to express my feelings of profound mourning for all victims, both at home and abroad, of that history.

Building from our deep remorse on this occasion of the 50th anniversary of the end of the war, Japan must eliminate self-righteous nationalism, promote international coordination as a responsible member of the international community and, thereby, advance the principles of peace and democracy. At the same time, as the only country to have experienced the devastation of atomic bombing, Japan, with a view to the ultimate elimination of nuclear weapons, must actively strive to further global disarmament in areas such as the strengthening of the nuclear non-proliferation regime. It is my conviction that in this way alone can Japan atone for its past and lay to rest the spirits of those who perished.

It is said that one can rely on good faith. And so, at this time of remembrance, I declare to the people of Japan and abroad my intention to make good faith the foundation of our Government policy, and this is my vow.

From the Ministry of Foreign Affairs web site: *www.mofa.go.jp*

DOCUMENT 8   **RECOVERING THE RIGHT TO BE PART OF ASIA (KENZABURO OE)**

Oe won the Nobel Prize for Literature in 1994. He is a prominent progressive intellectual, often vilified by conservatives and harassed by right-wing activists. He has steadfastly criticized Japan's heightened sense of war victimization and failure to come to terms with its own victimization of regional neighbors. Here he points out that people around the region and in Japan suffered from Japanese aggression in World War II and calls on the government to promote reconciliation by making a clear apology and offering compensation to Japan's victims.

The basic attitude of the Japanese government – that China hated what the military of Japan had done, but not the Japanese people – was maintained with thorough consistency. Needless to say, it was a gigantic fiction. The Chinese remember their brutal experiences and their stories of that time told from generation to generation. ...

For the Japanese to be able to regard 21st century Asia not as a new economic power rivaling the West but as a region in which Japan can be a true partner, they must first set up a basis that would enable them to criticize their neighbors and be criticized in turn. For this, Japan must apologize for its aggression and offer compensation. This is the basic condition, and most Japanese with a conscience have been for it. But a coalition of conservative parties, bureaucrats and business leaders opposes it. The resolution of remorse for Japanese conduct during WWII was supposed to apologize for the calamities that war brought to Asian nations, but it was watered down. And this most likely confirmed distrust of Japan.

But the feelings of the Japanese people are expressed by a 75-year-old woman. Her husband left her pregnant 10 months after they were married and was killed in Burma where some of the fiercest battles were fought. Her house and everything she possessed were then destroyed in an air raid. She wrote to a newspaper, 'The Association of the Families of the War Dead and the opposition groups in the Diet say things like, "This was a war of self-defense that Japan fought against its will" and "If we admit that we were the invaders, we are saying that those killed in battle died useless deaths." But our husbands were persuaded by the militarists that they were dying for the Emperor and for the country, and were herded into battlefields without knowing they were engaged in an invasion. The government committed aggression; our husbands were its victims.'

From Kenzaburo Oe, 'Recovering the Right to be Part of Asia',
Japan Times, 16 August 1995, p. 17.

DOCUMENT 9   **GOVERNMENT CENSORSHIP AND THE VETTING OF TEXTBOOKS**

Ienaga has opposed government censorship and Ministry of Education certification of school textbooks for the last four decades of the twentieth century, arguing that the educational reforms introduced by the Americans during the Occupation precluded such interventions. Certification is a vetting process by the Ministry of Education that enables it to suggest revisions in the texts and withhold approval from texts that do not meet its standards or expectations. He maintains that the Ministry has tried to whitewash Japan's history and believes that this does a disservice to the nation's honor, to its students and to the process of reconciliation with regional victims of Japanese aggression. His long crusade in the courts has featured both setbacks and victories, but he has succeeded in forcing a more open system of vetting textbooks.

Certification was extremely lax until the 1950s and there were almost no cases in which textbooks which disagreed with government ideology were excluded. The contents of textbooks were of course markedly changed as compared with the prewar period. Principles of democracy and peace were extolled instead of the emperor-system morality. Textbooks on Japanese history no longer began from the tales of the 'age of the gods' but from life in the stone age. As the emphasis shifted from emperor-, nobility-, and warrior-centered history to broader fields of society, economy, and culture Japanese history gave much more space to activities of common people.

It became possible to deal with such anti-Establishment movements as peasant revolts, the labor movement, the socialist movement, pacifism, and the truth about the Korean annexation and the invasion of China. Postwar historical education set out with the new aim, not of history as a means of cultivating anti-foreign or nationalist feelings, but of looking unflinchingly at both the bright and dark sides of a people's past, and of trying to help in the creation of future history.

Unfortunately, postwar reforms in education began to crumble in a few short years. Along with the intensification of the Cold War, the American occupation army abandoned the policies of democratization and demilitarization and began reviving Japan as part of the anticommunist camp. Japan's conservative government, which has maintained a semi-permanent majority of seats in the National Diet, welcomed the military alliance with the United States and pressed forward with policies of rearmament, undoing the democratic reforms and strengthening monopoly capital. These have been the fundamental factors in bringing about the abandonment of democratization in educational content.

The government 'course of study' has undergone repeated retrogressive revisions, and, as time has passed, democratic, pacifistic, and scientific hues have faded and such things as the obligation of serving the country, rearming, or of approving of military cooperation with the United States, and unscientific, 'emotional' patriotism, have come to be emphasized.

Measures to strengthen the power of educational administration, which have been advanced one after another in spite of strong opposition from teachers' unions, intellectuals, and others, have moved in the direction of government control of education.

Why have such policies, which run counter to the ideals of postwar educational reform, been steadily achieved? The basic reasons must be sought in such broad historical conditions as the continuation of the conservative government's firm rule, the establishment of the Japanese–American security treaty system, and the people's loss of political concern due to 'economic prosperity' within this system.

* * *

Especially during the wartime period, which lasted fifteen years from 1931, any scientific study of Japanese history was extremely difficult because of the harsh restrictions on freedom of thought and expression. There were taboos in all fields.

In accordance with my ideal plan I wrote a textbook of Japanese history for high schools. This textbook has been used constantly for two decades. ... In 1963 when my textbook failed to be approved, an official of the Education Ministry verbally notified the publisher and me of the reasons for its rejection. Reluctantly, I altered some points in the book and submitted the draft, which was then approved in 1964 on the condition that I modify almost 300 items.

Looking at all the items used as the pretext for the rejection and demanded modification, we can clearly see the tendency of the Education Ministry to control the content of historical education through the enforcement of state certification...

From Saburo Ienaga, 'The Historical Significance of the Japanese Textbook Lawsuit',
Bulletin of Concerned Asia Scholars, II:4 (Fall 1970), pp. 5–8.

DOCUMENT 10   THE NANKING MASSACRE

Conservatives still challenge established historical accounts of Japan's rampage through Asia between 1931 and 1945, arguing that this record has been falsified and distorted to discredit Japan and to extract concessions and reparations. They maintain that negative accounts of the Imperial armed forces reflect a 'victor's' history that demeans the sacrifices endured by Japanese on behalf of other Asians in trying to overturn the Western colonial order. Iris Chang's The Rape of Nanking *(1997) introduced this topic in a sensational manner to a wide audience, provoking the ire of Japanese conservatives who have either denied the massacre altogether or seek to minimize the atrocities. Honda (1999) presents a detailed account about the nature and extent of atrocities committed by Japanese troops based on interviews with Chinese survivors, Japanese soldiers, their diaries, contemporary media accounts and eyewitness reports by Europeans and Americans. Fogel (2000) and Brook (1999) provide additional evidence that belie assertions by Japanese conservatives that the Nanking Massacre is a myth. For a thoughtful comparison of how Germany and Japan have coped with the legacy of* World War II, *see Buruma (1994).*

A conference intended to play down Japan's record of atrocities during its occupation of China has unleashed a storm of criticism from Beijing and drawn strong condemnation from some historians and others in Japan.

The topic of the one-day conference, scheduled for Sunday in Japan's second largest city, Osaka, is the 1937 Nanjing Massacre, which organizers have provocatively called 'the biggest myth of the 20th century.'

The site selected for the meeting further stoked the ire of many in Japan. The conference will be in the city's International Peace Center, which houses permanent exhibits on war, including the American atomic bombing of Japan in World War II and Japan's brutal military campaign in China in the 1930s.

For several days running, the Chinese government and news media have bitterly attacked the conference as the work of people eager to falsify history and raise tensions between the two countries.

'By planning the rally, Japanese rightists want to distort history, paper over the aggression and undermine Sino-Japanese friendship,' said a Chinese foreign ministry spokesman, Zhu Bangzao, in a statement published in the official China Daily.

Ryutaro Nakakita, an Osaka lawyer opposed to the event, said that the organizers' intention was 'to bring chaos to a hall that was meant to promote peace, and to muddle history.' City officials say, however, that the Peace Center is a public place and that to refuse to allow the conference to be held there would be an infringement on free speech.

The organizers deny that the conference is meant to stir up trouble. They say it was conceived as a debate between experts who accept conventional accounts of the fall of Nanjing, which say that Japanese soldiers butchered as many as 300,000 people, and those who deny any large-scale atrocities took place.

'Originally, we had planned for a forum between the two sides, in order to verify the facts,' said Yasuhiko Yoshida, one of the organizers. 'But those who have claimed that there was a massacre declined to participate.'

Mainstream Japanese historians of the 1930s and 1940s, the period of Japan's aggressive militarism, say that to accept such an invitation is akin to legitimating the views of German extremists or others who would deny the existence of the Holocaust.

Although casualty estimates vary, it is widely accepted among scholars that after the sudden collapse of the Chinese defense of Nanjing in December 1937, rampaging Japanese soldiers executed thousands of prisoners of war, men suspected of being soldiers and civilians, and burned the homes of Chinese to keep warm. Thousands of Chinese women are also believed to have been raped.

In discussing this history, parallels with Germany are inevitably strained. Germany has broadly owned up to the horrors of its wartime past and has paid compensation to many of its victims. But Japan as a society has generally avoided any deep reflection and contrition over a period in which its army ran roughshod over much of Asia. It has generally refused to compensate its war victims and has even avoided paying veterans' benefits to Korean citizens forced to fight in Japan's defense.

Japan's aggression and the atrocities it entailed are treated only cursorily in most schools here. Even recent concessions to textbook reform in this area, like mention of the rape and sexual slavery of thousands of Korean and Chinese women, is under attack by conservatives, who cast doubt on the accounts and say these subjects should not be taught to young Japanese.

'The people claiming there was no Nanjing Massacre, including the organizers of this conference, are the people who would maintain that Japan's war in China was legitimate, that it was not an invasion,' said Tokushi Kasahara, a professor of Chinese modern history at Tsuru University in Tokyo. 'Many Japanese do not know much about these events, and the people of this camp are trying to influence them.'

But while fringe figures who deny the Holocaust exist in Germany and elsewhere, voices here dismissing or greatly playing down Japan's wartime crimes are regularly heard from the political, academic and media establishment. The governor of Tokyo, Shintaro Ishihara, for one, has frequently called the Nanjing Massacre a lie.

'People think by analogy that because Germans committed a Holocaust, that Japanese must have done something like that too,' said Dr. Shudo Higashinakano, a historian of social thought at Asia University in Tokyo. 'But you must look at the facts.'

Dr. Higashinakano, who is scheduled to speak at the Osaka conference, said the Nanjing Massacre, also commonly known as the Rape of Nanjing, was 'groundless war propaganda.'

From Howard W. French, 'Japanese Call '37 Massacre a War Myth, Stirring Storm', *New York Times*, 23 January 2000, p. 4.

DOCUMENT 11   THE ODA CHARTER

Japan has been the world's leading donor of Official Development Assistance (ODA) throughout the 1990s. The government developed a set of criteria for determining the provision of aid in order to clarify under what conditions ODA might be withheld from a recipient nation. Critics have argued that Japan has not rigorously applied its own principles as articulated in the ODA Charter. This document from the Ministry of Foreign Affairs explains the government of Japan's position on aid, discussing various cases that illustrate the flexible, case-by-case application of the criteria set forth in the ODA Charter.

Adopted as a cabinet decision in June 1992, Japan's ODA Charter demands the observance of several important principles with a bearing on the provision of aid. Though decisions on aid should be based on a comprehensive assessment of aid requests, economic and social conditions, bilateral relations, and other factors, the Charter also urges consideration of four key factors: namely, (i) pursuit in tandem of environmental conservation and development, (ii) avoidance of any use of ODA for military purposes or for aggravation of international conflicts, (iii) full attention to trends in recipient countries' military expenditures, their development and production of weapons of mass destruction and missiles and their export and import of arms, etc. and (iv) full attention to efforts for promoting democratization and introduction of a market-oriented economy, and the situation regarding securing basic human rights and freedoms in the recipient country.

In keeping with the principles of its ODA Charter, Japan has actively provided assistance to Mongolia, Vietnam, and several countries in Central Asia because they have all demonstrated acceptable progress in terms of democratization and the transition to free-market economic systems.

By contrast, the nuclear tests that India and Pakistan conducted in May 1998 forced Japan, in consideration of its ODA Charter, to adopt strict countermeasures. To be sure, the nuclear policies of both those countries had been in question for some time. Working through bilateral forums on aid, nuclear non-proliferation, and other policy dialogues, Japan and other countries concerned had urged that India and Pakistan rein in their nuclear weapons and missile development programs and sign the Non-Proliferation Treaty (NPT) as well as the Comprehensive Test Ban Treaty (CTBT). However, the Vajpayee Administration that assumed power in March 1998 raised further doubts about India's nuclear policies by declaring a policy guideline of the coalition government, in which India would exercise the option to become a nuclear-armed state. Though the Japanese government urged through high-level channels that it assume a policy of restraint, India decided instead to conduct underground nuclear tests in May 1998, going thus against the global trend toward a comprehensive ban on nuclear testing. Japan immediately and strongly protested, and, in consideration of the principles of its ODA Charter, decided to halt the provision of new grant aid (other than grant assistance for grassroots projects or of an emergency, humanitarian nature) and new yen loans, and to carefully consider any loans for India through multilateral development banks.

Following the Indian nuclear tests, Japan sent a Prime Minister's envoy to Pakistan and enlisted additional governmental channels to encourage Pakistan to exercise self-restraint. In late May, however, Pakistan also went ahead with underground nuclear tests, and Japan responded accordingly by imposing essentially the same measures it had taken against India.

Given that India and Pakistan are countries with which Japan has traditionally maintained friendly ties, it is disappointing that both have decided to act counter to the interests of the non-proliferation regime. It is expected that both countries will adopt revised nuclear policies that include abandoning the development of nuclear weapons.

China has actively pursued steps in openness and reform policy, and has also continued to show welcome progress toward a market-oriented economy. However, in 1995 it engaged in nuclear tests despite repeated requests from Japan. As a consequence, in August that year, Japan imposed a freeze on all grant aid to China other than aid of an emergency, humanitarian nature or for grassroots assistance. In July 1996, China enacted a moratorium on further nuclear testing and later signed the CTBT, thus prompting Japan to resume grant aid to the country in March 1997. Japan has also taken various opportunities to explain the position outlined in its ODA Charter on military spending and related issues, and has urged that China adopt a more transparent set of military policies, while China has taken some steps toward improved transparency, such as the publication of a document on Chinese arms control and disarmament in 1995 and another on national defense policy in July 1998.

With regard to Myanmar, Japan provides aid on a case-by-case basis, albeit with attention to trends regarding democratization and human rights, mainly for ongoing projects and other ventures in the area of basic human needs that can be expected to benefit the general public. Since Myanmar authorities have yet to demonstrate much progress in adopting democratic principles or, for that matter, a positive stance on respect for human rights, Japan is not yet in a position to provide significant levels of aid. However, in March 1998, it decided to furnish a 2.5 billion yen loan on grounds that it was urgently necessary, but only for safety-related restoration and repair work as part of the Yangon International Airport Expansion Project, an ongoing project formerly funded by Japanese aid. Furthermore, Japan provided Myanmar grant aid for increased food production the following July as a measure mainly aimed at fighting the drug problem.

From the Ministry of Foreign Affairs web site: *www.mofa.go.jp*

DOCUMENT 12   **BEYOND THE ASIAN CRISIS: SPEECH BY MR KIICHI MIYAZAWA ON THE OCCASION OF THE APEC FINANCE MINISTERS' MEETING, LANGKAWI, MALAYSIA, 15 MAY 1999**

Finance Minister Miyazawa discusses how the Japanese government has responded to the severe Asian financial crisis in 1997 that triggered extraordinary currency devaluations, bankruptcies and a devastating regional recession. This is an important speech because Japan has differed with the US and the International Monetary Fund on how to deal with the crisis, arguing for a regional stabilization fund and capital controls at odds with the market-oriented solutions favored in Washington. Japan's approach was initially rejected out of hand, but after the austerity measures advocated by the IMF were criticized for worsening the crisis, Japan's initiatives have gained more support, especially within the region.

The global economic crisis, which began in Thailand in July 1997 and spread rapidly throughout Asia, and then to Russia and Latin America, seems to have subsided, and it may be safe to say the immediate crisis is over. Now that we have entered a period of relative calm, it probably behooves [*sic*] us to look back and analyze what really happened and to come up with a perspective for the global economy, the Asia-Pacific economy in particular, for the next century.

The crisis caught most of us, particularly in this region, off-guard. Despite some earlier signs of vulnerability, market participants and analysts failed to predict the crisis from Thailand to South Korea. Risk premia for loans remained low, and rating agencies such as Standard & Poor's and Moody's maintained their relatively high ratings of sovereign bonds until the onset of the crisis. Many analysts and financiers argued, particularly at the outset of the crisis, that a lack of proper disclosure or an insufficient degree of transparency hampered a proper assessment of the risk. Objective evidence and data would seem to indicate, however, that the pertinent information, including real effective exchange rates, private sector short-term foreign debt, current account balances, and banking sector balance sheets, was largely available. The problem was, this information was not appropriately incorporated into the market risk assessment. An analysis of factors involving the behavior of hedge funds, pension funds and other non-bank financial institutions suggests that a herd mentality prevailed over the otherwise rational, detailed calculation of emerging market risk.

Thus, a more objective study of the circumstances surrounding these crises reveals that, in the globalized financial system we now have, sudden reversals of market confidence can cause periodic panics of varying magnitude and duration. Indeed, the substantial liberalization in 1993 and thereafter of the capital accounts of five Asian economies – South Korea, Indonesia, Malaysia, Thailand, and the Philippines – led to the inflow of approximately $220 billion in private capital into the region during the three-year period from 1994 to 1996. The reversal of flows that occurred in 1997 as a result of a sudden shift in confidence amounted to roughly $100 billion. No economy or region can withstand this kind of sudden shift in market sentiment, from euphoria to panic, and the resulting huge reversal of private flows.

These shifts in capital flows interacted with the affected economies' domestic financial systems, which in hindsight, were grossly inadequate to

deal with such an enormous amount of financial intermediation in such a
short period of time. Looking at the crisis from the perspective of recipient
economies, the problem was essentially one of a fund mismatch in currencies
and maturities compounded by ineffective intermediation. Asia, which has
quite strong economic fundamentals, including a high saving ratio and a
diligent labor force, has traditionally invested most of its savings outside the
region, mainly in the United States and in Europe. Funds flowed back to
Asia in the form of foreign direct investment and, increasingly in recent
years, in portfolio investment and bank loans with short maturities. In
other words, Asia remained on the periphery of the global financial system,
providing the bulk of the funds to the system while suffering from a
mismatch in obtaining refunding from the center.

In this context, I would like to report that Japan has created a $3 billion
guarantee fund in the Asian Development Bank, as well as providing ¥27.5
billion or $230 million, to subsidize interest payments. In addition, we
passed legislation last month that will allow the Export-Import Bank of
Japan to guarantee sovereign bonds to be issued by emerging economies, or
to purchase them directly. With these new instruments, it is expected that a
total of ¥2 trillion, or approximately $17 billion, of long-term sovereign
debt could be raised from the markets. Although there have been some
significant withdrawals of Japanese bank loans from the region in recent
years because of the restructuring of Japanese banks, I expect a large amount
of Japanese money primarily from institutional investors to flow back to
Asia through these long-term debt instruments.

Given the diversity of cultures, races, histories and developmental stages
of the Asian economies, it would clearly be extremely difficult to achieve
unification of the European type in Asia. Nor would it be possible for Japan
to play the type of role the US plays in the American continents.

In early October of last year, I came up with an initiative to provide $30
billion in financial assistance, short-term and medium- to long-term, to five
crisis-hit economies in Asia, Thailand, Malaysia, the Philippines, Indonesia,
and Korea. As of now, approximately two thirds of this assistance has been
committed. Japan intends to continue to implement and even enhance this
initiative both in substance and in scope in the coming years. In this
context, we plan to extend financial support to Vietnam as well, apart from
the $30 billion previously announced.

Having said that, let me emphasize that it has become increasingly
important to help channel private money to Asia, particularly since it is
expected that many of the South East and East Asian economies will
rebound and achieve positive growth in 1999. Speculative short-term
money is not welcome but sound medium- to long-term direct investment
and portfolio investment are very important. The guarantee scheme for
mobilizing an additional ¥2 trillion from the market that I have described

earlier would accelerate the return of private money and develop a healthy market in Asia for intermediating private money.

As the world enters the 21st century, the trend of 'globalization' would be accelerated. The 'globalization,' however, should be pursued with the due respect to the cultural and religious diversity on the globe. Achieving globalization amid diversity is a challenging task facing all of us.

From the Economic Planning Agency web site: *www.epa.go.jp*

DOCUMENT 13   JAPAN AND THE DEPLOYMENT OF NUCLEAR WEAPONS

Japan, as the only country to experience atomic bombings, has been a staunch advocate for nuclear disarmament. Throughout the Cold War, the principles of non-nuclear Japan coexisted uncomfortably with the realities of the US–Japan Security Treaty. Unable to exercise control over what the US military did on its bases in Japan, the Japanese government publicly maintained that it was not aware of US nuclear weapons deployment in Japan and expressed confidence that the US would respect its non-nuclear principles and not introduce such weapons into Japan. This article reveals that this trust was misplaced and that in fact the Japanese government was aware of, and had accommodated, extensive deployment of nuclear weapons and related infrastructure on Japanese soil.

If there is any country that has had a 'nuclear allergy,' it is Japan. Its defeat in World War II and occupation by the United States led to Article 9 of its 1947 constitution, in which Japan renounced war and the maintenance of 'land, sea, and air forces.' The Diet has interpreted Article 9 as permitting military alliances deemed necessary for national security, but even in that case, there is an undeviating rejection of nuclear weapons. The cornerstone of that rejection: the three non-nuclear principles – 'no production, no possession, and no introduction.' These principles date from 1959, when Prime Minister Nobusuke Kishi stated that Japan would neither develop nuclear weapons nor permit them on its territory.

But when these non-nuclear principles were being enunciated, Japanese territory was already fully compromised, in spirit if not in letter. Although actual nuclear weapons were removed from Iwo Jima at the end of 1959, Chichi Jima, which had the same legal status, continued to house warheads with their nuclear materials until 1965. And Okinawa, of course, was chock-a-block full of nuclear weapons of all types until 1972. Nuclear-armed ships moored at US Navy bases in Japan, and others called at Japanese ports without restriction.

Yet, as compromised as it was, Japan's non-nuclear policy was not wholly fictitious. The Pentagon never commanded nuclear storage rights on the main islands, and it had to withdraw nuclear weapons from Okinawa in 1972.

Historical circumstances forced Washington to accept some constraints. First, the experience of Hiroshima and Nagasaki created such strong feelings among the Japanese about nuclear weapons that every administration in Tokyo and Washington had to make accommodations. Second, Tokyo wanted to immunize the nation from the potential effects of a nuclear war between the superpowers. Such a goal was difficult for any nation to advance during the Cold War. For the Japanese nation and Japanese political leaders, the elaborate stratagem maintained the illusion of nuclear purity. Japanese political leaders could either deny everything or plead ignorance.

Undoubtedly, Japanese rulers firmly believed that the compromises they made with Washington were necessary for Japanese security during the dark days of the Cold War. Through it all, nonetheless, 'non-nuclear Japan' was a sentiment, not a reality.

From Robert S. Norris, William M. Arkin and William Burr, 'How Much Did Japan Know?', The Bulletin of Atomic Scientists, 56:1 (2000), pp. 11–13, 78–9.

DOCUMENT 14   SHINTARO ISHIHARA ON JAPAN'S RELATIONSHIP WITH THE US

Ishihara, a conservative political maverick who has served in the Diet and is Governor of Tokyo, is an unabashed nationalist who argues that Japan has been too deferential to the US and has thus not effectively promoted its own interests. His book came out in Japanese during the Bubble era (1989) when many Japanese were confident, assertive and tired of the unequal relationship with the US. His book tapped into this disaffection and the resentments fueled by US pressures on Japan to open its markets. In the US, the translation caused a sensation because of the frank message, assertive tone and implicit threats. Ishihara's view that Japan was being forced continually to make unilateral concessions to the US came as a surprise to Americans more accustomed to reading about Japan's trading policies being neo-mercantilist and any concessions as grudging, limited and soon forgotten.

The United States has not sufficiently appreciated Japan and even taken us all that seriously because, since 1945, we have been under Uncle Sam's thumb. Today, Americans may feel that Japan is getting out of hand. My own view is that Japan should not immediately disassociate itself from the US security system. For our sake and that of the whole Pacific region, the special Tokyo–Washington relationship must be preserved. A breakup could destroy the budding new developments in that region. Japan should play an expanded role in the post-Cold War world order. Effective use of our economic power – technology, management skills, and financial resources – at our own initiative can be the key to stable progress.

The economic dimension of the next era is already unfolding. That communism, a political doctrine no longer meaningful or functional, has remained powerful until recently is an irony of history. ... To Japanese, as a pragmatic people inclined towards craftsmanship rather than metaphysics, the end of ideology is good news.

History shows that technology creates civilization and determines the scale and level of its economic and industrial development. Eastern Europe and the Soviet Union want state-of-the-art technology and financial aid to make them productive. What country can provide them? Only Japan.

The conflicts among nations will be increasingly economic in nature. With the Cold War over, friction on trade and investment will inevitably intensify. Over the next few years, Japan-bashing in the US will become even more virulent. Although I see the bilateral relationship as the dominant force in the next century, before we reach that level of cooperation, US policy towards Japan will approximate the stance against the Soviet Union at the height of the Cold War.

If we try to bend with the wind, making concessions and patchwork compromises as usual, the tempest will abate for a while, only to recur with even greater force. We must not flinch in the face of pressure. The only way to withstand foreign demands is to hold our ground courageously. No more temporizing. When justified, we must keep saying no and be undaunted by the reaction, however furious. A prolonged standoff forces both sides to find areas of agreement. That is the best way to resolve disputes, not unilateral concessions by Japan, which leave the other party unaware of how we really feel. Our lack of assertiveness in the past has led to disparaging epithets like 'the faceless people.'

A deal with the Soviet Union over semiconductors cannot be completely ruled out. As I have noted, microchips determine the accuracy of weapons systems and are the key to military power. US strategists count on Japan's ability to mass-produce quality chips. Yet some Japanese businessmen believe that if Moscow returns the Northern Territories, we should terminate the security treaty and become neutral. They hope then that Japan would receive exclusive rights to develop Siberia.

From Shintaro Ishihara, *The Japan That Can Say No: Why Japan Will Become First Among Equals*, New York: Simon & Schuster, 1991, pp. 103–19.

DOCUMENT 15   ON THE REVISION OF THE US–JAPAN SECURITY TREATY, 1960

Nishi articulates the concerns of many Japanese about Japan being dragged into war against its wishes because of its alliance with the US. His remarks capture the ambiance of the Cold War and the threat perceptions that prevailed at that time. His opposition to revision of the Security Treaty was based on his belief that this would be interpreted as a provocation by the Soviet Union and the People's Republic of China with potentially dire consequences for Japan. His view that the Security Treaty actually increased Japan's security threats and vulnerability was widely shared by domestic critics of government policy, some of whom advocated neutrality rather than choosing sides in the Cold War.

I consider the proposed Security Treaty revision to contain enormous danger for our country when viewed from the perspective of our relations with the Soviet Union and China. The Soviet Union has steadfastly maintained that the Security Treaty was imposed on powerless Japan by the US at the time of the conclusion of the peace treaty. She has not condemned Japan on this account. However, the proposed revision of the pact will be carried out by the free will of Japan. ... We must be prepared to face a protest coming from the Soviet Union and Communist China. ... It goes without saying that the Soviet Union and Communist China will hold Japan responsible for all the provisions of the treaty, not just those articles that are being revised ..... the problem that concerns me most is the fact that US soldiers can embark from bases located within Japan. As it has been reported, after the treaty revision, consultation with or consent of the Japanese government will be required in this matter, and thus the American military's freedom of action will be somewhat more restricted than before. However within the limitation thus set on the action of the American military, Japan will become equally responsible in that she is party to the American action. In this sense there is potentially a great danger. For example, if the crisis over Qemoy and Matsu (Taiwanese islands) of last year is revisited, or the situation governing North and South Korea becomes worsened, it is conceivable that the American military will adopt a far stronger military measure to cope with the situation. And in this connection if American soldiers must take off from bases in Japan, we must be prepared to face a charge of joint responsibility in the military action that can be levied against us from the Soviet Union and Communist China ... We must always bear in mind that once the US accepts defense of Japan as an obligation under a treaty, the Soviet Union and Communist China will regard the treaty revision as merely a means to strengthen military cooperation between the US and Japan, and they may begin putting pressure on Japan. ... In an emergency, would it not be more likely that the Security Treaty will give an excuse for the Soviet Union and Communist China to invade Japan by terming us a common enemy along with the US? ... The national power of Japan, compared to the prewar era, has been reduced to such a level that if we commit one false move, we can even be completely annihilated. The country that will be exposed to that kind of danger as a result of the Security Treaty revision is Japan and not the US.

From *Haruhiko Nishi Kaiso no Nihongaiko* (*Reminiscences on Japanese Diplomacy*),
Tokyo: Iwanami Shoten, 1965, pp. 183–9. As cited in David J. Lu, *Japan: A Documentary
History*, vol. II, Armonk, NY: M.E. Sharpe, 1997, pp. 520–4.

DOCUMENT 16   THE GUIDELINES FOR US–JAPAN DEFENSE COOPERATION (ABRIDGED), 23 SEPTEMBER 1997

The new defense guidelines were passed in the Diet in 1999 with minimal public debate or opposition, indicating just how much Japan has changed since the 1960 anti-Security Treaty demonstrations. There were growing concerns in Washington that in the event of a crisis the Japanese government would be paralyzed and unable to act swiftly enough to authorize Japanese participation in any military operations, thus compromising combat effectiveness. The new guidelines also aim to avert a scenario in which US forces based in Japan would come under fire, but not receive any assistance from its ally. The potential threats of China and North Korea in the region created an impetus to clarify Japan's willingness to participate in collective defense by providing rear area support that does not violate the prevailing interpretation of Article Nine in the Constitution.

II. BASIC PREMISES AND PRINCIPLES

The Guidelines and programs under the Guidelines are consistent with the following basic premises and principles.

1. The rights and obligations under the Treaty of Mutual Cooperation and Security between the United States of America and Japan (the U.S.–Japan Security Treaty) and its related arrangements, as well as the fundamental framework of the U.S.–Japan alliance, will remain unchanged.
2. Japan will conduct all its actions within the limitations of its Constitution and in accordance with such basic positions as the maintenance of its exclusively defense-oriented policy and its three non-nuclear principles.
3. All actions taken by the United States and Japan will be consistent with basic principles of international law, including the peaceful settlement of disputes and sovereign equality, and relevant international agreements such as the Charter of the United Nations.

4. The Guidelines and programs under the Guidelines will not obligate either Government to take legislative, budgetary or administrative measures. However, since the objective of the Guidelines and programs under the Guidelines is to establish an effective framework for bilateral cooperation, the two Governments are expected to reflect in an appropriate way the results of these efforts, based on their own judgements, in their specific policies and measures. All actions taken by Japan will be consistent with its laws and regulations then in effect.

V. COOPERATION IN SITUATIONS IN AREAS SURROUNDING JAPAN THAT WILL HAVE AN IMPORTANT INFLUENCE ON JAPAN'S PEACE AND SECURITY

Situations in areas surrounding Japan will have an important influence on Japan's peace and security. The concept, situations in areas surrounding Japan, is not geographical but situational. The two Governments will make every effort, including diplomatic measures, to prevent such situations from occurring. When the two Governments reach a common assessment of the state of each situation, they will effectively coordinate their activities. In responding to such situations, measures taken may differ depending on circumstances.

1. When a Situation in Areas Surrounding Japan is Anticipated

When a situation in areas surrounding Japan is anticipated,

the two Governments will intensify information and intelligence sharing and policy consultations, including efforts to reach a common assessment of the situation.

At the same time, they will make every effort, including

diplomatic efforts, to prevent further deterioration of the situation, while initiating at an early stage the operation of a bilateral coordination mechanism, including use of a bilateral coordination center. Cooperating as appropriate, they will make preparations necessary for ensuring coordinated responses according to the readiness stage selected by mutual agreement. As circumstances change, they will also increase intelligence gathering and surveillance, and enhance their readiness to respond to the circumstances.

2. Responses to Situations in Areas Surrounding Japan

(b) Rear Area Support

Japan will provide rear area support to those U.S. Forces that are conducting operations for the purpose of achieving the objectives of the U.S.–Japan Security Treaty. The primary aim of this rear area support is to enable U.S. Forces to use facilities and conduct operations in an effective manner. By its very nature, Japan's rear area support will be provided primarily in Japanese territory. It may also be provided on the high seas and international airspace around Japan which are distinguished from areas where combat operations are being conducted.

In providing rear area support, Japan will make appropriate use of authorities and assets of the central and local government agencies, as well as private sector assets. The Self-Defense Forces, as appropriate, will provide such support consistent with their mission for the defense of Japan and the maintenance of public order.

> Defense Agency, Completion of the Review of the Guidelines for US–Japan Defense
> Cooperation, US – Japan Security Consultative Committee, New York,
> 23 September 1997. From the Defense Agency web site: *www.jda.go.jp*

DOCUMENT 17 MORIHIRO HOSOKAWA ON THE NEW SECURITY GUIDELINES, 5 MARCH 1999

Former Prime Minister Hosokawa (1993–94), the first non-LDP prime minister (actually he withdrew from the LDP to form an opposition party) since the formation of the party in 1955, has been one of the few prominent political leaders to speak out against the new defense guidelines, arguing that they represent a revision of the Security Treaty and significantly expand Japan's defense commitments. In view of the Constitutional ramifications, he laments the lack of public debate about the new guidelines.

The Japan–U.S. Security Treaty, signed in 1951, is understood to be an arrangement whereby the United States, in exchange for the use of military bases in Japan, is committed to the rescue of this nation in the event of external aggression. Japan, with its 'war-renouncing' Constitution, follows a policy of non-involvement in foreign disputes …

However, the new laws governing the Japan–U.S. defense cooperation guidelines allow this nation to cooperate with U.S. forces beyond the framework of the (revised) 1960 treaty. … It is clear to everyone that these laws …. represent a de facto revision of the security treaty. The security treaty has changed in qualitative terms; therefore, a full dress debate should be conducted on security issues, including not only those issues that involve the Constitution but also those pertaining to the modalities of the Japan–U.S. alliance.

[However] … the guidelines bills were passed after just two months of cursory discussions. The Diet, it must be said, betrayed the trust that the people place in the nation's highest deliberative body.

It also worries me that there is a growing trend toward neonationalism in the country, as evidenced ... by abrupt moves to legalize the Hinomaru flag and the 'Kimigayo' anthem and by the establishment of a parliamentary review panel on the Constitution. We must remember history's lesson that the bud of nationalism may blossom into ultranationalism.

Many Japanese have one simple critical question: Why despite the end of the Cold War, is Japan strengthening its military cooperation with the U.S. to prepare for contingencies in surrounding areas? So far the question has not been answered in convincing and clear-cut terms.

From Morihiro Hosokawa, 'A De Facto Treaty Revision',
Japan Times, 31 May 1999, p. 18.

DOCUMENT 18   **NIXON ON US RELATIONS WITH JAPAN DURING THE COLD WAR**

Nixon articulated the Cold War logic of the US changing its position on Japanese disarmament, arguing that it was an honest mistake based on a miscalculation of communist intentions. At the time that the US wrote the constitutional prohibition on maintaining Japanese armed forces in Article Nine, disarming Japan was a reaction to its wartime aggression and a desire to prevent a recurrence.

If Japan falls under communist domination, all of Asia falls. There is no question about it and from Japan's standpoint, if the rest of Asia falls under communist domination, Japan will also fall under communist domination; and therefore if Japan desires to be free, desires to be independent, it is essential that they work with the free nations in maintaining adequate defenses and adequate strength – strength which will ensure that the communist aggression goes no further than it has already gone in this section of the world.

It must be admitted that the primary responsibility for Japan's defense must rest upon Japan and the Japanese people. It is true that there are grave problems. The nation's economic capabilities have been sapped by the war through which it has gone, but it is essential, if Japan is to survive as a free and independent nation, that we recognize frankly that its defense forces must be increased eventually to an adequate level...

There are those who say the US is taking a very inconsistent position about the rearmament of Japan. They might say: In 1946 who was it that insisted that Japan disarm? It wasn't the Japanese, although they were willing to embark on that program, but it was at the insistence of the US that Japan disarmed.

Now if disarmament was right in 1946, why is it wrong in 1953? ... I am going to admit right here that the US did make a mistake in 1946.

We made a mistake because we misjudged the intentions of Soviet leaders. It was an honest mistake. We believe now as we believed then in the principle of disarmament.

In other words, in 1946, both in the US, in Japan and in most of the free world, we looked ahead to the future hoping against hope that it would be possible at long last to reduce the armaments of nations to a minimum level. But since that time, the communist threat has gained in power, wars have been begun – witness the one in Korea – and the threat has become so great that as we analyze it today we must change our opinion.

Richard M. Nixon, 'To the Japanese People', *Contemporary Japan*, XXII:7–9 (1953),

pp. 369–71, as excerpted in Jon Livingston, Joe Moore and Felicia Oldfeather (eds),

Postwar Japan: 1945 to the Present, New York: Pantheon, 1973, pp. 263–4.

DOCUMENT 19   JAPAN'S ROLE IN THE INTERNATIONAL COMMUNITY

Ozawa called on his nation to rethink how it participates in the international community, criticizing what he termed a selfish, inward-looking pacifism that shifted the difficult burdens and responsibilities on to other nations. He was responding to the reluctance of Japan to contribute anything but money to the Gulf War conflict and the opposition to legislation authorizing the government to commit troops to peace-keeping operations (PKOs) overseas because it flouted Article Nine of the Constitution.

What is a 'normal nation'? First it is a nation that willingly shoulders those responsibilities regarded as natural in the international community. It does not refuse such burdens on account of domestic political difficulties. Nor does it take action unwillingly as a result of 'international pressure'. This is especially relevant where national security is concerned. We don't need to return to the Gulf War or PKO bill debates to see how suddenly eloquent we become in self-righteous arguments about the constitution and other laws whenever security issues arise. We look for ways, however fallacious, to avoid a responsible role. The contradiction is clear: how can Japan, which so depends on world peace and stability, seek to exclude a security role from its international contributions? For many people, the thought of Japan playing any sort of role in the security arena conjures up images of a rearmed, militarist Japan. But this is, quite simply, not an issue of militarization or aspirations to military superpower status. It is a question of Japan's responsible behavior in the international community.

A second requirement of a 'normal nation' is that it cooperate fully with other nations in their efforts to build prosperous and stable lives for their people. It must do so on issues that affect all nations, such as environmental preservation. While Japan has made significant progress in this area, we still have a great deal to offer and can lead a worldwide effort toward making our planet more sustainable.

From Ichiro Ozawa, *Blueprint for a New Japan: The Rethinking of a Nation*,
Tokyo: Kodansha International, 1994, pp. 94–5.

DOCUMENT 20   THE GOVERNMENT'S POSITION ON ARTICLE NINE OF THE CONSTITUTION

Article Nine has been the source of considerable controversy, not least because it appears to render the Self-Defense Forces (SDF) unconstitutional. The Japanese government and higher courts have held that the wording does indeed permit Japan to maintain forces sufficient for self-defense. This interpretation is questioned both in Japan and by international jurists. This document conveys the government's position on this issue.

A. Self-Defense Capability Permitted to Be Possessed.

The self-defense capability that Japan is permitted to possess is limited to the minimum necessary by the constitutional limitations.

The specific limit of the minimum necessary level of armed strength for self-defense varies depending on the prevailing international situation, the standards of military technology and various other conditions. However, whether or not the said armed strength corresponds to 'war potential' stipulated in paragraph 2 of Article 9 of the Constitution is an issue regarding the total strength that Japan possesses. Accordingly, whether the SDF are allowed to possess some specific armaments depends on the judgment whether its total strength will or will not exceed constitutional limitations by possessing such armaments.

But in any case in Japan, it is unconstitutional to possess what is referred to as offensive weapons that, from their performance, are to be used exclusively for total destruction of other countries, since it immediately exceeds the limit of the minimum necessary level of self-defense. Therefore, for instance, the SDF is not allowed to possess ICBMs [inter-continental ballistic missiles], long-range strategic bombers or offensive aircraft carriers.

B. Conditions for Exercise of Right of Self-Defense.

The exercise of the right of self-defense is restricted to the following so-called three requisite conditions:

(i)   there is an imminent and illegitimate act of aggression against Japan;

(ii) there is no appropriate means to deal with this aggression other than resort to the right of self-defense; and

(iii) the use of armed strength is confined to the minimum necessary level.

C. Geographical Scope of Exercise of Right of Self-Defense.

The use of minimum necessary force to defend Japan as employed in the execution of its self-defense is not necessarily confined to the geographic scope of Japanese territorial land, sea and airspace. Generally speaking, however, it is difficult to make a wholesale definition of exactly how far this geographic area stretches because it would vary with separate individual situations.

Nevertheless, the government believes that the Constitution does not permit it to dispatch armed forces to foreign territorial land, sea and airspace for the purpose of using force, because such an overseas deployment of troops generally exceeds the limit of minimum necessary level of self-defense.

D. Right of Collective Self-Defense.

Under international law, it is understood that a state has the right of collective self-defense, that is, the right to use force to stop armed attack on a foreign country with which it has close relations, even when the state itself is not under direct attack. It is beyond doubt that as a sovereign state, Japan has the right of collective self-defense under existing international law. The government, however, is of the view that the exercise of the right of self-defense as permissible under Article 9 of the Constitution is authorized only when the act of self-defense is within the limit of the minimum necessary level for the defense of the nation. The government, therefore, believes that the exercise of the right of collective self-defense exceeds that limit and is constitutionally not permissible.

E. Right of Belligerency.

Paragraph 2 of Article 9 of the Constitution provides that 'the right of belligerency of the state will not be recognized.' As already mentioned, however, it is recognized as a matter of course that Japan can make use of the minimum force necessary for self-defense and that the use of such force is quite different from exercising the right of belligerency.

From the Defense Agency web site: *www.jda.go.jp*

DOCUMENT 21   FRANCIS FUKUYAMA ON THE CONSEQUENCES OF
THE CONTRACEPTIVE PILL

*Fukuyama, famous for his 'End of History' thesis, here sketches what he
believes to be the negative social consequences of the contraceptive pill in
the West as a basis for criticizing the government's decision to legalize its
use in Japan. Is the pill the root of various social problems in the US and
will its use have such dire consequences in Japan? Fukuyama's essay raises
questions about the necessary conditions for stable families and what are
the threats to that stability.*

By giving women in the West the means to prevent pregnancy, the pill freed
men from the social responsibility of dealing with the consequences of sex.
... The fatherless household that emerged contributed to a host of other
social ills, such as poverty, crime, poor educational achievement and drug
use.

Japan (along with South Korea) stands out among developed countries
as lacking many social dysfunctions that have plagued Western societies. In
the decades after WWII, violent crime rates in Japan actually declined,
during a period when they were rising rapidly in the United States. Divorce
has increased only slightly in the past 40 years, while single-parent families
remain very rare.

There are no extremes of poverty, drug use or teenage pregnancy, despite
the fact that Japan has a minimal welfare state when compared with North
America and Europe. While much of the so-called Asian values debate has
been discredited by the Asian economic crisis, it is true that Asian societies
have been more orderly than their Western counterparts in large measure
because they have stronger and more stable families. And the stability of the
traditional family rests, in Asia as elsewhere, on a sexual division of labor.

... There are many reasons for thinking that the Japanese family, and
thus vaunted social stability, will face disruption over the next generation.

Japan is beginning to de-industrialize as the United States and Britain did
a generation ago, with male workers losing jobs to smart machines and
cheap foreign labor. Because of Japan's historically low fertility, the country
will face a severe labor shortage as it loses well over 1 percent of its population each year in the 21st century. This shortage can be met either by
importing foreign workers, something that Japan has resisted strongly, or
by encouraging more women to work.

Together with the pill, these factors will undercut the social bargain on
which Japanese society has traditionally rested, in which male resources
were exchanged for female fertility.

Japan will be embarking on a fascinating social science experiment when
it finally legalizes the pill. We will see if this bit of medical technology will

produce consequences similar to ones that occurred in the West. That, more than the introduction of the Internet or the globalization of the economy, may produce a convergence between societies East and West.

From Francis Fukuyama, 'Why Japan Has Been Right to Wonder about the Pill',
New York Times, 9 June 1999, p. 29.

DOCUMENT 22 THE SEXUAL EXPLOITATION OF WOMEN IN JAPAN

The sexual exploitation of women in Japan and a pervasive pornographic culture are a source of concern to many Japanese, but social disapprobation has not dampened growth in this flourishing industry. This essay represents a feminist critique of pornography and its influence on how women are treated and perceived in society.

Since 1985 a new genre of sexually oriented literature has emerged called 'Lolita eros'. This style of comic magazine emphasizes sex with young girls and often features on its covers a cute young teenage girl in swimwear. From cover to cover the 'Lolita' magazines abound in straightforward sex, exhibiting young girls in various positions and postures intended for visual rape. There is hardly any element of storytelling but, instead, portrayals of individual and gang rape, featuring violence and maltreatment of young girls. Furthermore, girls who have been raped are described as getting home not only unperturbed by their experience but even grateful for the ecstasy accorded them by their rapist. The writers completely ignore the fact that numerous girls who are actually raped have suffered traumatic consequences for the rest of their lives. There are, moreover, numerous scenes in which girls are bound and beaten without any dialogue...

The following features are characteristic of sexual descriptions contained in male-oriented comics:

1. Male writers describe the woman or girl's body as a commodity, as if it were a toy. Pictures of enlarged breasts and genitals are presented with no more respect than if they were pieces of meat.
2. Male and female roles are stereotyped, with the former as the rapist and voyeur and the latter the raped and the exhibit.
3. The female is portrayed as, by nature, a masochist. She is stimulated by being raped and awakened to her desires and becomes a 'sex maniac'. Her sexual passivity is emphasized.
4. The so-called 'Lolita eros' magazines present the female body as the man's possession and young girls in particular are at his mercy.

While it is important to look at the great extent to which pornographic culture pervades contemporary Japan, it is also important to stress that women in Japan have been actively protesting the production of such images, and are trying to change the situation.

In 1991 the Japanese Foundation for AIDS Prevention produced a set of posters to be displayed at train stations and city halls for World AIDS Awareness Day. These posters are interesting in terms of what they reveal about the prevailing attitudes concerning sexuality. One of these posters shows a businessman hiding his face with a Japanese passport, and the ad copy reads (both in Japanese and English): 'Have a nice trip! But be careful of AIDS.' Another poster features a naked woman enveloped in an enormous condom, with the caption, 'Thin, but strong enough for AIDS.'. ... Through our efforts these posters were withdrawn.

> Kuniko Funabashi, 'Pornographic Culture and Sexual Violence', in Kumiko Fujimura-
> Fanselow and Atsuko Kameda (eds), *Japanese Women: New Feminist Perspectives on the
> Past, Present, and Future*, New York: The Feminist Press, 1995, pp. 255–63.

DOCUMENT 23   SOCIAL POLICY FOR AN AGING POPULATION

Japan's demographic time-bomb is generating concern that the nation is ill-prepared to cope with the financial consequences of this transformation. This document sketches some of the government programs that have been implemented to deal with elderly care needs and the rising costs of pensions, medical care and facilities for the elderly.

1. OVERALL SITUATION

Progress of the Fewer Children and an Aging Population

- The rate of progress of fewer children and an aging population in Japan is at a speed unprecedented in other nations. The population age 65 and older in 1995 was 14.8 per cent; it is predicted that it will be at the highest level of anywhere in the world in 2010, 15 years later. At the same time, the total fertility rate (which indicates the number of children borne to a woman throughout her lifetime) had fallen to 1.43 in 1995. The form of the family is undergoing a transformation, with women's participation in society and the scaling down of the family. In the midst of this transformation, the role which social security must play is expected to grow to include support for long-term care needs and child care.

Transforming Economic Conditions

- In recent years, the growth of the economy in Japan has been transforming into a slow-growth one, and at the same time, a structural reform is called for to cope with the 'hollowing out' of industry and globalization of the economy among other issues.

- In addition, in the future, the labor force is expected to shrink. As may be observed with the large amount of government bonds which have been issued to make up for the deficit, both nationally and locally, Japan's finances are in a grave situation. Amidst such a state, concerns are beginning to emerge that the burden of whatever scale the future of social security takes may likely become a limiting factor in maintaining an energetic society and economy.

2. INTEGRATED DEVELOPMENT OF HEALTH, MEDICAL CARE AND WELFARE

Formulating and Promoting the Three Plans for Health and Welfare

- To deal with the growing and diversifying needs for social security, it is necessary to enhance services in the welfare area, achieve the inter-cooperation of health, medical care and welfare, and develop integrated measures with a medium- to long-term perspective. For this, the Golden Plan, the Angel Plan and the Plan for People With Disabilities were formulated, and health and welfare measures are being promoted both systematically and in an integrated fashion.

a. Golden Plan and New Golden Plan
In 1989, the Ten-Year Strategy to Promote Health Care and Welfare for the Elderly (the Golden Plan) was established. This plan was made for establishing a long-term care service system to allow elderly people requiring long-term care to be independent as much as possible and continue to live in their accustomed homes and communities. It was decided to enhance in-home and institutional welfare services as well as to prevent bedridden elderly under this plan. In 1990, welfare service administration was shifted to municipalities, and the establishment of the Local Health and Welfare Plan for the Elderly became mandatory. Later, in 1994, in order to meet the expanded needs after the Golden Plan implementation, the New Golden Plan was established, under which the foundation of elderly long-term care services are being built.

b. Angel Plan
In recent years, the total fertility rate has fallen, accompanying an increase in late marriages among other factors, and the trend toward fewer children has continued. For this reason, the Angel Plan was established in 1994. Under this plan, comprehensive measures are being promoted, such as: a)

support for simultaneous child rearing and work, b) support for child rearing at home, c) arrangements for housing and living environments, d) actualization of a relaxed education and a healthy maturation, and e) reduction of child rearing costs.

In addition, urgent measures are being taken under this plan to meet diversified child care needs such as child care for younger children and nighttime child care.

3. STRUCTURAL REFORM OF SOCIAL SECURITY AND EFFORTS TOWARDS THE CREATION OF LONG-TERM CARE INSURANCE

Structural Reform of Social Security

• We are in the midst of an ongoing trend towards population aging with fewer children, the changes in the basic economic condition, and a more serious fiscal condition among other phenomena. Under these circumstances, it is necessary for Japan to resolve the public concern over the future of social security and to form a social security system which matches the needs of a mature society and economy. To this end, the time has come when the structure of social security has to be reviewed towards the 21st century while reaffirming its role. Considered significant is the goal of under 50 per cent for the ratio of taxation and social security burden, which is a percentage of taxes and social insurance premiums against national income.

Efforts Towards the Creation of Long-Term Care Insurance

• Today, the long-term care issue is the largest cause for concern of the Japanese people about their postretirement life. In the year 2025, the continually aging population is predicted to make the number of people requiring long-term care to 2.6 times that in 1997, or 5.2 million people. Also, the period of time long-term care is required and the age of those caring for the elderly will increase. Therefore, long-term care for bedridden and senile elderly people will become a critical issue.

Ministry of Health and Welfare, *Structural Reform of the Social Security Programs for an Aged Society with Fewer Children: 1990–present* (2000). From the Ministry of Health and Welfare web site: *www.mhw.go.jp*

DOCUMENT 24   JAPAN'S DEMOGRAPHIC CRISIS: THE SOCIAL AND ECONOMIC IMPLICATIONS

The complex consequences of a rapidly aging society pose many challenges to Japanese society in the twenty-first century. Japan's success in dealing with these interwoven challenges will significantly influence the quality of life of all of its citizens. This lengthy excerpt from a 1995 Ministry of Health and Welfare report focuses on the nature of Japan's demographic crisis and the implications for the family and the economy.

SECTION 7. CHANGES IN THE CIRCUMSTANCES SURROUNDING THE ELDERLY

The transformation of the family after the war has had the greatest impact on the elderly. As society has grown increasingly oriented toward nuclear families, the percentage of households where children and the elderly live under the same roof has been decreasing, and 40 per cent of the elderly now live either alone or as a couple. Attitudes toward supporting elderly parents have also changed significantly. It is becoming increasingly difficult to expect that families will provide support, and the problems of illness and long-term care are the greatest concern of the elderly.

1. The Increase in Longevity and the Advancement of the Aging of Society

(1)   The Average Life Expectancy in Japan Is the Longest in the World.
After the war, economic growth led to an improved standard of living. As standards of hygiene improved and medical science and technology advanced, the average life span in Japan increased markedly. In 1947, shortly after the end of the war, the average life span in Japan was 50.06 years for men and 53.96 years for women. The average life span in 1994 rose to 76.57 for men and 82.98 for women, increasing 26.51 and 29.02 years respectively in the 50 years after the war.

Compared with other countries, the average life span is literally the longest in the world.

(2)   The 21st century Will Be the 'Century of the Elderly.'
The elderly population is increasing sharply as life span increases. The 65 and older population increased from 4.16 million in 1950 to 17.59 million in 1994. In this 44-year time period, the actual number of the elderly increased by 13.44 million, a 4.2-fold increase. The increase in the population of the latter-stage elderly (75 and older) was particularly marked. In the same 44-year time period, this population increased from 1.07 million to 6.87 million. The actual number increased by 5.80 million, a 6.4-fold increase.

The aging of society in Japan is characterized first by the fact that the

advancement of the aging of society is a comparatively recent phenomenon since the 1970s. Secondly, Japan is the most rapidly aging society
in the world. In 15 years from now, around the year 2010, Japan will
have the highest aging rate (ratio of the population 65 and older) in the
world. Thirdly, the increase in the number of the latter-stage elderly is
conspicuous. Consequently, of the 27.75 million elderly people 65 years of
age or over in the year 2010 when the aging rate will be the highest in the
world at 21.3 per cent, it is estimated that the 75 and older latter-stage
elderly will number 13.02 million, or 47 per cent of all of the elderly.

Based on the medium variant in the Institute of Population Problems'
'Population Projections for Japan' (Provisional data of Sept. 1992), the
aging rate in Japan will surpass 25 per cent in 2018, and then will
continue to rise after an initial peak of 25.8 per cent in 2025, reaching a
peak of 28.4 per cent around 2045. Subsequently, the rate is projected to
stay in the 27 to 28 per cent range and then drop below 25 per cent in
2090. Thus, a state in which one out of every four citizens is elderly will
continue for about a century, making the 21st century the 'century of the
elderly.'

2. Changes in the Relationship Between Adult Children and Parents

(1) Increase in the Length of the Contemporaneous Period for
Parents and Children
(a) The Contemporaneous Period for Parents and Children Is Lengthening Due to the Increase in Longevity.
The contemporaneous period for parents and children, i.e., the period of
time during which both a parent and child are alive, is lengthening due
to the effect of the increase in longevity. Assuming the case in which both
parents live together with their son's family, and making calculations based
on the model of a 20 year old son and a 50 year old father, the period
during which both father and son were alive was 16.7 years from 1926
to 1930, but lengthened to 27.8 years in 1989, an increase of 11.1 years.
This period is projected to lengthen further to 29.0 years in 2025, the
year of the first peak in the aging of society.
(b) The Contemporaneous Period for Daughters-in-Law and Mothers-
in-Law Is Lengthening Due to the Increase in Longevity.
The period of time during which both a daughter-in-law and mother-in-
law are alive is lengthening due to the increase in the average life span.
According to calculations based on a model of a 25 year old daughter-
in-law and a 55 year old mother-in-law, the contemporaneous period
was 16.3 years from 1926 to 1930, but lengthened to 28.2 years in
1989, an increase of 12 years. This means that if a parent becomes in
need of long-term care, the period of such care provided by daughters-
in-law may become even longer unless something is done to improve the

present situation in which women bear the majority of the burden of long-term care for the elderly living at home.

(2)   Decrease in the Ratio of the Elderly Living Together With Their Children

(a)   The Ratio of the Elderly Living Together With Their Children Is Falling.

If we examine how the ratio of living together is changing for the elderly age 65 and older as the contemporaneous period for parent and child is lengthening, we find that the ratio was 68 per cent in 1975, but declined to 55.3 per cent in 1994.

(b)   The Ratio of Living Together in Japan Is Extremely High Compared to Other Countries.

Making an international comparison of the ratio of living together for the elderly and their children, we find that the ratio is still higher in Japan than in other countries. In the case of a parent needing long-term care, it is highly probable that the burden of that care falls first on the family members living together with the parent.

(c)   The Trend Toward Living Together Is Still Strong in Japan.

The high ratio of living together in Japan is also substantiated by an international comparison of attitudes toward how the elderly associate with their families. The ratio of elderly who think 'it would be good if I could always live together with my children and grandchildren' is 53.6 per cent, second only to Korea. In contrast, the ratios in other industrialized countries are comparatively lower at 15.4 per cent in Germany, 3.9 per cent in the U.K. and 3.4 per cent in the United States.

When married women were asked whether 'it would be good for elderly parents to live together with their son's family,' the ratio of those agreeing exceeded 50 per cent regardless of their age group. This illustrates the strong trend for many women who often bear the burden of long-term care to live together with their husband's parents. However, nearly 50 per cent of women in their 30s disagreed with the above proposition. Further, among those actually living together with their husband's parents or living in a not densely populated district, the ratio of those who think positively about living together with their husband's parents is higher.

(d)   Signs Can Be Seen of Changing From Living Together With the Son's Family to Living Together With Either the Son's or Daughter's Family.

When we examine the circumstances of parents actually living together with their children, it can be seen that the ratio is trending upwards for parents living together with their daughter's family. As couples have fewer children, the ratio of couples without a son is rising. On the other hand, the normative viewpoint that a male must succeed the family is also changing. Further, the employment of women is on the rise and the housing situation in the cities is beset with difficulties. All of these factors are contributing to a change among the elderly from living together with their son's family to living together with either the son's or daughter's family.

(e) The Ratio of Those Living Together With a Parent Increases as Children Grow Older.

When viewing the ratio of those living together with a parent by the age group of the children, we find that the ratio of those living together with the parent of the greatest income earner of the household (generally, the husband) rises as the children grow older. This trend is the same for the parent of the spouse of the greatest income earner of the household (generally, the wife). In this case, however, it is characteristic that the rate of living together with the parent of the spouse of the greatest income earner increases as the children enter their 40s and 50s when they have their own home.

Since this survey examined the circumstances of parents living together or apart from their children based on the greatest income earner of the household, regardless of the parents' age, the rate of living together is lower than that in the survey taken from the perspective of the elderly.

(f) The Majority of Children Living Apart From Their Parents Live Within an Hour's Distance.

When we examine how far away, in terms of time, parents living apart from their children reside, we find that 35.6 per cent of parents of the greatest income earner of the household live under 30 minutes away, while 14.3 per cent live between 30 and 59 minutes away. Combined, 49.9 per cent of these parents live less than an hour away from their children's residence.

Examining the location of the residence of the parents of the spouse of the greatest income earner of the household, a similar trend is found, with 36.9 per cent living under 30 minutes away and 17.3 per cent living from 30 to 59 minutes away. Combined, 54.2 per cent of these parents live less than an hour away from their children's residence.

As shown above, although the rate of children living together with their parents is declining, about half are choosing to live nearby, less than one hour away.

(3) Changes in Attitudes Toward Support for Elderly Parents

(a) Attitudes Toward the Support of Elderly Parents Are Changing Significantly.

A survey on the support of elderly parents reveals a precipitous decline since the second half of the 1980s in the ratio of those who agree with the idea that such support is a 'natural obligation of a child,' and the ratio of those who think it 'can't be helped because of an inadequate system and facilities' is rising sharply. If we consider this trend in combination with the attitudes discussed earlier on living together with parents as well as the maturing of the pension system from which parents receive payments, we find that the younger generation is beginning to think about the question of living together with their parents and the question of supporting their parents as separate issues.

(b) Fifty-five Percent of the Income of Elderly Households Comes From 'Pensions and Public Servant's Pensions.'

Examining the trends in the breakdown of income by type in elderly households, it can be seen that the ratio of all household income occupied by 'pensions and public servants' pensions' was a mere 26.2 per cent in 1975, but rose to 54.8 per cent in 1993.

(c) The Orientation Is Changing From Personal Support to Social Support Based on the Pension Programs.

When various age groups, not limited to the elderly, were asked what they expect to be the sources of their income during their elderly life, the ratio of those who replied 'public pensions' was nearly 80 per cent. As the relative weight of the pension in supporting the elderly rises, economic support of the elderly is shifting from personal support within the family to social support based on the pension system, and this shift is apparent even in people's attitudes.

3. **Changes in Circumstances of the Elderly**

(1) Forty Percent of the Elderly Are Living Alone or With an Elderly Spouse.

As was discussed in Section 1, the number of single-member households has been rising markedly in Japan since the end of the war and the family has become more individualized. In the midst of these changes, the increase in the number of elderly single-member households is particularly conspicuous. Examining the age distribution in the ratio of those who comprised a single-member household (ratio of the heads of single-member households) in 1970, 1980 and 1990, we find that the number of those who form a single-member household increases with the years during elderly life for both men and women. Overall, however, this trend is marked for women. Further, the ratio of men who form a single-member household is high for those 80 years of age or older.

Among the elderly, there were 3,740,000 households as of 1993 that were either single-member households or comprised only an elderly couple. This amounts to a state in which 40 per cent of all the elderly are either living alone or living only with their spouse.

(2) The Economic Status of Households in Which the Head of the Household Is Elderly Is Not Inferior on Average When Compared to Other Households.

Examining the economic status of households by age group of the head of the household reveals that the income per household of households in which the head is elderly is somewhat low when compared to those in their 30s to 50s. Nonetheless, the income per household member is nearly the same as for other age groups. However, the savings balance is largest for those households in which the head of the household is 65 years of age or older. When we consider that over 80 per cent of households with the elderly 65 years of age or older own their own home, we can see that the economic status of households in which the head of the household is elderly is not inferior compared to other households.

(3)   Elderly Households Have a Large Income Differential.

Examining the income status of elderly households by income level, it can be seen that the ratio of low-income elderly households is high compared to all households, substantiating the large differential between the haves and the have-nots. The burdens of the elderly must be much more carefully considered than those of younger people.

(4)   The Employment Rate of the Elderly Is Falling.

Examining the trends in the employment rate of the elderly 65 years of age or older, we discover that the rate was 38.1 per cent in 1962, but that rate declined to 24.3 per cent in 1994. The ratio of agricultural and forestry workers, which was heavily weighted in 1962, significantly dropped in 1994. Although the number of workers outside of agriculture and forestry is increasing, the ratio of the elderly in this area is mostly trending sideways.

(5)   The Desire to Work During Elderly Life Is Rising.

As of 1991, a survey that asked people if they want to work after the age of 60 reveals that 54.9 per cent 'want to work as long as possible,' 13.0 per cent 'want to work until around age 65' and 3.9 per cent 'want to work until age 70.' Combining these ratios reveals that more than 70 per cent want to work even after the age of 60. Comparing this result with a survey conducted in 1986, it can be seen that the desire to work during elderly life is on the rise.

(6)   The Greatest Fears in Elderly Life Are the Problems of Illness and Long-Term Care.

As the economic status of the elderly improves, the greatest fears regarding elderly life are the problems of illness and long-term care. A survey on attitudes during elderly life shows that 90 per cent responded 'sometimes am fearful.' A description of their fears revealed that the responses 'that my spouse or I will become weak and prone to illness' and 'that my spouse or I will become bedridden or become senile and require long-term care' were each 50 per cent.

On the other hand, the number of elderly living either alone or as a couple continues to increase. Even in families with three generations living together, it is becoming extremely problematic, as women continue to enter the work force, for families to provide long-term care on their own if their elderly become bedridden or senile. Further, the changing attitudes toward support for the elderly since the 1980s indicate that it is becoming difficult to expect the support of the family even from the standpoint of their stated attitudes.

Ministry of Health and Welfare (1995). From the Ministry of
Health and Welfare web site: *www.mhw.go.jp*

DOCUMENT 25   **RICHARD KATZ ON THE RISE AND FALL OF JAPAN'S ECONOMIC MIRACLE**

In the following extract, from a contribution to the Japan Times, *Katz (author of* Japan: The System that Soured*) explores the reasons for Japan's economic success and the current malaise. He argues that overdue reforms have not been implemented because they would harm the vested interests that benefit from the existing arrangements and practices. He expresses pessimism about the prospects for reform, despite the urgency thereof, due to the political realities of economic policy.*

In all likelihood, the era that began with the collapse of the bubble economy in 1990 will turn out to be the third great transition in Japan's modern history. By 1990, the political-economic system previously responsible for Japan's economic miracle had turned into the country's biggest ball and chain. The Catch-22 is that the very features that now obstruct economic growth also serve as pillars of Japan's political system. Consider the informal cartels pervading private industry. They not only sap efficiency; they also create high prices that siphon off consumer demand. ... The political difficulty is that cartels, structural protectionism and high prices serve as disguised employment and income redistribution for moribund sectors like farming, construction, paper, glass and a host of others. Eliminating inefficiency in these sectors would also eliminate 10 million jobs. Sure, reform would eventually create even more new jobs. That, however, would take time and Japan has a thin social safety net. Hence the very things that make reform necessary also make it difficult.

Once Japan reached maturity in the early 1970s, there were no more infant industries. 'Developmentalist' techniques should have been ended. Instead, they were reinforced, with one big difference: In the high growth era, Japan primarily promoted future winners; after 1973, it protected losers.

The trigger for this shift was the oil shock of 1973. For a full decade, zero growth plagued industries accounting for half of Japan's manufacturing output and a third of its factory workers. Rather than accepting downsizing, companies and workers cried out for relief. The government gave it to them.

Gradually, Japan turned into a deformed dual economy – a dysfunctional hybrid of super- strong exporting industries and super-weak domestic sectors. ... By the late 1980s, the exporters could no longer support the burden. They were caught in a squeeze between high costs at home and a rising yen, which made it more difficult to pass on those costs overseas. In response, the exporters fled. Today, Japan produces more cars outside of Japan than inside Japan; more consumer electronics outside Japan than inside Japan. As this flight progressed, the productivity of the entire economy was steadily dragged down to the level of the stagnant sectors.

Richard Katz, 'Japan in the Midst of a Third Great Transition',
Japan Times, 27 June 1999, p. 1.

DOCUMENT 26   **THE DESTINY OF SALARIED WORKERS**

Sakaiya, as of 2000 the Director of the Economic Planning Agency, was one of the first commentators to point out the need for transforming Japan's economic paradigm. At a time when Western observers were penning best-selling books about the secrets of Japan's economic success, he warned about the high costs and inefficiency of white-collar workers and the burdens of a bureaucratic and stifling managerial culture. His ideas about merit- and performance-based pay and promotion were anathema at the time, but have now become mainstream ideas in a society gingerly approaching corporate restructuring.

During the era of rapid economic growth, Japan was a country where salaried workers had things pretty much their way. Protected by lifetime employment and with a pay scale that gave them steady increases in income every year as they advanced in seniority, most secured a status befitting their age throughout their careers. As soon as they reached a certain level in the hierarchy, elite salaried workers were also granted one of the perquisites of the corporate scene: The authority to use 'entertainment funds.' This type of expense account was unknown in prewar Japan and much more lavish than expense accounts in other countries, and with it these workers would wine and dine the company's clientele.

The past few decades of Japanese history have been, in other words, a paradise for salaried workers. Not surprisingly, large numbers of youths left their home towns and family businesses to work for leading companies. But the good old days are over, or will be soon.

It was the hallmark of good management to have the stage set for imple-mentation as soon as a company consensus had been reached. The patience with which consensus was awaited was not, however, the monopoly of top management; it was shared by management at every level from headquarters to individual sections. What evolved was a sort of waiting game style of management. The foremost requirement of any manager was bureaucratic-style administrative ability. ...

In line with the reigning trend toward formalism and bureaucratic control of society, the worth of a salaried worker was judged chiefly on the basis of personal self-sacrifice. The number of hours and the amount of effort devoted to a job were more important than how a job turned out. It was the process, not the outcome, that counted.

Without doubt, the privileges of salaried workers in big business will disappear with the arrival of the new age. Specifically, the systems of seniority-based wages and lifetime employment will be gradually dismantled.

It will no longer be possible merely to wait one's turn to become a department chief. As the age factor decreases in importance, only those who steadily improve their performance on the job will rise to key positions and be rewarded accordingly. Performance will be judged by three elements of business acumen: foresight, decisiveness and dynamism. The self-sacrifice demanded of salaried workers in the past will no longer be needed; the test will be the ability to devise new lines of business and make them profitable.

Taichi Sakaiya, 'New Role Models, for the Work Force', in *Economic Views from Japan:
Selections from Economic Eye*, Tokyo: Keizai Toho Center, 1986, pp. 166–73. Mr Sakaiya's
article originally appeared in the March 1984 issue of *Chuo Koron*. As quoted in David J. Lu,
Japan: A Documentary History, Vol. II, Armonk, NY: M.E. Sharpe, 1997, pp. 547–50.

DOCUMENT 27 ECONOMIC LIBERALIZATION AND REFORM: JAPAN'S 'BIG BANG'

The costs of protectionism and exclusionary, non-reciprocal international economic interactions are most evident in Japan's beleaguered financial services industry. The woeful performance of Japanese companies in this sector, pressure from trading partners to accommodate enhanced foreign participation and the need to generate higher returns on investments led the Ministry of Finance to cobble together a package of liberalization and reform measures into a Japanese 'Big Bang'. The gradual implementation of these measures over an extended period of time means that the 'bang' has been muted. However, considered as a whole, the reform measures do promise considerable deregulation, liberalization and a revival of what had become a moribund sector. It remains to be seen if this promise can be realized.

An efficient and competitive financial sector is absolutely essential for the vitality of the Japanese economy in the 21st century. The Financial System Reform, 'Japanese Big Bang', was commenced in November 1996 under the three principles of 'free, fair and global', aiming to rebuild the Japanese

financial market into an international market comparable to the New York
and London markets.

As the first step, the revised Foreign Exchange Law was changed to totally
liberalize cross-border transactions in April 1998. Then, the Financial System
Reform Law, a package of revisions of laws including the Banking Law, the
Securities and Exchange Law, and the Insurance Business Law, that were
required to implement the Financial System Reform, was enforced in
December 1998.

... [E]fforts were made to provide attractive services through vital inter-
mediary activities, such as promoting entry of banks, securities companies and
insurance companies into each other's business, switching from the licensing
system to a registration system for securities companies, liberalizing cross-
border capital transactions and foreign exchange business, fully liberalizing
brokerage commissions, and eliminating the obligation to use premium
rates set by the non-life insurance rating organization.

...[D]iversified markets and channels for fund raising were created by
abolishing the requirements to trade stocks only through stock exchanges,
and introducing proprietary trading systems (electronic trading systems).
The Tokyo Stock Exchange established a new market for promising start-
ups, so called Mothers (Market of High Growth and Emerging Stocks), in
November 1999, and there is a plan to establish NASDAQ Japan stock
market at the Osaka Stock Exchange in June 2000.

...[A] framework for reliable trading was established by improving the
disclosure system, setting up fair trading rules, such as stricter insider trading
control, and protecting customers in times of failure of financial institutions.
Since the accounting period ending March 1999, financial institutions are
required by law to disclose information on their non-performing assets on a
consolidated base according to standards equivalent to the ones set by the
Securities and Exchange Commission of the United States, with possible
penalties for non-compliance.

As a result of the financial system reform as well as ongoing restructuring,
the Japanese financial sector has entered a new era of competition; from the
competition within the same field of business to the one that transcends the
business field and national borders. In these circumstances, reorganization of
the financial sector through mergers and establishment of holding companies
are rapidly promoted and foreign institutions are increasingly penetrating into
the Japanese market. The inward foreign direct investment in the financial and
insurance sectors almost tripled to reach the record high in FY1998. It is
expected that efficiency and profitability of financial institutions will improve,
allowing them to make new strategic investments for financial innovations,
and thus offering advanced and diversified financial services to customers.

Ministry of Finance, *Japanese Big Bang*. From the Ministry of Finance web site:
www.mof.go.jp

*In this speech, Prime Minister Keizo Obuchi (1998–2000) clearly enunciates
what many Japanese people also think – Japan is commencing a third great
transformation and the patterns and policies of the past are no longer
appropriate for the challenges of the new century. Unusual in a policy
speech, he calls for the 'fulfillment of our souls'. The five bridges to the
twenty-first century outlined in his speech represent government thinking
about how to make the most of this period of transition while coping with
the immediate problems that confront the nation.*

It seems to me that Japan is now experiencing a Third Reform, which
follows the great reforms effected during the Meiji Restoration and the
Post-War era. In the years following the Meiji Restoration our nation, both
government and private sector, made great efforts which gave birth to the
foundations upon which a modern state was built. The amazing economic
growth achieved by Japan, and the prosperity which we now enjoy, are the
fruits of those efforts. However, we are unable to merely idle forward in
peace and security using only the morals of our past successes. As our very
values diversify and the world undergoes great transformation, the systems
and decision-making processes which once allowed us to effectively manage
our country are now pulling us down as shackles.

The reforms achieved during the Meiji Restoration and in the period
after World War II involved great difficulty, still we must not forget that it
was the bravery and resolve of our forefathers which made that possible.
Therein lie the difficulties which we must now overcome in realizing reform.
As a society, we must change our very consciousness.

We must remember that in addition to removing that which holds us
back, we must build new systems to replace them, and at the same time we
should make an effort to keep that which is good and wonderful in our
society. It must certainly be clear to all that this Third Reform can not be
realized only through the will of politicians. Indeed, nothing can succeed
unless there is a reform in the consciousness of the people and unless the
people participate in the process.

Of foremost importance is that we create a society which provides each
and every one of our people with a safe and affluent lifestyle. There is no
way that our nation can be a great nation unless her people are happy. Still,
at the same time the time has passed when a society in which the people
look to government to provide for them can be considered a sound society.
For more than a half century after the War we engaged in a single-minded
pursuit of abundance. Although we have certainly met to some degree our
target of becoming an abundant nation, no one would deny that we have

conversely tended to forget that which is of ultimate importance to us as human beings – fulfillment of our souls.

Since taking the reins of power, on many occasions I have stressed that our nation must be an abundant one with great virtue. Sound capitalism can not be maintained based purely on pursuit of profit. This precept rings clear in the words of the German sociologist Max Weber, as well as philosophers the world over. Unless our nation is a moral one enriched with great aspirations, there is no way that we can continue as an abundant nation and we most certainly will not gain the trust of the world.

(The Five Bridges Which Lead to the 21st Century)

I believe that the foundation of our national policy toward the 21st Century should be the following five bridges. We must build first of all a bridge to the world, secondly, a bridge to prosperity, thirdly, a bridge to safety, fourthly, a bridge to security, and fifthly, a bridge to the future. I would now like to outline my basic views along the paths of these five bridges. Please forgive me if I do not provide sufficient detail on specific measures for the policies.

(A Bridge to the World)

In the world of today no nation can stand alone. We must think first of all of ensuring our national security and our prosperity. Next, our nation must earn the respect of the international community and carry out responsibilities commensurate with its position therein. I will build a bridge to the world as we enter the 21st Century.

In considering our national security we must foremost strengthen even further the relations between Japan and the United States. In that regard, it is of vital importance that the laws related to the Guidelines for Japan–US Defense Cooperation be enacted at the earliest date possible. Furthermore, with the understanding and cooperation of Okinawa Prefecture, I intend to seriously address the various issues faced by Okinawa, an area in which there is a concentration of facilities and areas used by the United States.

Next, it is important that we build stable relations with the Russian Federation and the People's Republic of China – nations of regional importance on a par with the United States. In particular, I will continue to do my utmost to deepen relations across the entire spectrum with the Russian Federation, as I seek to conclude a peace treaty by next year based on the Tokyo Declaration and the Moscow Declaration, and achieve full normalization in our bilateral relations. Furthermore, in Japan–People's Republic of China relations, reflecting the fact that we have entered a new phase as a result of last year's visit to Japan by President Jiang Zemin, I intend to develop this bilateral relationship so that we can work toward common goals both together and within the international community.

The situation on the Korean Peninsula exerts a great influence on the national security of Japan. As a result of the discussions with President Kim Dae Jung of the Republic of Korea last autumn, our two countries have settled all past issues and moved forward to become true neighbors both geographically and in spirit.

However, regarding North Korea, I intend to continue to coordinate closely with the United States and the Republic of Korea in order to resolve the international concerns about last year's missile launch, and the suspected secret nuclear facilities, and to resolve the various issues outstanding in Japan's relations with North Korea. Provided that North Korea indicates that it is ready to take a constructive approach, Japan is ready to achieve improvements in its dialogues and exchanges with North Korea.

The prosperity of Japan is premised upon the stability of the world economy. In particular, given that our nation accounts for two thirds of the economy of Asia, it is our own responsibility to actively contribute to stabilizing the currencies and economies of Asia. A single currency, the euro, has been introduced in Europe and the world economic and monetary systems are entering a new age. I reaffirm my conviction that we must fully consider the interdependence between our economy and the world economy as we actively participate in the creation of new frameworks and rules for the global economy, and promote greater internationalization of the yen as a global currency.

Moreover, as our country builds a bridge to the world it is only natural that we continue to appropriately contribute to the international community. I intend to strive to gain the full understanding of the Japanese people for even greater cooperation by Japan in terms of assistance to developing countries and assistance for United Nations peace-keeping operations (PKO), including the lifting, of restrictions on involvement in peace-keeping force (PKF) activities.

(A Bridge to Prosperity)

Economic prosperity is made up of the realization of an abundant and comfortable lifestyle for the people, and development of society and the nation. I will focus the very life of this Cabinet on creating a bridge to prosperity.

Since assuming the reins of power as Prime Minister in July 1998, I have focused on the key issue of revitalization of our financial system, with the unceasing cooperation of the Diet. We have promptly taken bold measures through the enactment of the two laws related to financial revitalization and the implementation of measures to provide government guarantees, as well as by taking steps to ease the difficulties of small and medium enterprises facing the credit crunch. Indeed, we have heard from many small and medium enterprises around the country that they have somehow managed to overcome the greatest of the difficulties. Those words are etched deeply in the minds of all who work so hard, and we intend to continue to concentrate all our efforts on resolving the issues that remain.

I am confident that with the synergy created by these measures and the serious efforts being taken by the private sector, the Japanese economy in FY1999 will recover to real economic growth of approximately 0.5 per cent. Our nation stands firmly on a foundation which, by international standards, is extremely sound, sustained by great foreign assets and individual savings, a powerful manufacturing sector supported by advanced technologies and a diligent populous. I christen this year as the year of economic revitalization, and intend to do my utmost to ensure the revitalization of our economy.

With the outstanding balance of public debt expected to reach 327 trillion yen, Japan faces an extremely difficult fiscal situation. When I think of the next generation, I am keenly aware of the grave responsibility which I bear to effect fiscal structural reform. Once the Japanese economy is soundly on the road to recovery, we must broadly and thoroughly consider, from the medium- to long-term perspective, what we can do to address the various challenges which remain in the fiscal and tax systems. Indeed, it is our duty to show the people the way forward.

To do so, we must further promote deregulation and decentralization and reconsider the respective roles of the public and private sectors, and thereby thoroughly review the involvement of government in the lives of the people and the activities of corporations. Indeed, the realization of a smaller, more streamlined government is of utmost importance.

(A Bridge to Safety)

Today many of the people of Japan enjoy that which humanity has sought since ancient times – a long life. However, at the same time many of our people are concerned about how they will support their lifestyles after they retire. Looking ahead to a 21st Century in which we will be an aging society with a diminished population, we must begin now to create a bridge to safety so that we can build a bright and dynamic society for our nation.

If we look around our society we see many instances in which the systems and practices created in an age in which life expectancy was 50, still remain without having been reformed to meet current life expectancies of 80 years. As the lifestyles of the Japanese people change we must change the structures of our society, and the ways in which our people think, by promoting employment opportunities for the elderly and creating an environment in which the elderly can live active lives, so that all of our people can enjoy lifelong good health and fulfillment. Moreover, the arrival of an aged society will create a class of abundant consumers with diverse needs, which will inherently offer new business opportunities for economic development.

As we review the overall structures of our society, it is imperative that we forcefully promote structural reform of those systems which make up the social safety net, including the pension, health, and nursing systems, so that stable administration can be guaranteed into the future. In order to ensure the necessary provision of those services while considering the burden to be born by future generations, and at the same time maintain the dynamism in our society and our economy, we must achieve a balance between provision and burden ratios while at the same time expanding the choices of users, including introducing private sector service providers as we increase the efficiency and rationality of our systems. In particular, regarding pension and health care, I will focus on tax reform so that we can establish trust-worthy and stable systems which can respond to changes in the environment.

The rapidly decreasing population of our country has a great influence on our economic society. I recently received a proposal from the panel of eminent persons to consider responses to the falling birth rate that our entire society must be united in addressing the need to create an environment in which our people can hold dear the dream of raising children and of having a family. I intend to do my utmost to take a broad-based approach encompassing all people by establishing a Citizens' Council composed of representatives of all sectors, in order to appropriately address this challenge. The Fundamental Law Designed to Promote a Gender-Equal Society will be submitted to this session of the Diet, and I am certain that it will provide great momentum toward achieving these goals.

(A Bridge to Security)

Preserving life and ensuring a safe way of life, which can otherwise be spoken of as ensuring human security, is one more important duty which we bear. I am committed to building a bridge to security until we are able to guarantee the security of every one of our citizens, and to preserve the environment of our climate.

A society of mass production and mass consumption generates massive waste and places a great burden on the global environment. One of our most weighty responsibilities is to pass on to our children, and to their children, a beautiful and stable environment by creating a renewable economic society. In order to carry out this responsibility I intend to address global environment issues, to promote increased energy efficiency and further develop nuclear energy utilization and new sources of energy and promote their use and to strive for the creation of recycling systems which can process specific needs. Furthermore, I will see to the creation of a new legislative framework to preserve the environment by addressing the problem of so-called 'environmental hormones' by reducing emissions of dioxin and promoting the control of chemical substances. Japan will lead the way in creating a society which respects nature and preserves natural resources in order to defend our irreplaceable earth.

The creation of social capital and providing a state in which the people can live at ease is an issue which the government must continue to address. Learning from the lessons of the Great Hanshin Awaji Earthquake and the damage from the repeated torrential rains last year, I will do my utmost to expand disaster prevention measures and crisis management capacity. Furthermore, the development of a nation is supported by a good social order and I will deal resolutely with malicious high-tech crime which makes use of advanced telecommunication technologies, and the criminal use of poisons to threaten the lives and safety of the people, as well as organized crime and the increasingly serious transnational problem of narcotics.

(A Bridge to the Future)

If we think about our society in the 21st Century, it is clear that there are many issues which must be addressed, and that we must build a bridge to the future.

In the coming century there will be even more scientific and technological development and it is clear that the use of information and technology will expand rapidly. Science and technology and the use of information technologies will provide the driving force for economic development and improvement in the lifestyle of our people in the future. In order to maintain a leading edge in global technology, government and the private sector must unite in order to promote science and technology and to realize an advanced telecommunications society. At the same time we must address the Y2K problem, and take other appropriate measures such as preventing improper access to computer networks.

In preparation for a wide-spread, aging society with a diminishing population we must create a social infrastructure upon which each and every one of our people can dream for the future, and can feel assured that they will be able to live the rest of their lives at ease.

I also intend to continue to focus efforts on educational reform which will allow diversification and choice in our school systems, and will foster the creation of unique schools in which a spirit of individuality and autonomy is respected. We must also continue to effect reform of our educational systems, including sweeping reform of our universities in order to bring them up to the international standards for universities.

The morals which have been formed over many years in our homes, in our communities and at our places of work, and the spirit of warm and friendly relations among people, as well as our excellent culture and traditions, are precious assets which must be handed down and continued on into the future by the next generation. Moreover, we must realize a society where the human rights of each individual are respected and build a judicial system which the people feel a part of.

Policy speech by Prime Minister Keizo Obuchi to the 145th session of the Diet, 19 January 1999 (abridged). From the Ministry of Foreign Affairs web site: *www.mofa.go.jp*

DOCUMENT 29   MASAO MIYAMOTO ON BUREAUCRACY AND CONFORMITY IN JAPAN

Miyamoto, a psychiatrist who worked in the Ministry of Health and Welfare, was an outspoken critic of the bureaucracy and its role in promoting groupism and conformity through the educational system and deflecting pressures for change. His columns in the mass media proved enormously popular, tapping into growing public distrust and skepticism towards the government.

The following points crystallize some of the major aspects of the Japanese bureaucracy, the ultimate microcosm of Japanese society.

- The bureaucracy is the biggest trade barrier to entry into the Japanese market, since the bureaucracy controls the entire market through a system of regulations and permits. If the market were truly open, it would enrich the lives of consumers in both Japan and the West. But this would mean downsizing and restructuring, to which the bureaucrats would never agree. Therefore do not expect any meaningful deregulation in the future.
- The interests of producers are consistently given priority over those of consumers because the bureaucrats see the enlargement of Japan Inc., as their overriding goal.
- To expand Japan Inc., the bureaucracy introduced the philosophy of *messhi hoko*, or self-sacrifice for the sake of the group. This philosophy requires the subordination of individual lives to the good of the whole. Since all Japanese invariably belong to some sort of group, through this philosophy they end up sacrificing their personal lives, voluntarily or otherwise.

  It is difficult to say no to *messhi hoko* and look for another job, since most Japanese companies are based on this philosophy. A person who rejects the concept of self-sacrifice can expect total isolation from the group. The fear of ostracism evokes strong anxiety in most Japanese, therefore the threat of removal from the group exerts a strong controlling influence on individual behavior.
- In psychological terms, the stimulation of masochistic tendencies equals pleasure. The more you lose your personal life, the more pleasure you get, and as it is very difficult to resist the centripetal force of *messhi*

hoko, this philosophy has become a very efficient way to control people. It has infiltrated the daily lives of the Japanese, particularly through the education system, which the bureaucrats control.

- The Japanese are educated so that even if they are frustrated or unhappy, they will resign themselves to the situation. This education is very important since, if people do not complain, it is easier to propagate the philosophy of *messhi hoko*.
- To accomplish the goal that every Japanese embrace the philosophy of *messhi hoko*, the bureaucrats introduced an educational program based on the idea that all Japanese should look, think, and act alike. This type of education does not allow for individual differences, and as a result, creativity is severely curtailed. From a psychiatrist's point of view, the bureaucrats are asking the people to embrace an illusion.
- Ultimately the bureaucracy does not want people to be independent. Being independent means that a person expresses his thoughts openly, develops a capacity to say no, and questions the status quo. *Messhi hoko* prevents people from becoming independent. What this means in terms of personality structure is that a person's pride is fragile, and can be easily injured.
- The bureaucrats announce to the world that Japan is a democracy with a free-market economy. But because Japanese society functions like a totalitarian country because, even though the separation of the three branches of government is constitutionally guaranteed, bureaucratic control of all forms of power is nearly absolute. Once you belong to a group, freedom of expression disappears. Open expression of critical thoughts is not tolerated without approval by the entire group. ...

What distinguishes Japan's 'totalitarianism' is that there is no observable Big Brother figure. It is the structure itself that functions as Big Brother. This kind of structure makes it almost impossible to change the system.

> From Masao Miyamoto, *The Staitjacket Society: An Insider's Irreverent View of Bureaucratic Japan*, Tokyo: Kodansha International, 1994, pp. 20–4.

DOCUMENT 30   MULTI-ETHNICITY IN JAPAN

The myth of ethnic homogeneity is widespread and implicit in Japan. The government and media contribute to this misconception as do the social values of conformity and uniformity. In addition, ethnic diversity is not as visually apparent in Japan as in some other societies because most of its minorities are also Asian. This essay introduces some key features of Japan's multi-ethnicity.

Japan is a society with many ethnic and social minority groups and a large majority population of heterogeneous origins. Anthropological evidence describes a migration from Southeast Asia and later from East Asia, probably over land bridges that once existed. The early settlers in the Jomon era included the Ainu and Ryukyuan peoples, and were followed by immigrants of the Yayoi era. The Ryukyuans lived in Okinawa and the other Ryukyu islands, and had their own distinctive language and culture and strong ties with China before their independent kingdom was forcibly incorporated into the expanding Japanese nation. The Ainu maintained their ethnic characteristics by moving north, but the Yayoi-era people either exterminated or absorbed the Jomon, people with whom they came into contact. It was these Yayoi people who eventually formed the Yamato state in the fifth century.

Invasion and migration from China and Korea continued until the ninth century, by which time nearly one-third of the aristocratic clans in the Chinese-style Heian capital (present-day Kyoto) were of Korean or Chinese ethnicity. Immigrants were well received as they were recognized as bearers of a superior cultural tradition, not only as nobility but as craftsmen, priests, and educated professionals. Their traditions in literature, art, and religion were absorbed and became a foundation on which much of Japanese culture was based.

The sixteenth-century plunder of Korea by military forces under Hideyoshi included the capture of artisans and scholars who were brought to Japan *en masse* for their advanced skills in pottery and printing. In more recent times, large numbers of people from Korea and Taiwan, who were at that time colonial subjects and Japanese nationals, settled in Japan or were pressed into prewar or wartime labor there. Despite efforts to repatriate them after the war, many stayed in Japan but lost their Japanese nationality when the postwar San Francisco Peace Treaty of 1952 designated them as foreigners. The Allied Occupation brought hundreds of thousands of people to Japan, mostly American men, and the maintenance of military facilities has led to the continued presence of a significant number of American military personnel. Most of this population has been transient, but some have left behind offspring while others have settled permanently in the country and married Japanese women.

In today's Japan, in addition to at least twenty-four thousand Ainu and a million Okinawans, ethnic minorities holding citizenship include recently naturalized persons from various ethnic backgrounds, particularly Korean. In addition, there are persons of mixed ethnic ancestry, such as the offspring of Korean–Japanese or American–Japanese parentage. There are also nearly a million resident foreigners, the majority of whom are Koreans, with smaller numbers of Chinese, Filipinos, Americans, and others.

In recent years, the ethnic composition of foreigners in Japan has changed dramatically with a flood of workers and students from around the world seeking opportunity in Japan. Businessmen, laborers, entertainers, and English teachers have flocked to Japan to participate in the economic miracle. Students, mainly from China and other parts of Asia, are also rushing to Japan in rapidly increasing numbers to fill the government's stated goal of 100,000 by the year 2000, although many use their student status simply to enter the country to work. Some of these newcomers choose to stay in Japan for extended periods or permanently. Ironically, these immigrants include former Japanese nationals (and their descendants) who once left Japan to seek their fortune elsewhere. Aided by favorable treatment in the new immigration law of 1990, their U-turn has already reached 150,000 and is growing.

The largest minority in Japan, the *burakumin*, are physically and linguistically indistinguishable from majority Japanese but exhibit the political and cultural traits of an ethnic group. They are the as many as three million descendants of the *eta*, a subclass legally distinguished during the Tokugawa period (1600–1868) and until their emancipation in 1871. The atomic bomb survivors of Hiroshima and Nagasaki, the *hibakusha*, and their descendants are a new minority group who, like the *burakumin*, may be plagued by fears that they are genetically defective or contaminated.

In all, about five percent of the Japanese population, or some six-million persons, are minorities who suffer much the same fate that ethnic and other minorities do in America and Europe. While they each have their own unique history of separation and oppression, and distinct cultural, class, or genetic background, all have encountered barriers of discrimination in employment and marriage. This discrimination limits their opportunities in life and encourages those who can hide their identity to 'pass' as majorities. Most of Japan's minority groups have higher rates of unemployment, welfare, and crime, and lower levels of income and educational attainment, than the majority population.

From Stephen Murphy-Shigematsu, 'Multiethnic Japan and the Monoethnic myth',
MELUS, 18:4 (Winter 1993), pp. 63–80.

DOCUMENT 31   **JAPAN IN THE 1990S: ICHIRO OZAWA'S FIVE FREEDOMS**

Ozawa is a conservative politician who was once a protégé of Prime Minister Tanaka. Coming from this milieu of shady deals and money politics, he is an unlikely champion of reform and the progressive ideas he expresses in this book. While acknowledging that Japan enjoys wealth and stability, Ozawa is an outspoken critic of what he terms an anachronistic socio-economic system that does not serve the interests of the people. He articulates a widespread dissatisfaction among both conservatives and progressives about the state of Japan in the 1990s. His proposal for five freedoms is a direct challenge to the patterns of behavior and the values that have permeated postwar society.

The counterpart to these blessings is the poverty of the lives of citizens. Our economy and society are beginning to show signs of strain. The economy continues to grow, while the people – the very essence of the economy – are robbed of their freedom. Why is this? It is because Japan has become a society dedicated solely to its corporations. The people have become mere cogs in the Japanese corporate wheel.

Japanese people work long hours and are almost completely subject to the will of their companies. Companies retain most of the fruits of economic growth; the portion left to individuals is small by comparison. We may have nominally attained the world's highest income, but we continue to struggle with small residences, lengthy commutes, and extreme urban concentration.

I would like to see Japan strive toward the goal of 'five freedoms'.

- *Freedom from Tokyo* requires reversing the extreme concentration of population and resources in Tokyo and making the transition from urban overcrowding and rural depopulation to a more balanced development policy.
- *Freedom from companies* means placing the individual rather than the company at the center of the social and economic framework, so that each citizen can approach his or her work more freely and place greater value on his or her own individual life.
- *Freedom from overwork* requires steps that will aggressively reduce work hours so that people may work with greater ease and plan their own futures. We must also alter the excessively competitive examination system.
- *Freedom from ageism and sexism* means enabling the growing number of senior citizens to participate more fully in society, and building a society in which women can play more active and varied roles.
- *Freedom from regulation* entails abolishing anachronistic and meaningless rules. It also means allowing individuals and companies more freedom.

From Ichiro Ozawa, *Blueprint for a New Japan: The Rethinking of a Nation*, Tokyo: Kodansha International, 1994, pp. 156–7.

CHRONOLOGY

1952   US Occupation ends and San Francisco Peace Treaty comes into effect. Yen is pegged at 360:$1.

1953   Japanese government begins to roll back and dilute Occupation reforms. First outbreak of Minamata mercury poisoning. Korean War ends.

1954   Self-Defense Forces are established. Reparations agreement is signed with Burma.

1955   Liberal Democratic Party is formed. Population is 89 million. Japan joins the General Agreement on Trade and Tariffs (GATT). Era of high-speed growth begins.

1956   Japan joins the United Nations. Reparations agreement is signed with the Philippines.

1957   Nobusuke Kishi, an indicted class 'A' war criminal, becomes prime minister.

1958   There are popular protests against the revision of National Police Law. Reparations agreement is signed with Indonesia.

1959   Democratic Socialist Party is established. Reparations agreement is signed with South Vietnam.

1960   Massive street protests against the renewal of the Security Treaty with the US forces the cancellation of President Eisenhower's visit and leads to the ousting of Prime Minister Kishi. Hayato Ikeda becomes Prime Minister and announces the income doubling plan.

1961   Farmers constitute 29% of the workforce. Basic Agricultural Law is passed.

1962   First Japanese-made atomic reactor commences operating. Active trade agenda is aimed at lowering tariffs on a mutual basis with key trading partners.

1963   Japan becomes a member of the Organization for Economic Cooperation and Development (OECD).

1964   Olympic Games are held in Tokyo. Japan enters the International Monetary Fund (IMF). These events symbolize Japan's rehabilitation and reintegration into the world community.

1965   Population reaches 98 million. Japan–Korea Basic Treaty is signed.

1966	Inaugural meeting of Asian Development Bank is held in Tokyo.
1967	Farmers constitute 19% of the workforce. Basic Law on Environmental Pollution is passed, spurred by large anti-pollution citizens' movement.
1968	Japan's GNP ranks second in the world after the US. Beginning of trade disputes with the US. Consumers aspire to own the three Cs: car, air conditioner (cooler) and color television. Japan becomes the world's leading producer of televisions. Yasunari Kawabata receives the Nobel Prize in Literature.
1969	President Nixon pledges to return Okinawa to Japanese sovereignty in 1972. Students and police clash on university campuses.
1970	Environmental Agency is established, responding to public anxiety over horrific pollution incidents. Osaka hosts the first world fair held in Asia. Yukio Mishima, noted author and flamboyant rightist, commits suicide.
1971	Emperor Hirohito tours Europe. Nixon halts dollar/gold convertibility. UN votes Peking in and Taipei out.
1972	Okinawa reverts to Japan. US normalizes ties with the People's Republic of China (PRC) without prior notification, stunning the Japanese government. Prime Minister Tanaka then normalizes relations with PRC amid strident criticism from within the LDP by party members loyal to Taiwan. Winter Olympics held in Sapporo. Yen rises to 272:$1. Japanese terrorists strike in Tel Aviv.
1973	Organization of Petroleum Exporting Countries (OPEC) drives up oil prices and triggers global slowdown in economic growth. This sparks inflation and panic buying in Japan. Anti-pollution legislation is incorporated into the Criminal Code.
1974	Prime Minister Tanaka is greeted by anti-Japanese riots in Bangkok and Jakarta. Former Prime Minister Eisaku Sato wins the Nobel Peace Prize.
1975	Government sponsors recession cartels and unveils other programs aimed at the 'sunset' industries, such as shipbuilding, steel, textiles, etc. There is a record number of bankruptcies. Population is 112 million.
1976	Lockheed scandal is exposed and former Prime Minister Tanaka is arrested on suspicion of taking bribes related to the purchase of planes by a domestic airline from Lockheed.
1977	Japanese average life expectancy rises to age 73, the highest in the world. Prime Minister Fukuda initiates 'heart-to-heart' diplomacy with nations of the Association of South-East Asia (ASEAN), involving aid for

industrialization and diplomacy aimed at promoting reconciliation with Indochina. Unemployment reaches 1.1 million.

1978   Government agrees to 'voluntary' restraints on car exports to the US to cope with growing trade tensions. Yen rises to 185=$1.

1979   G-7 Summit is hosted by Tokyo. Textile trade dispute with the US is resolved.

1980   Prime Minister Masayoshi Ohira dies in office on the eve of parliamentary elections, helping his LDP win a large victory from the sympathy vote.

1981   Government continues 'voluntary' restraints on car exports. Government establishes Commission on Administrative Reform aimed at privatizing state-owned enterprises.

1982   Korea and China protest about Japanese high school textbooks, complaining that atrocities and excesses are glossed over.
        Six Japanese are arrested and another eleven are charged for industrial espionage in the US (Silicon Valley).

1983   Former Prime Minister Tanaka is found guilty of corruption. Prime Minister Nakasone makes the first official postwar visit of a Japanese prime minister to South Korea.

1984   Trade agreements with the US on citrus and meat imports.
        The over-65 population reaches 10% of the total population.
        President Chun Doo Hwan of Korea visits Japan and the Emperor expresses regret about the annexation of Korea in 1910.

1985   Agreement with the US on steel trade.
        Government telecommunication and railway monopolies are privatized.
        520 Japanese die in a domestic plane crash.
        The Plaza Accord paves the way for endakka (sharp appreciation of the yen).

1986   Doi Takako becomes the first woman to lead a political party, the Japan Socialist Party.
        Retirement age is raised to 60 years from 55.
        High yen dampens exports.

1987   Japan National Railway is broken up and privatized.
        Rengo, an umbrella labor union federation, is formed.
        The defense budget exceeds 1% of GNP.
        The US announces economic sanctions against Japan.
        Diplomatic dispute erupts with South Korea over Japanese textbooks' treatment of their shared past.

1988   Trade surplus with US hits a record high. Japan's overseas foreign direct investment is the highest in world.
        Trade negotiations with the US focus on construction. With the completion of new tunnels and bridges, the four main islands are connected by rail services.

1989   Emperor Hirohito dies, ending the Showa Era (1926–89). The Heisei Emperor, Akihito, ascends to the throne.

Recruit scandal engulfs political and bureaucratic elite.
Unpopular consumption tax (3%) is implemented. Prime Minister Noboru Takeshita resigns.

1990   GDP grows by 7.5%, but economic bubble bursts with the implosion of prices for stocks and land. Decade-long recession begins.

1991   Gulf War débâcle as Japan is embarrassed by the appearance of exercising checkbook diplomacy while letting other nations assume the risks and burdens.

1992   Severe economic downturn.
New political reform parties emerge in response to public disenchantment with corruption and the mismanagement of economic policies.
Government passes a controversial peace-keeping law that allows Japanese armed forces to participate in UN peace-keeping in Cambodia, their first return to the region since World War II and their first overseas duty since the re-establishment of the military in 1954.

1993   The LDP is defeated in the House of Representatives elections for first time since 1955 and a non-LDP coalition takes power.
Government underwrites the UN Transitional Authority in Cambodia and attempts to stage democratic elections.
Prime Minister Hosokawa makes a specific apology to South Korea about abuses during colonial rule.
Crown Prince marries.

1994   Major electoral political reform legislation is enacted. Two non-LDP coalition governments fall and the LDP, in coalition with the Socialist Party, regains power.
Justice Minister resigns over denying the Nanking Massacre happened.

1995   Kobe earthquake, the nation's worst since the 1923 Tokyo earthquake, devastates the city.
Aum Shinrikyo unleashes nerve gas attacks on subways in Tokyo. Spiritual leader Shoko Asahara and other members are arrested.
Yen reaches postwar peak at 79:$1.
Population is 126 million.
Less than a majority of the Diet passes an equivocal apology resolution commemorating the fiftieth anniversary of the end of World War II.
Former comedians win gubernatorial elections in Tokyo and Osaka.

1996   LDP wins election under the new electoral rules and forms a government.
Bureaucrats' reputation is sullied by a series of revelations about incompetence and corruption.
Japan and South Korea dispute sovereignty over a small island.
Rogue traders lose Daiwa bank $1.1 billion and Sumitomo Corporation $2.4 billion.
Personal computer ownership per capita is less than one half of the US figure.

1997   Prime Minister Hashimoto increases consumption tax, dampening
          consumer spending and hopes for economic recovery. Financial 'Big
          Bang' initiated.
          17 million Japanese travel overseas, doubling departures registered in
          1988.
          Japan leads the bailout of Southeast Asian economies felled by regional
          currency crisis.
          Kyoto hosts global Environmental Summit.

1998   Banking crisis persists and the government mounts a $600-billion
          taxpayer-funded bailout despite the unpopularity of this program.
          Long Term Credit Bank bankruptcy leads to its temporary
          nationalization.
          LDP forms a coalition government with a former LDP maverick in the
          Liberal Party and Komeito, a party affiliated with Sokka Gakkai, a
          religious organization.
          North Korea launches a missile over Japan's main island.

1999   Tokaimura nuclear accident shakes public confidence in nuclear power
          and government competence.
          Japan–US defense guidelines bill is approved by the Diet.
          Defense vice-minister resigns over remarks supporting nuclear
          rearmament.
          Legislation conferring legal status on a national flag and national
          anthem is passed amid controversy over the conservative shift in national
          politics.

2000   Unemployment stands at 3 million. Prime Minister Obuchi dies in office.
          His successor, Yoshiro Mori, stirs controversy with reference to Japan
          being a divine country centered on the Emperor because of links with
          wartime ultra-nationalist sentiments.
          Government establishes a parliamentary commission for revising the
          Constitution.

GLOSSARY

Amakudari Descent from Heaven. A reference to the common practice of retired senior bureaucrats moving to well-paid, sinecure positions in firms that they dealt with in the course of their government duties. Often criticized as a source of collusive relations between bureaucrats and the firms they hope to join upon retiring.

Article Nine The article in the Japanese Constitution that bans the development of military forces and the resort to war to settle international disputes.

ASEAN Regional Forum (ARF) This forum focuses on security issues in the Asia-Pacific area.

Asia-Pacific Economic Cooperation (APEC) APEC was established in 1989 as an informal dialogue group in response to the dynamism, growth and accelerating integration among member economies. Over the years APEC has developed into the primary regional vehicle for promoting open trade and investment and regional economic cooperation. APEC's twenty-one members include Australia, Brunei, Canada, Chile, People's Republic of China, Hong Kong (China), Indonesia, Japan, Republic of Korea, Malaysia, Mexico, New Zealand, Papua New Guinea, Peru, the Philippines, Russia, Singapore, Chinese Taipei, Thailand, the US and Vietnam. The combined economies account for approximately 45 percent of world trade. The Association of Southeast Asian Nations (ASEAN), the Pacific Economic Cooperation Council (PECC) and the South Pacific Forum (SPF) have observer status. The APEC Secretariat was established in 1993 and is located in Singapore.

Asian values A thesis popularized in the early 1990s that the traditional family and community-centered values of Asian societies explain their superior economic performance and social cohesion. Critics point out the rich variety of traditions and values in Asia and suggest that the assertion of Asian values by governments was motivated by a reluctance to accommodate the political consequences of economic development. Proponents of Asian values often criticize advocates of democracy and human rights for embracing values alien to Asia, while these advocates counter by pointing out that Asian religions and philosophies are consistent with democracy and human rights. The economic crisis that hit Asian economies in 1997 was interpreted as discrediting some of the major assertions of proponents of Asian values.

Association of Southeast Asian Nations (ASEAN) A regional organization established in 1967, including ten nations of Southeast Asia – Brunei, Cambodia, Indonesia, Laos, Malaysia, Myanmar (Burma), the Philippines, Singapore, Thailand and Vietnam.

Aum Shinrikyo (Supreme Truth Sect). A new religion centered on the teachings of Shoko Asahara. It staged an attack on Tokyo subways in 1995 using sarin gas.

Big Bang Financial deregulation program initiated by the government of Prime Minister Ryutaro Hashimoto in 1996 often characterized by the media as the 'little whimper' for failing to meet expectations for sweeping liberalization.

Burakumin 'Hamlet people' is term used to refer to some 1 million Japanese today. Visually indistinguishable from other Japanese, 'hamlet people' suffer discrimination in jobs, housing, marriage, etc. because they are identified as being members of this class. During the Tokugawa era (1603–1868) this class became hereditary and was linked to 'polluting' activities such as slaughtering animals.

Diet The parliament in Japan which is composed of an elected upper and lower house.

Dokken kokka Construction state. A reference to the vast spending on public works projects equivalent to US defense budget with implications of environmental devastation and political corruption.

Enjo kosai Compensated dating, usually between junior or high school girls and middle-aged men, often involving sex.

Fukoku kyohei Literally 'rich nation, strong military'. This was the rallying slogan of the Meiji era government (1868–1911).

Gaiatsu Foreign pressure. This term refers to the pressures put on the Japanese government by other governments to modify various policies. In some cases, such pressures are actually welcomed as a way to overcome a domestic political impasse that is preventing necessary reforms desired by the government. However, inviting or staging *gaiatsu* as a means of overcoming political inertia has nurtured public resentments about what is portrayed in the mass media as high-handed tactics by other nations, notably the US.

Gaijin Foreigner(s).

Gengo The Imperial system of periodization based on making the first year of an Emperor's reign Year 1 and so on. Official dates in Japan and even rail passes are commonly based on this system.

Giri An obligation one incurs to conform to social expectations.

Gyosei shido Administrative guidance. A reference to the informal manner in which bureaucrats wield their broad regulatory and discretionary powers to ensure corporate compliance with government goals and policies. Implicit is the threat to use those powers in a manner harmful to those who do not comply.

Habatsu Factions within the LDP.

Heisei Era of 'achieving of peace' (1990–present) under the reign of Emperor Akihito.

Hinomaru The national flag with a red circle in the middle of a white background.

Honne Inner feelings, usually unexpressed because they do not conform to social norms and expectations.

Ie The patriarchal family system that denied women independence and legal rights. The Constitution sought to correct this bias with decidedly mixed results. Many Japanese women today still bridle under what they see as the legacy of this male-oriented system in the home, in society and at work. Conservatives often blame current social problems on the decline of the *ie* system.

Ijime Bullying is a pervasive practice in society that is aimed at imposing conformity within a specific group and ostracizing those who do not conform or meet expectations. High-profile suicides among students show this problem to be especially evident in schools.

Iron Triangle The nexus of power involving big business, the bureaucracy and the Liberal Democratic Party (LDP) that is said to control Japan in the post-WWII era.

Japan, Inc. A term coined to characterize the close relationship between the government and big business in Japan and the government's focus on economic issues.

Jusen Real estate lending subsidiaries of banks that incurred massive unrecoverable loans in the wake of the bubble, threatening the collapse of the Japanese financial system in the mid-1990s and forcing a government bailout despite strong public criticism.

Kanson mimpi Bureaucratic arrogance towards the public.

Keiretsu Bank-centered, industrial conglomerates that dominate the Japanese economy, many of which have strong links with the pre-World War II *zaibatsu*. The exclusionary business practices and conflicts of interest within the *keiretsu* have come under scrutiny as a source of trade friction.

Kimigayo Your Majesty's Reign. The national anthem is controversial because of its apparent reference to the days when the Emperor was an absolute monarch, making it a divisive political issue between conservatives and progressives.

Koenkai Local political support organizations that mobilize voters and funds for politicians.

Kokusaika Internationalization. A concept that is frequently invoked with mixed results to broaden horizons among Japanese and inculcate a positive value for interaction with foreigners and their cultures.

Koseki A family register, maintained over the generations with information about births, deaths, marriages, etc.

LDP (Liberal Democratic Party) Formed by a merger of the Liberal Party and the Democratic Party in 1955. It is the conservative political party that has dominated post-World War II Japanese politics.

Messhi hoko Self-sacrifice.

Mura hachibu Village ostracization imposed on those who do not meet social expectations in rural Japan.

Narikin The nouveau riche who emerged during the bubble at the end of the 1980s who engaged in conspicuous and often garish consumption fueled by wealth generated by spiraling land and stock prices.

Nenko The seniority employment system that has determined wages and pro- motions, but is now no longer sacrosanct as firms shift towards a more merit- oriented system.

Nopan shabushabu Notorious restaurants featuring beef, mirrored floors and waitresses wearing short skirts and no panties. The wining and dining of Ministry of Finance bureaucrats at such establishments by businessmen under their jurisdiction provoked public outrage in the late 1990s and became symbolic of the collusion between corporate Japan and the government, and the special favors involved.

Omoiyari yosan Literally 'sympathy budget'. A reference to the money the Japanese government pays to base US troops in Japan. This amounted to approximately $2.5 billion in 2000.

On A personal sense of social debt or obligation created in a relationship by a benevolent act.

Red Purge The US-controlled SCAP and the conservative Japanese government initiated a crackdown beginning in 1947 on left-wing activists, radicals, unions, etc. as a consequence of the Cold War-inspired reverse course. The purge was a response to shared concerns that prevailing socio-economic conditions left Japan vulnerable to the appeal of communism, a prospect feared by the US and their conservative allies in the Japanese government.

Reverse course After 1947, the US Occupation in Japan became influenced by the Cold War between the US and the USSR. Punitive policies were replaced by an emphasis on rebuilding Japan into a showcase for American-style democracy and capitalism. The progressive New Deal policies implemented between 1945 and 1947 were in many cases 'reversed' by more conservative policies. Prior to 1947, SCAP and the Japanese government sought to prosecute right-wing militarists, but after 1947 the government engaged in what is known as the Red Purge, cracking down on left-wing unions and activists.

Salarymen (sararimen) Salaried white-collar workers who are often the subject or object of both mockery and respect. Their image is of hard working, extremely loyal company employees who place greater emphasis on work than on the family and personal desires.

SCAP (Supreme Command of the Allied Powers) During the US Occupation of Japan (1945–52) this organization was nominally a multilateral institution that governed the country and sought to realize the goals of demilitarization, democratization and decentralization. In fact, the US and General Douglas MacArthur controlled SCAP.

SDF (Self-Defense Forces) (Jietai in Japanese) The military forces of Japan.

Shinjinrui New species. A negative reference by older people used when criticizing the various presumed failings of the younger generation.

Showa Era of 'enlightened peace' (1926–89) under the reign of Emperor Hirohito.

Soapland An establishment where men pay for sexual services.

Sokaiya Corporate extortionists linked with the *yakuza* who threaten to expose company secrets and disrupt shareholder meetings unless they are paid substantial sums. The government and firms have tried to curb this widespread practice.

Tatemae Public behavior conforming to acceptable norms.

Yakuza Organized crime syndicates in Japan.

Ubasteyama A traditional practice/legend that involved abandoning elderly people in remote mountain areas to die as a way of coping with limited food and allowing the younger generation to marry and carry on the family line.

Yoshida Doctrine The policy of Prime Minister Shigeru Yoshida (1946–47, 1949–54), emphasizing the need of Japan to concentrate resources on economic recovery as a way to deflect US demands that it rearm in the early 1950s.

Zaibatsu Family-owned industrial conglomerates that dominated the pre-World War II Japanese economy. Initially, these were targeted for dissolution by SCAP because they were held to be responsible for supporting and abetting the 1931–45 military rampage through Asia. However, after the reverse course, SCAP did not aggressively proceed with the dissolution. During the Occupation the ownership and structure of these conglomerates was transformed and the pre-World War II *zaibatsu* became the post-World War II *keiretsu*.

Zaitech The speculative activities by corporations in land and stock unrelated to core business activities.

PRIME MINISTERS SINCE 1952

(Family name first as is custom in Japan)

Yoshida Shigeru (1948–54)
Hatoyama Ichiro (1954–56)
Ishibashi Tanzan (1957)
Kishi Nobusuke (1957–60)
Ikeda Hayato (1960–64)
Sato Eisaku (1964–72)
Tanaka Kakuei (1972–74)
Miki Takeo (1974–76)
Fukuda Takeo (1976–78)
Ohira Masayoshi (1978–80)
Suzuki Zenko (1980–82)
Nakasone Yasuhiro (1982–87)
Takeshita Noboru (1987–89)
Uno Sosuke (1989)
Kaifu Toshiki (1989–91)
Miyazawa Kiichi (1991–93)
Hosokawa Morihiro (1993–94)
Hata Tsutomu (1994)
Murayama Tomoiichi (1994–96)
Hashimoto Ryutaro (1996–98)
Obuchi Keizo (1998–2000)
Mori Yoshiro (2000)

WHO'S WHO

This is a shortlist of some of the people who made history in Japan's post-World War II era. It aims to provide brief bio data for readers about key figures mentioned in the text or who were influential in their fields. By definition, such a list focuses on prominent figures, but this should not be construed as to exaggerate their importance or to minimize the importance of ordinary citizens. The lack of women on this list does not imply that they have not played a crucial role in contemporary Japan, but it is a telling absence that reflects prevailing realities. As is the custom in Japan, the family name comes first.

Abe Kobo (1924–93) He is one of the best-known Japanese literary figures in the postwar era. He focuses on themes of alienation and identity, often with Kafka-esque scenarios. *Women in the Dunes* (1962) is his most acclaimed novel. He wrote plays, formed his own theater group and in later years wrote in an absurdist vein.

Emperor Hirohito (1901–89) The Emperor reigned for 62 years, longer than any other Japanese Emperor, ascending to the throne in 1926. His era is known as Showa (Enlightened Peace). The first twenty years of his reign witnessed aggressive colonial expansion and war, leading to widespread devastation in Asia, and eventually the destruction of Japan's cities and the death of an estimated 3 million Japanese. Debate over his role in and responsibility for the war persists. Recent scholarship indicates that he was much more involved in, and aware of, government and military plans and actions during the wartime era (1931–45) than is usually depicted in official textbooks that emphasize the traditional constraints on his office and exercise of power. He is credited with bringing an end to the war, casting the deciding vote when the Supreme War Council evenly split over surrender in August 1945. He was spared prosecution for war crimes because SCAP deemed him to be more useful alive, both in lending support to Occupation era reforms and out of concern that as a dead martyr he would serve as a rallying point for ultra-nationalists. He repudiated his presumed divinity among Japanese in 1946 and supported the new Constitution drafted by SCAP that made him the symbol of the state and the unity of the people. He died a popular figure, known to most Japanese for his keen interest in marine biology and for his self-effacing style. The outpouring of international condolences and the large attendance of foreign dignitaries at his funeral indicate how far Japan was rehabilitated and reintegrated into the community of nations following World War II.

Ienaga Saburo (1913–) Controversial professor emeritus from the University of Tokyo who has waged court battles in a series of lawsuits since 1965 that challenge the constitutionality and legality of the government's school textbook review system, conducted by the Ministry of Education. He has protested the government efforts to force him to modify his depiction of Japan's brutal wartime actions during the 1931–45 period and maintains that the textbook review system amounts to censorship. His views of history have been vindicated over time, but the court rulings on the textbook review system have been mixed. As a result of his actions, the review process has become more open to public scrutiny. In addition, the court ruled that the Ministry of Education has been excessive in wielding its review powers and the public has become more aware of the politics of history.

Ikeda Hayato (1899–1965) Former elite bureaucrat in the Ministry of Finance turned politician, he served as prime minister as a member of the LDP from 1960 to 1964. He is remembered for his income doubling plan and his success in refocusing public attention towards economic growth rather than the controversial security ties with the US that polarized politics in 1960. He sought to maximize Japan's growth potential by expanding public spending, lowering interest rates and cutting taxes. He also forged closer ties with the US by promoting three major cooperative agreements in economic, cultural and scientific fields with President Kennedy.

Ishihara Shintaro (1932–) Celebrated novelist and outspoken conservative politician who served in the Diet from 1968 as a member of the LDP. His novel, *Season of the Sun* (1955), won literary prizes for its depiction of alienated youth rejecting established mores and values. He is famous for expressing frustrations with the bilateral US–Japan relationship in his book, *The Japan That Can Say No* (1989), and his blunt nationalistic rhetoric. He was elected Governor of Tokyo in 1999 and has continued to be controversial, calling on the government to tilt towards Taiwan in its relations with China, requesting the US to vacate an airbase in Tokyo, and calling on the SDF to be vigilant about foreigners in the event of an earthquake.

Kawabata Yasunari (1899–1972) The most famous and widely translated Japanese novelist, he was the first to win the Nobel Prize for Literature (1968). His novels are often termed quintessentially Japanese because of their conscious evocation of traditions, aesthetics and relationships that conjure up a world disappearing under the onslaught of modernization. Many of his masterpieces were written before World War II, but among his post-war novels *Sound of the Mountain* and *Thousand Cranes* are notable. He committed suicide.

Kurosawa Akira (1910–98) Japan's most internationally renowned film director and script writer won a lifetime achievement Oscar in 1990. His most famous movies are his samurai epics such as *Seven Samurai* (1954), *Throne of Blood* (1957), *Kagemusha* (1980) and *Ran* (1985), while film critics favor his early *Rashomon* (1950) and *Ikiru* (1952). *No Regrets for Our Youth* (1946) explores political oppression during wartime Japan. *The Bad Sleep Well* (1960) is a classic depiction of the collusion between big business, politicians and bureaucrats. Acclaimed overseas, he had limited critical and commercial success at home.

Mishima Yukio (1925–70) Prolific author of fiction, drama and essays, his real name was Hiraoka Kimitake. His novels are some of the best post-World War II literature in Japan, fusing Japanese traditions and Western influences. His homosexuality and ritual suicide, calling for a revival of militarism and the Emperor system, have overshadowed his literary accomplishments among a Japanese public that, in general, does not accord him the same stature he enjoys among international audiences.

Miyazawa Kiichi (1920–) A former elite Finance Ministry bureaucrat and a third-generation Diet legislator, he has been in the mainstream of Japan's politics ever since he was first elected to the Diet in 1953. As a member of the LDP, he served as prime minister (1991–93), but resigned due to political machinations within his party and the fallout of money politics. At 80 years of age he was reappointed as Minister of Finance due to his experience and the reassurance he offers to international financial markets as Japan attempts to recover from a decade-long recession. Entering the twenty-first century, he is Japan's leading elder statesman and a strong voice in favor of internationalism.

Morita Akio (1921–99) Founder of SONY and Japan's most famous post-war businessman, he contributed to Japan's internationalization in many ways. Fluent in English, he served as an articulate and savvy spokesman for Japan. He made SONY the first Japanese company to list its shares on the New York stock exchange and was a pioneer in setting up plants in the US. He played a key role in trying to ease US–Japan trade frictions through his participation in various fora. During his leadership of SONY, Japanese products shed their image as shoddy, cheap merchandise and became synonymous with high-quality and cutting-edge technology.

Murayama Tomoiichi (1924–) Entering a historic coalition government with the LDP, this chairman of the Japan Socialist Party became the first socialist prime minister (1994–96) in the post-Occupation era. His government replaced the first non-LDP government since the party's formation in 1955. His ascendancy to power also marked the decline of the Socialists because his tie-up with the LDP alienated the party faithful who were concerned that the key principles of the party had been compromised as the price of coalition. During his administration, the twin tragedies of the Kobe Earthquake and the Aum Shinrikyo subway gas attacks rocked Japan.

Nakasone Yasuhiro (1918–) Conservative politician, member of the LDP until his resignation from the party in 1989 due to scandal, he served as prime minister (1982–87) under the aegis of Kakuei Tanaka, his most important supporter. His cabinets were referred to as the Tanakasone governments in recognition of his mentor's power behind the scenes. He was known overseas as a personable and straightforward statesman who enjoyed close relations with President Ronald Reagan and Prime Minister Margaret Thatcher. A hawk on security issues, he played a significant role in expanding Japan's defense profile. He oversaw ambitious fiscal and administrative reforms and the privatization of government-operated monopolies in telecommunications and the railways.

Ozu Yasujiro (1903–63) Film director noted for his depictions of contemporary family life and the corrupting influence of postwar modernization. *Tokyo Story* (1953) is his most famous film, evoking a timeless melancholy about what was fading quickly in a transforming Japan. The elegant simplicity of his films is evident in laconic dialogue and the everyday situations with which ordinary Japanese could identify. Low, tatami-level camera angles are his trademark. His films are no longer popular, but at the time were valued for reassuring viewers that their losses and tribulations were shared. As with Kawabata for literature, Ozu is considered the quintessentially Japanese film director.

Takeshita Noboru (1924–2000) Leading protégé of Tanaka Kakuei who served as prime minister (1987–89) and held numerous cabinet portfolios in a Diet career that began in 1958. Like his mentor, he resigned from office under the cloud of scandal. He was also unpopular for introducing the consumption tax in 1989. During the 1990s, his control of what had been the Tanaka faction, the largest in the LDP, gave him unrivalled political influence as the party's kingmaker.

Tanaka Kakuei (1918–93) Conservative politician first elected in 1947, he acted as kingpin of the LDP during the 1970s and 1980s. He served as prime minister (1972–74) but resigned in the Lockheed corruption scandal, was arrested in 1976, sentenced to jail in 1983 and died while appealing his sentence in 1993, eight years after he suffered a debilitating stroke. He is remembered for his idea of remodeling the Japanese archipelago, an effort to spread the fruits of development to backwater areas such as Niigata, where he was born. He personified money politics in Japan and was the fixers' fixer. From the early 1970s he controlled the largest faction in the LDP until his resignation from politics in 1990, effectively using his power behind the scenes even after his fall from grace. His protégés, Noboru Takeshita, Shin Kanemaru and Ichiro Ozawa, dominated national politics in the 1990s.

Yoshida Shigeru (1878–1967) The second most influential postwar politician after Kakuei Tanaka, he twice served as prime minister (1946–47, 1948–54). He grudgingly enacted liberal Occupation era reforms and resisted US pressures to rearm, arguing that Japan's precarious economic situation precluded reviving military forces. He oversaw the end of the Occupation, the consolidation of conservative power in Japan and forged close security ties with the US. Towards the end of World War II he was briefly arrested by the military police for his role in trying to bring a cessation of hostilities.

BIBLIOGRAPHY

REFERENCE WORKS

Allinson, G.D., *The Columbia Guide to Modern Japanese History*, Columbia University Press, New York, 1999.
Dower, J., *Japanese History and Culture from Ancient to Modern Times: Vol. 7. Basic Bibliographies*, Markus Weiner Publishing, New York, 1986a.
Duus, P. (ed.), *The Cambridge History of Japan: Vol. 6. The Twentieth Century*, Cambridge University Press, Cambridge, 1988.
International Society for Understanding Japan, *Japanese Chronology*, International Society for Educational Information, Tokyo, 1989.
Kodansha Encyclopedia of Japan (9 vols), Kodansha International, Tokyo, 1983.
Livingston, J., J. Moore and F. Oldfather (eds), *Postwar Japan 1945 to the Present*, Pantheon Books, New York, 1973.
Lu, D.J., *Japan: A Documentary History. The Late Tokugawa Period to the Present*, M.E. Sharpe, Armonk, New York, 1997.
Starr, D. (ed.), *Japan: A Cultural and Historical Dictionary*, Curzon Press, Richmond, UK, 2000.

GENERAL WORKS

Allinson, G.D., *Japan's Postwar History*, Cornell University Press, Ithaca, New York, 1997.
Buckley, R., *Japan Today* (third edition), Cambridge University Press, Cambridge, 1999.
Chapman, W., *Inventing Japan*, Prentice-Hall, New York, 1991.
Dower, J., *Japan in War and Peace*, New Press, New York, 1993.
Duus, P., *Modern Japan* (second edition), Houghton Mifflin, Boston, MA, 1998.
Field, N., *In the Realm of the Dying Emperor: Japan at Century's End*, Vintage, New York, 1993.
Gluck, C. and S. Graubard (eds), *Showa: The Japan of Hirohito*, W.W. Norton, New York, 1992.
Gordon, A. (ed.), *Postwar Japan as History*, University of California Press, Berkeley, CA, 1993.
Hane, M., *Eastern Phoenix: Japan since 1945*, Westview Press, Boulder, CO, 1996.
McCormack, G., *The Emptiness of Japanese Affluence*, M.E. Sharpe, Armonk, New York, 1996.
Naff, C., *About Face: How I Stumbled onto Japan's Social Revolution*, Kodansha International, Tokyo, 1994.
Reischauer, E., *The Japanese*, Harvard University Press, Cambridge, MA, 1977.
Smith, P., *Japan: A Reinterpretation*, Pantheon Books, New York, 1997.

AGING

Campbell, J., *How Policies Change: The Japanese Government and the Aging Society*, Princeton University Press, Princeton, NJ, 1992.

Harris, P.B. and S.O. Long, 'Husbands and Sons in the U.S. and Japan: Cultural Expectations and Caregiving Experiences', *Journal of Aging Studies*, 13:3 (Fall 1999), pp. 241–67.

Hurd, M. and N. Yashiro (eds), *The Economic Effects of Aging and the US and Japan*, University of Chicago Press, Chicago, IL, 1997.

Long, S.O. (ed.), *Caring for the Elderly in Japan and the US*, Routledge, London, 2000.

Noguchi, Y. and D. Wise (eds), *Aging in the United States and Japan*, University of Chicago Press, Chicago, IL, 1994.

Ohtake, F., 'Aging Society and Inequality', *Japan Labor Bulletin*, 38:9 (July 1999), 5–11.

Yamamoto, N., 'The Continuation of Family Caregiving in Japan', *Journal of Health and Social Behaviour*, 38:2 (June 1997), 164–176.

ECONOMY

Chalmers, N., *Industrial Relations in Japan: The Peripheral Workforce*, Routledge, London, 1989.

Cole, R., *Japanese Blue-Collar*, University of California Press, Berkeley, CA, 1971.

Dore, R., *British Factory, Japanese Factory: The Origins of Diversity in Industrial Relations*, University of California Press, Berkeley, CA, 1973.

Emmott, B., *The Sun Also Sets: Why Japan Will Not Be Number One*, Simon & Schuster, New York, 1989.

Fallows, J., *Looking at the Sun: The Rise of the New East Asian Economic and Political System*, Pantheon Books, New York, 1994.

Fingelton, E., *Blindside: Why Japan is Still on Track to Overtake the U.S. by the Year 2000*, Simon & Schuster, New York, 1995.

Garon, S., *The State and Labor in Modern Japan*, University of California Press, Berkeley, CA, 1987.

Gordon, A., *The Wages of Affluence: Labor and Management in Postwar Japan*, Harvard University Press, Cambridge, MA, 1998.

Hein, L., *Fueling Growth: The Energy Revolution and Economic Policy in Postwar Japan*, Harvard University Press, Cambridge, MA, 1990.

Johnson, C., *MITI and the Japanese Miracle*, Stanford University Press, Stanford, CA, 1982.

Katz, R., *Japan: The System that Soured – The Rise and Fall of the Japanese Miracle*, M.E.Sharpe, Armonk, New York, 1998.

Krugman, P., 'The Myth of the Asian Miracle', *Foreign Affairs*, Nov.–Dec., 1994, pp. 62–78.

Lincoln, E., *Japan's Unequal Trade*, Brookings, Washington, DC, 1990.

Murphy, R., *The Weight of the Yen*, W.W. Norton, New York, 1996.

Murphy, R., 'Japan's Economic Crisis', *New Left Review*, Jan.–Feb., 2000, pp. 25–52.

Nakamura, T., *The Postwar Japanese Economy: Its Development and Structure*, University of Tokyo Press, Tokyo, 1981.

Nikkeiren (Japan Federation of Employers' Association), *Creating a Dynamic and Appealing Society*, Nikkeiren, Tokyo, 1999.

Nikkeiren, *Toward a Market Economy with a Human Face*, Nikkeiren, Tokyo, 2000.

Okimoto, D., *Between MITI and the Market: Japanese Industrial Policy for High Technology*, Stanford University Press, Stanford, CA, 1989.

Okita, S., *Postwar Reconstruction of the Japanese Economy*, University of Tokyo Press, Tokyo, 1992.

Prestowitz, C., *Trading Places*, Basic Books, New York, 1990.

Ries, P., *The Asian Storm: The Economic Crisis Examined*, Charles Tuttle, Tokyo, 2000.

Sato, K. (ed.), *The Transformation of the Japanese Economy*, M.E. Sharpe, Armonk, NY, 1999.

Tachibanaki, T., *Wage Determination and Distribution in Japan*, Clarendon Press, Oxford, 1996.

Uriu, R., *Troubled Industries: The Political Economy of Industrial Adjustment in Japan*, Cornell University Press, Ithaca, New York, 1998.

Wood, C., *The Bubble Economy: The Japanese Economic Collapse*, Charles Tuttle, Tokyo, 1993.

Yamamura, K. and Y. Yasuba (eds), *The Political Economy of Japan* (Vol. 1), Stanford University Press, Stanford, CA, 1987.

FOREIGN POLICY

Arase, D., *Buying Power: The Political Economy of Japan's Foreign Aid*, Lynne Reinner, Boulder, CO, 1995.

Buckley, R., *US–Japan Alliance Diplomacy 1945–1990*, Cambridge University Press, Cambridge, 1992.

Calder, K., *Asia's Deadly Triangle: How Arms, Energy and Growth Threaten to Destabilize the Asia-Pacific*, Nicholas Brealey, London, 1997.

Curtis, G. (ed.), *Japan's Foreign Policy after the Cold War: Coping with Change*, M.E. Sharpe, Armonk, New York, 1993.

Dore, R., *Japan, Internationalism and the UN*, Routledge, London, 1997.

Green, M.J., *Arming Japan: Defense Production, Alliance Politics and the Postwar Search for Autonomy*, Columbia University Press, New York, 1995.

Inoguchi, T., *Japan's Foreign Policy in an Era of Global Change*, Pinter, London, 1993.

Johnson, C. (ed.), *Okinawa: Cold War Island*, Japan Policy Research Institute, Cardiff, CA, 1999.

Koppel, B.M. and R.M. Orr, Jr. (eds), *Japan's Foreign Aid: Power and Policy in a New Era*, Westview Press, Boulder, CO, 1993.

Matthews, R. and K. Matsuyama (eds), *Japan's Military Renaissance?* Macmillan, London, 1993.

Orr, R., *The Emergence of Japan's Foreign Aid Power*, Columbia University Press, New York, 1990.

Rix, A., *Japan's Foreign Aid Challenge*, Routledge, London, 1993.

JAPAN AND ASIA

Brook, T. (ed.), *Documents on the Rape of Nanking*, University of Michigan Press, Ann Arbor, MI, 1999.

Buruma, I., *The Wages of Guilt: Memories of War in Germany and Japan*, Farrar Strauss Giroux, New York, 1994.

Chang, Iris, *The Rape of Nanking: The Forgotten Holocaust of World War II*, Basic Books, New York, 1997.

Curtis, G. (ed.), *The United States, Japan and Asia: Challenges for US Policy*, W.W. Norton, New York, 1994.

Fogel, J., *The Nanjing Massacre in History and Historiography*, University of California Press, Berkeley, CA, 2000.

Goto, K., *Returning to Asia*, Ryukei Shyosha, Tokyo, 1997.

Hatch, W. and K. Yamamura, *Asia in Japan's Embrace: Building a Regional Production Alliance*, Cambridge University Press, Cambridge, 1996.

Havens, T., *Fire across the Sea: The Vietnam War and Japan*, Princeton University Press, Princeton, NJ, 1987.

Hein, L. and M. Selden (eds), *Censoring History: Citizenship and Memory in Japan, Germany and the United States*, M.E. Sharpe, Armonk, New York, 2000.

Hicks, G., *The Comfort Women*, Yen Books, Tokyo, 1995.

Honda, K., *The Nanjing Massacre*, M.E. Sharpe, Armonk, NY, 1999.

International Public Hearing Report (ed.), *War Victimization and Japan*, Toho Shuppan, Osaka, 1993.

Katzenstein, P. and T. Shiraishi (eds), *Network Power: Japan and Asia*, Cornell University Press, Ithaca, New York, 1997.

Marshall, J., *To Have and Have Not: Southeast Asia's Raw Materials and the Origins of the Pacific War*, University of California Press, Berkeley, CA, 1995.

Reader, I. and M. Soderberg (eds), *Japanese Influences and Presences in Asia*, Curzon Press, Richmond, UK, 2000.

Sato, S., *War, Nationalism and Peasants: Java under the Japanese Occupation, 1942–45*, M.E. Sharpe, Armonk, New York, 1997.

Toer, P., *The Mute's Soliloquy*, Hyperion East, New York, 1999.

Young, L., *Japan's Total Empire: Manchuria and the Culture of Wartime Imperialism*, University of California Press, Berkeley, CA, 1998.

Wakamiya, Y., *The Postwar Conservative View of Asia*, LTCB International Library Foundation, Tokyo, 1999.

POLITICS

Allinson, G. and Y. Sone (eds), *Political Dynamics in Contemporary Japan*, Cornell University Press, Ithaca, New York, 1993.

Broadbent, J., *Environmental Politics in Japan: Networks of Power and Protest*, Cambridge University Press, Cambridge, 1998.

Calder, K., *Crisis and Compensation: Public Policy and Political Stability in Japan, 1949–1986*, Princeton University Press, Princeton, NJ, 1991.

Curtis, G., *The Japanese Way of Politics*, Columbia University Press, New York, 1988.

Curtis, G., *The Logic of Japanese Politics: Leaders, Institutions and the Limits of Change*, Columbia University Press, New York, 1999.

Hartcher, P., *The Ministry: The Inside Story of Japan's Ministry of Finance*, Harper Collins, London, 1997.

Masumi, J., *Contemporary Politics in Japan*, University of California Press, Berkeley, CA, 1995.

Otake, H., *Power Shuffles and Policy Processes: Coalition Government in Japan in the 1990s*, Tokyo: Japan Center for International Exchange, 2000.

Ozawa, I., *Blueprint for a New Japan*, Kodansha International, Tokyo, 1994.

Packard, G., *Protest in Tokyo*, Princeton University Press, Princeton, NJ, 1966.

Pempel, T. (ed.), *Uncommon Democracies*, Cornell University Press, Ithaca, New York, 1990.

Pempel, T., *Regime Shift: Comparative Dynamics of the Japanese Political Economy*, Cornell University Press, Ithaca, New York, 1998.

Ramsayer, M. and F. Rosenbluth, *Japan's Political Marketplace*, Harvard University Press, Cambridge, MA, 1993.

Richardson, B., *Japanese Democracy: Power, Coordination and Performance*, Yale University Press, New Haven, CT, 1997.

Schlesinger, J., *Shadow Shoguns: The Rise and Fall of Japan's Postwar Political Machine*, Simon & Schuster, New York, 1997.

Schoppa, L., *Bargaining with Japan: What American Pressure Can and Can Not Do*, Columbia University Press, New York, 1997.

Stockwin, J., *Governing Japan: Divided Politics in a Major Economy*, Blackwell, London, 1998.

von Wolferen, K., *The Enigma of Japanese Power*, Macmillan, London, 1989.

Whiting, R., *Tokyo Underworld*, Pantheon Books, New York, 1999.

SOCIETY

Bornoff, N., *Pink Samurai*, Grafton, London, 1991.

Cummings, W., *Education and Equality in Japan*, Princeton University Press, Princeton, NJ, 1980.

Dale, P., *The Myth of Japanese Uniqueness*, Routledge, London, 1986.

Davis, W., *Japanese Religion and Society*, SUNY Press, Albany, New York, 1992.

DeVos, G. et al., *Japan's Minorities*, Minority Rights Group, London, 1983.

Doi, T., *The Anatomy of Dependence*, Kodansha International, Tokyo, 1973.

Douglass, M. and G. Roberts (eds), *Japan and Global Migration*, Routledge, London, 2000.

Freeman, L., *Closing the Shop: Information Cartels and Japan's Mass Media*, Princeton University Press, Princeton, NJ, 2000.

Greenfield, T., *Speed Tribes: Days and Nights with Japan's Next Generation*, Harper Collins, New York, 1994.

Hall, I., *Cartels of the Mind*, W.W. Norton, New York, 1997.

Ishida, H., *Social Mobility in Contemporary Japan*, Stanford University Press, Stanford, CA, 1993.

Kaplan, D. and A. Dubro, *Yakuza*, Addison-Wesley, Reading, MA, 1986.

Kitaguchi, S. and A. McLauchlan, *An Introduction to the Buraku Issue*, Japan Library, Richmond, UK, 2000.

Lebra, T. (ed.), *Japanese Social Organization*, University Press of Hawaii, Honolulu, 1992.

Lee, C. and G. DeVos, *Koreans in Japan*, University of California Press, Berkeley, CA, 1981.

Lifton, R., *Destroying the World to Save It: Aum Shinrikyo, Apocalyptic Violence and the New Global Terrorism*, Metropolitan Books, New York, 1999.

Mouer, R. and Y. Sugimoto, *Images of Japanese Society*, KPI, London, 1986.

Nakane, C., *Japanese Society*, University of California Press, Berkeley, CA, 1970.

Rauch, J., *The Outnation: A Search for the Soul of Japan*, Harvard Business School Press, Cambridge, MA, 1992.

Reader, I., *Religion in Contemporary Japan*, Macmillan Press, Basingstoke, 1991.

Reader, I., *A Poisonous Cocktail? Aum Shinrikyo's Path to Violence*, Nordic Institute of Asian Studies, Copenhagen, 1996.

Richie, D., *The Inland Sea*, Weatherhill, Tokyo, 1971.

Richie, D., *A Lateral View: Essays on Culture and Style in Contemporary Japan*, Stonebridge Press, Berkeley, CA, 1992.

Rohlen, T., *Japan's High Schools*, University of California Press, Berkeley, CA, 1983.

Shimada, H., *Japan's 'Guest Workers': Issues and Public Policies*, University of Tokyo Press, Tokyo, 1994.

Upham, F., *Law and Social Change in Postwar Japan*, Harvard University Press, Cambridge, MA, 1987.

Vogel, E., *Japan as Number One*, Charles Tuttle, Tokyo, 1980.

Weiner, M. (ed.), *Japan's Minorities: Illusions of Homogeneity*, Routledge, London, 1997.

WAR AND OCCUPATION

Barnhardt, M., *Japan Prepares for Total War*, Cornell University Press, Ithaca, New York, 1988.

Bix, H., *Hirohito and the Making of Modern Japan*, HarperCollins, New York, 2000.

Cohen, T., *Remaking Japan: The American Occupation as New Deal*, Free Press, New York, 1987.

Davis, G., *An Occupation Without Troops*, Charles Tuttle, Tokyo, 1997.

Dower, J., *War Without Mercy: Race and Power in the Pacific War*, Pantheon, New York, 1986b.

Dower, J., *Embracing Defeat: Japan in the Wake of World War II*, W.W. Norton, New York, 1999.

Finn, R., *Winners in Peace: MacArthur, Yoshida and Postwar Japan*, University of California Press, Berkeley, CA, 1992.

Forsberg, A., *America and the Japanese Miracle: The Cold War Context of Japan's Postwar Economic Revival 1950–1960*, University of North Carolina Press, Chapel Hill, NC, 2000.

Frank, R., *Downfall: The End of the Imperial Japanese Empire*, Random House, New York, 1999.

Gold, H., *Unit 731: Japan's Wartime Human Experimentation Program*, Yen Books, Tokyo, 1996.

Harvey, R., *The Undefeated: The Rise, Fall and Rise of Greater Japan*, Macmillan, London, 1994.

Hein, L. and M. Selden (eds), *Living with the Bomb: American and Japanese Cultural Conflicts in the Nuclear Age*, M.E. Sharpe, Armonk, New York, 1997.

Norris, R., et al., *The Bulletin of Atomic Scientists*, Jan.–Feb., 2000 (*www.thebulletin.org*)

Schaller, M., *The American Occupation of Japan: The Origins of the Cold War in Asia*, Oxford University Press, Oxford, 1985.

Tanaka, Y., *Hidden Horrors: Japanese War Crimes in World War II*, Westview, Boulder, CO, 1998.

WOMEN

Bernstein, G., *Haruko's World: A Japanese Farm Woman and Her Community*, Stanford University Press, Stanford, CA, 1983.

Brinton, M., *Women and the Economic Miracle: Gender and Work in Postwar Japan*, University of California Press, Berkeley, CA, 1993.

Condon, J., *A Half Step Behind: Japanese Women of the 1980s*, Dodd, Mead, New York, 1985.

Cook, A. and H. Hayashi, *Working Women in Japan: Discrimination, Resistance and Reform*, New York State School of Industrial and Labor Relations, Ithaca, New York, 1980.

Dalby, L., *Geisha*, Vintage Books, New York, 1983.

Imamura, A., *Urban Japanese Housewives: At Home and in the Community*, University of Hawaii Press, Honolulu, 1987.

Iwai, S., *The Japanese Woman: Traditional Image and Changing Reality*, Free Press, New York, 1993.

Jolivet, M., *Japan: The Childless Society?*, Routledge, London, 1997.

Kondo, D., *Crafting Selves: Power, Gender and Discourses of Identity in a Japanese Workplace*, University of Chicago Press, Chicago, IL, 1990.

Lam, A., *Women and Japanese Management*, Routledge, London, 1992.

Mercier, R., 'Power, Not Sex, Behind Pornography', *Japan Times*, 12 July 1999, p. 16.

Ogasawara, Y., *Office Ladies and Salaried Men*, University of California Press, Berkeley, CA, 1998.

Osawa, M., 'Working Mothers: Changing Patterns of Employment and Fertility in Japan', *Economic Development and Cultural Change*, 36:4 (1988), 623–50.

Roberts, G., *Staying on the Line: Blue Collar Women in Contemporary Japan*, University of Hawaii Press, Honolulu, 1994.

Saso, M., *Women in the Japanese Workplace*, Shipman, London, 1990.

Smith, R., 'Gender Inequality in Contemporary Japan', *Journal of Japanese Studies*, 13:1 (1987), 1–25.

Smith, R. and E. Wiswell, *The Women of Suye Mura*, University of Chicago Press, Chicago, IL, 1982.

LITERATURE

(Date of publication in Japanese in parenthesis.)

Abe, K., *The Woman in the Dunes* (1962), Vintage, New York, 1991.

Ariyoshi, S., *Twilight Years* (1972), Kodansha International, Tokyo, 1984.

Birnbaum, A., *Monkey Brain Sushi: New Tastes in Japanese Fiction*, Kodansha International, Tokyo, 1991.

Dazai, O., *The Setting Sun* (1956), Charles Tuttle, Tokyo, 1981.

Endo, S., *The Sea and Poison* (1957), New Directions, New York, 1992.

Gessel, V. and T. Matsumoto (eds), *The Showa Anthology: Modern Japanese Short Stories* (2 vols), Kodansha International, Tokyo, 1985.

Kaiko, T., *Darkness in Summer* (1972), Charles Tuttle, Tokyo, 1974.

Kawabata, Y., *Beauty and Sadness* (1961), Vintage Books, New York, 1996.

Mishima, Y., *Forbidden Colors* (1968), Charles Tuttle, Tokyo, 1969.

Mitsios, H. (ed.), *New Japanese Voices: The Best Contemporary Fiction from Japan*, Atlantic Monthly Press, New York, 1991.

Miyabe, M., *For All She is Worth* (1992), Kodansha International, Tokyo, 1996.

Murakami, H., *Norwegian Wood* (1987), Kodansha International, Tokyo, 1989

Murakami, R., *Almost Transparent Blue*, Kodansha International, Tokyo, 1992.

Oe, K., *A Personal Matter* (1964), Grove Press, New York, 1969.

Shimazaki, T., *The Broken Commandment* (1906), Columbia University Press, New York, 1987.

Sumii, S., *The River With No Bridge*, Charles Tuttle, Tokyo, 1990.

Tanizaki, J., *Some Prefer Nettles* (1955), Perigree, New York, 1981.

Yamasaki, T., *The Barren Zone* (1976), Kodansha International, Tokyo, 1987.

VIDEOS

(Available with English Subtitles; * = original in English.)

Capra, F., *Know Your Enemy: Japan* (1945)*

Center For New American Media, *The Japanese Version* (1991)*

Choy & Tong (Filmmakers Library), *In the Name of the Emperor* (1995)*

Hatta, K., *Picture Bride* (1996)*

Higashi, Y., *Village of Dreams* (1996)

Ichikawa, K., *Fires on the Plain* (1959)

Imamura, S., *The Insect Woman* (1963)

Imamura, S., *The Ballad of Narayama* (1983)

Itami, J., *The Funeral* (1987)

Itami, J., *Tampopo* (1987)

Itami, J., *The Taxing Woman* (1987)

Itami, J., *Minbo* (1992)

Kobayashi, M., *The Human Condition* (3 parts: 1958–61)

Kumai, K., *Sandakan 8* (1974)

Kurosawa, A., *No Regrets for Our Youth* (1946)

Kurosawa, A., *Stray Dog* (1949)

Kurosawa, A., *Ikiru (To Live)* (1952)

Kurosawa, A., *The Bad Sleep Well* (1960)

Kurosawa, A., *High and Low* (1963)
Logan, J., *Sayonara* (1957)*
Mann, D., *Teahouse of the August Moon* (1956)*
Morita, Y., *Family Game* (1983)
Okada, E., *Woman in the Dunes* (1964)
Oshima, N., *Cruel Story of Youth* (1960)
Ozu, Y., *Tokyo Story* (1953)
Pacific Century Series, Vol. 5: *Reinventing Japan*; Vol. 6: *Inside Japan, Inc.* (1992)*
PBS–Oregon, *Occupied Japan: An Experiment in Democracy* (1996)*
Suo, M., *Shall We Dance* (1996)
Tsukamoto, S., *Tetsuo: The Iron Man* (1988)
Yanagimachi, M., *Fire Festival* (1985)
http://www.homefilmfestival.com/foreign.html
http://www.facets.org/

INTERNET LINKS

http://www.elibrary.com/ (On-line Searchable Library of Articles)
http://www.bijapan.com/ (Business Insights Japan)
http://www.jinjapan.org/ (Japan Information Network)
http://csf.colorado.edu/bcas/ (Bulletin of Concerned Asian Scholars)
http://jin.jcic.or.jp/stat/index.html (Government Statistics)
http://www.newsonjapan.com/ (Current news on Japan culled from various sources)
http://www.jcer.or.jp/eng/index.html (Japan Center for Economic Research)
http://www.ibjs.co.jp/e/res_links/index.html (Industrial Bank of Japan Securities)
http://www.asahi.com/english/english.html (Asahi Newspaper)
http://www.bridgetojapan.org/ (Daiwa Foundation (UK) Information Resources)
http://fuji.stanford.edu/jguide/ (Stanford University Jguide – Info clearing house)
http://coombs.anu.edu.au/asia-www-monitor.html (Australian Asian Info Resources)
http://www.epa.go.jp/e-e/doc/menu.html (Economic Planning Agency)
http://www.ndl.go.jp/e/index.html (National Diet Library)
http://www.jpri.org/ (Japan Policy Research Institute)
http://www3.yomiuri.co.jp/main/main-e.html (Yomiuri Newspaper)
http://www.mainichi.co.jp/english/index.html (Mainichi Newspaper)
http://nias.ku.dk (Nordic Institute of Asian Studies)

PRINTED PUBLICATIONS

AMPO-Japan-American Quarterly
Asian Survey
Asian Wall Street Journal
Asia Watch
Asia Week
Economist
Far Eastern Economic Review
Japan Echo
Japan, Inc.

Japan Economic Institute Reports
Japan Policy Research Institute Reports
Japan Quarterly
Journal of Asian Studies
Journal of Japanese Studies
Look Japan
Oriental Economist
Pacific Affairs
Social Science Japan Journal
Tokyo Journal

INDEX

Abe, General, 32
Abe, Kobo, 201
ageing crisis *see* elderly
agriculture, 190
aid, foreign, 53, 54, 148–50
AIDS, 76, 166
Ainu, 119, 187
Akashi, Yoji, 63
Akihito, Emperor, 192, 196
amakudari (descent from heaven), 96, 195
Angel Plan, 167–8
anthem, Kimigayo, 116, 160, 194, 197
APEC (Asian Pacific Economic Cooperation), 55–6, 195
ARF (ASEAN Regional Forum), 55, 56, 1 95
Ariyoshi, Sawako
The Twilight Years, 81
armed forces
    demilitarization during US Occupation, 9, 12, 16, 22
    levels in Far East, xi (map)
    modernization of, 63
    number of, 66
    and SDF *see* SDF
Article Nine, 12, 22, 61, 65–6, 131, 132, 153, 157, 162–3, 195
Asahara, Shoko, 110–11, 112
Asahi Newspaper, 53
ASEAN (Association of Southeast Asian Nations), 54, 55, 56, 191, 195
ASEAN Regional Forum *see* ARF
Asia, 45–57
    anti-Japanese riots (1974), 54, 56
    and comfort women, 50–1
    contemporary ties with Japan, 53–5
    economic ties with Japan, 53–4
    failure to convey contrition over aggression and refusal to pay compensation, 7, 48, 147
    financial crisis (1997), 54–5, 60, 150–3, 194
    future, 56–7
    improvement in relations, 54
    Japan's expansionism in, 45
    motivation for invasion of southeast and justification for, 46–7
    multilateral participation by Japan in, 55–6
    and Murayama apology for atrocities caused, 46, 142–3

and Nanking Massacre, 48, 50, 51–3, 146–8, 193
Oe's call for apology for aggression by Japan towards, 47, 143–4
promotion of decolonization by Japan, 45
security problems and frictions, 62
textbook censorship relating to wartime conduct in, 45, 49–50, 146, 192, 201–2
and war apology resolution (1995), 45–6, 140–1
war crimes committed by Japanese military, 46
see also individual countries
Asia Women's Fund (AWF), 51
Asian Development Bank, 152, 191
Asian Pacific Economic Cooperation *see* APEC
Asian values, 195
Association of the Families of the War Dead, 144
Association of Southeast Asian Nations *see* ASEAN
Aum Shinrikyo (Supreme Trust Cult), 110–12, 193, 195, 203
AWF (Asia Women's Fund), 51

baby-boom generation, 86
Bad Sleep Well, The (film), 31, 202
bakumatsu period, 29
Ballad of Narayama (film), 80–1
Bangzao, Zhu, 147
bases, US military, 23, 58–9, 135, 156
Basic Agricultural Law, 190
Basic Law on Environmental Pollution, 191
behaviour, 3
Big Bang, 87, 97, 109, 177–8, 194, 195
birth control pill, 76, 164–5
birth rate decline, 70, 75, 76, 79, 183
'black mist' scandals (1960s), 30
Blaker, Michael, 60
Bretton Woods system, abandoning of by United States, 44
Brinton, M., 70, 73, 74
Broadbent, Jeffrey, 21, 26
Brook, T., 146
Bubble: What Could That Money Have Bought, The (Murakami), 110
Bubble (1980s), 44, 91, 105–10, 154
    collapse of, 96, 101–2, 105, 107, 175, 193
    impact of, 108–10

215

Bubble (1980s) (*continued*)
    and increase in wealth, 108
    reasons for occurrence, 105–6
Buckley, R., 23
bullying, 93, 117, 196
burakumin, 119, 188, 196
bureaucracy, 28, 37, 185–6

Calder, K., 21
Cambodia, 55, 63–4, 193
car exports, 192
cartels, 41, 44, 91, 175, 191
censorship
    during US Occupation, 15
    textbooks, 45, 49–50, 144–6, 192, 201–2
Chang, Iris
    The Rape of Nanking, 52, 146
chikan, 77
child care, 75
child pornography, 77, 118
Childcare Leave Law, 70
China, 10, 65, 143
    denouncement of Japan's revision of
        textbooks, 49
    expansion into by Japan, 11
    invasion of Manchuria and war with
        Japan, 11, 46
    Japanese military force levels in, xi (map)
    military budget, 65
    and Nanking Massacre, 48, 50, 51–3,
        146–8, 193
    nuclear tests, 150
    opposition to TMD, 64
    provision of aid by Japan, 150
    reasons for Japan's aggression in, 46–7
    refusal to sign San Francisco Treaty, 22
    relations with Japan, 56, 65, 180, 191 and
        US–Japan Security Treaty, 156–7
Chrysanthemum Club, 138
Chukakuha (Red Army Faction), 27
Chun Doo Hwan, President, 192
Cicero, 2
Citizen's Council, 183
Civil Code, 69
Clinton, President Bill, 62
Cold War, 13, 22, 156
    end of, 29, 62
comfort women, 50–1
Commission on Administrative Reform, 192
communism, 160, 198
Comprehensive Test Ban Treaty (CTBT),
    149, 150
Constitution (1947), 12, 131–4
    Article Nine, 12, 22, 61, 65–6, 131, 132,
        153, 157, 162–3, 195
    calls for revision, 66–7
    and women's rights, 12, 69
Constitution, Meiji (1889), 10, 11, 12, 131
construction, 25–6, 32 *see also, dokken
    kokka*

consumerism, rise in, 95
consumption tax, 83, 84, 193, 194, 204
contraceptive pill, 76, 164–5
corporate welfare, 92, 93
corruption, 25, 28, 30–1, 34, 96, 102, 127,
    193
crime, 117, 164, 184
Curtis, G., 27–8, 30

Dae Jung, President Kim, 181
Daiwa bank, 193
dango, 25, 96
date clubs, 117–18
defense
    budget and spending on, 12, 40–1, 62, 66,
        192
    new guidelines (1999), 61, 62, 65, 157–9,
        159–60, 180
    see also security
delinquency, 118
demilitarization during US Occupation, 9,
    12, 16, 22
democracy, 30
    assessment of today, 125–6
    during Taisho era, 11
    during US Occupation, 9–10, 12–13, 15,
        16, 134
Democratic Socialist Party, 190
demonstrations
    against renewal of Security Treaty (1960),
        24, 27, 135, 190
deregulation, 90, 92, 96, 97, 99, 101, 104,
    127, 182
discrimination, 118–20
    against ethnic minorities, 47, 118–19, 188
    against foreigners, 88, 118, 119–20
divorce, 69, 109, 164
dokken kokka (construction state), 25, 26,
    102, 196
Dore, Ronald, 72
Dower, John, 15, 56, 134–5
Dulles, John Foster, 22

e-commerce, 101
earthquake, 184
    Kanto (1923), 88
    Kobe (1995), 112–14, 184, 193, 203
Economist, The, 94
economy, 4, 36–44, 54, 90–103, 124–5,
    166–7, 175–6
    access to US market and technology as
        factor for growth, 38, 41
    and Asian financial crisis, 54–5, 150–3
    and Big Bang, 87, 97, 109, 177–8, 194,
        195
    and Bubble *see* Bubble
    and demise of Iron Triangle's influence,
        98–9, 124
    deregulation and liberalization of, 90, 92,
        96, 97, 99, 101, 104, 127, 182

economy (*continued*)
  dimming of during 1970s and reasons, 43–4
  during US Occupation, 37–8
  external forces changing, 99
  favorable factors for postwar recovery and growth, 37–41
  and FDI, 96, 97–8, 178
  growth, 3, 28, 36, 44, 90
  impact of Great Depression, 10
  and income disparities, 42, 85–6, 94, 126
  and income doubling plan, 25, 43, 139–40, 190, 202
  internal forces promoting change, 99–100
  and IT revolution, 100–1, 124
  and *keiretsu*, 14, 41, 54, 96–7, 99, 109, 197, 199
  lifetime employment, seniority wages and enterprise unions as factors of growth, 39–40
  and MITI sponsorship, 36
  Obuchi on bridge to prosperity, 181–2
  and oil crisis (1973), 41, 43, 175
  opening of market to foreign competition, 100
  policy paralysis, 102
  promotion of recovery and growth by LDP, 26
  and protectionism, 36, 41–2, 53–4, 91, 175
  reasons for malaise, 90–2, 175–6
  recession and malaise, 34, 43, 52, 72, 74, 90, 91, 96–7, 101, 106, 107, 193
  state-sponsored development as factor for growth, 36–7
  transformation and restructuring of, 95–8, 103, 124–5
  women workers as shock absorbers of, 43, 72
education, 38–9, 184, 186
  censorship and revision of textbooks, 45, 49–50, 144–6, 192, 201–2
  demand for change, 4
  during US Occupation, 13
  school system, 117
  and women, 73–4
Eisenhower, President, 23
elderly, 79–89
  changes in circumstances of, 173–5
  changes in relationship between adult children and parents, 170–3
  and employment, 93, 174
  family-based care for, 41, 80–2, 84, 169
  greatest fears of, 174
  impact of ageing crisis, 79–80
  increase in numbers, 79, 127, 166, 169–70, 192
  medical care, 85
  and nursing care insurance, 75, 83–5
  Obuchi on helping, 182–3
  and pensions, 85, 86, 87, 173, 183
  reasons for rising of numbers, 79
  and reforms in caring for, 86–7
  respect for, 80
  social and economic implications of demographic crisis, 169–75
  social policy, 41, 82–3, 166–8
  threatening of labor shortage by ageing, 87–8, 100
  widening income disparities due to ageing of society, 86
  women and caring for, 75, 81–2, 84, 171
Elderly Care Law (1998), 70
elections, 29 *see also* voting
electoral reform, 33–4
electronics, 39
Emmott, Bill, 44
employment, 93–4, 96
  changing paradigm of, 92–3
  and elderly, 93, 174
  fading of lifetime employment and seniority wages system, 92–3, 101
  labor shortage, 80, 87–8, 92, 94, 100, 128, 164, 167
  lifetime, 39–40, 42, 90, 92–3, 101, 176, 177
  reduction in full-time jobs, 92–3
  wage gap between men and women, 72–3
  and women, 43, 69–73, 74–5, 79, 88, 100, 128
  see also unemployment
enjo kosai, 117–18, 196
enterprise unions, 39, 40
environment, 25–6, 191
  impact of economic growth, 43
  impact of pork-barrel politics, 25
  improvement in air and water, 26
  need for international cooperation, 161–2
  Obuchi addressing issue of, 183–4
  and 'Pollution Diet', 26
Equal Employment Opportunity Law (1986), 70
ethnic minorities, 186–8
  discrimination against, 47, 118–19, 188
Export-Import Bank of Japan, 152
Ezoe, Hiromasu, 32

Fallows, J., 21
families, 164
  and caring for elderly, 41, 80–2, 84, 169
  losses during Bubble bursting, 109
  preference for smaller, 79, 166
  and women, 68, 69, 70
farmers, 190, 191
FDI (foreign direct investment), 96, 97–8, 178
financial services, 91
  deregulation of (Big Bang), 87, 97, 109, 177–8, 194, 195
Financial System Reform Law, 178

flag, national, 116, 160, 194
flag-and-anthem bill, 116
'floating voters', 29
Fogel, J., 146
foreign companies, 100
foreign direct investment *see* FDI
Foreign Exchange Law, 178
foreign policy
  defensive diplomacy and weakness of, 60,
    161–2
  see also international relations; security
foreign workers, 88–9, 103, 164
foreigners
  discrimination against, 88, 118, 119–20
Fujioka, Nobukatsu, 52
fukoku kyohei, 196
Fukuda, Prime Minister, 54, 191
Fukuyama, Francis, 76, 164–5
Fundamental Law Designed to Promote a
  Gender-Equal Society, 183

gaiatsu (foreign pressure), 60, 95, 196
gaijin see foreigners
Gap, The, 95
GDP, 90, 97, 193
General Agreement on Trades and Tariffs
  (GATT), 41, 190
gengo, 196
Germany, 48, 147
GNP, 96, 97, 139, 191
GNPism, 25, 26, 43, 139
Golden Plan, 167
Goto, K., 46
Great Depression, 10
Great Hanshin Awaji Earthquake *see* Kobe
  earthquake
Gulf War, 63, 161, 193
gyosei shido (administrative guidance), 36–7,
  196

Hall, Ivan, 120
'hamlet people' *see burakumin*
Hashimoto, Prime Minister Ryutaro, 45, 62,
  83, 194, 195
Hatch, W. and Yamamura, K., 54
Hayato, Ikeda, 202
Hein, L. and Selden, M., 48
Heisei era, 196
hibakusha, 188
Hideyoshi, 187
Higashinakano, Dr Shudo, 148
Hinomaru flag, 116, 160, 194
Hirohito, Emperor, 59, 191, 198
  absolving of for war crimes, 15–16, 201
  biographical details, 201
  death and funeral, 56, 104–5, 192
Hiroshima, 9, 17, 154, 188
homelessness, 109
Honda, 38, 42
Honda, Katsuichi, 53, 146

honne, 3, 196
Hosokawa, Prime Minister Morihiro, 61,
  159–60, 193
housing, 108, 109

ie system, 69, 196
Ienaga, Saburo, 50, 144, 201–2
ijime see bullying
Ikeda, Prime Minister Hayato, 25, 43, 139,
  190, 202
IMF (International Monetary Fund), 60,
  150, 151, 190
immigration, 88–9, 119, 188
income
  disparities, 42, 85–6, 94, 126
  doubling plan, 25, 43, 139–40, 190, 202
India, 149
Indonesia, 151, 152, 190
information technology, 124, 125, 126, 184
insurance scheme, nursing care, 75, 83–4
international community
  Ozawa on Japan's participation in, 161–2
  relations with, 11, 60, 161–2, 180–1
Internet, 101
Iron Triangle, 21, 98–9, 124, 197
Ishihara, Governor Shintaro, 51–2, 88, 148,
  154–5
IT revolution, 100–1, 103, 124, 128

Japan
  achievements and advances, 123
  ambivalence towards rapidity of change,
    124
  assessment of change, 126–8
  five bridges to 21st Century, 179–85
  image and stereotypes of, 3
  limits and constraints on postwar model,
    123–4
  reasons for problems in 1930s and 1940s,
    10–12
  transformation and change of, 1, 3, 4, 123
Japan Institute of Labor, 86
Japan Socialist Party *see* Socialist Party of
  Japan
Japan–Korea Basic Treaty (1965), 190
Japanese
  change in attitudes of individual, 96, 125
Japanese Communist Party, 14
Japanese Foundation for AIDS prevention,
  166
Japanese Society for New History Education,
  52
Johnson, Chalmers, 21, 36–7, 138–9
JSP (Japan Socialist Party) *see* Socialist Party
  of Japan
Jubaku: Archipelago of Rotten Money, 31,
  110
judiciary, 12, 126
jusen, 107, 197
justice, 126

kakahu hakkai, 95
Kamei, Shizuka, 84
Kanemaru, Shin, 33, 204
kanson mimpi, 95–6, 197
Kanto earthquake (1923), 88
Kasahara, Tokushi, 148
katatataki, 77
Katz, Richard, 90, 175–6
Kawabata, Yasunari, 191, 202
Keidanren, 99
keiretsu, 14, 41, 54, 96–7, 99, 109, 197, 199
Kennedy, President, 202
Kimigayo anthem, 116, 160, 194, 197
Kishi, Prime Minister Nobusuke, 25, 135, 153, 190
Kobayashi, Yoshinori, 52
Kobe earthquake (1995), 112–14, 184, 193, 203
koenkai, 25, 197
kokusaika, 120
Komeito, 194
Korea, 44, 49, 192
    and comfort women, 50
    Japanese colonialism in, 47
    migration to Japan from, 187
    relations with Japan, 47, 56, 190
    see also North Korea; South Korea
Korean War (1950–53), 22, 38, 56
Koreans
    in Japan, 47, 118–19, 187
koseki, 197
Kurosawa, Akira, 31, 33, 202
Kyubin, Sagawa, 31, 33, 34

labor
    conflict, 27, 40
    and foreign workers, 88–9, 103, 164
    shortage of, 80, 87–8, 92, 94, 100, 128, 164, 167
    see also unions
Lam, A., 72
land prices, 105, 106, 107, 108
land reform, 13, 38
LDP (Liberal Democratic Party), 23–6, 33, 193, 194, 197
    battles with progressive political forces, 24
    coalition government, 23, 28
    dominance of, 21, 23
    efforts to roll back American reforms, 24
    factions within, 24–5, 28
    focus on pork-barrel projects, 25–6
    formation, 23, 24, 190
    ideology of GNPism, 43
    and Kakuei Tanaka *see* Tanaka, Kakuei
    reinvention as catch-all party, 26–7, 28
    support of rural vote 34–5
    tackling of environment issues, 26
League of Nations
    withdrawal from (1933), 11

Lebra, T., 81
left
    purge of ('red purge'), 14–15, 198
    tension between conservative forces and radical, 24
Liberal Democratic Party *see* LDP
life expectancy, 79, 169, 182, 191
lifetime employment, 39–40, 42, 72, 90, 92–3, 101, 176, 177
literacy, 38
Lockheed corruption scandal (1976), 30–1, 31–2, 191, 204
'Lolita eros', 165
Long Term Credit Bank, 100, 194
long-term care insurance, 168

MacArthur, General, 12, 14, 61–2, 131, 135
McCormack, Gavan, 25, 48
Maekawa Report, 95
Malaysia, 151, 152
Manchuria, invasion of (1931), 11, 46
Mansfield, Mike, 60
marriage, 82
Marshall Plan, 38
Marxism, 24
maternity leave, 75
Matsu, 156
medical care, 85, 86, 167, 183
Meiji Constitution (1889), 10, 11, 12, 131
Meiji era/restoration (1868–1911), 10, 26, 29, 30, 37, 104, 127, 179
messhi hoko (self-sacrifice), 117, 185–6, 197
middle classes, 24, 28, 38
militarism, 10–11, 13, 59
military *see* armed forces; defense
military bases *see* bases, US military
Minamata mercury poisoning, 26, 190
Ministry of Education, 120, 144, 146, 201–2
Ministry of Finance, 110
Ministry of Health and Welfare, 76
    report (1995), 169–75
Ministry for International Trade and Industry (MITI), 21, 36
Mishima, Yukio, 191, 202–3
Miyamato, Masao, 185–6
Miyazawa, Kiichi, 32, 203
    speech (1999), 150–3
mobile phones, 101
Mongolia, 149
Monju nuclear accident (1995), 115
morality, 116, 180
Mori, Prime Minister Yoshiro, 67, 194
Morita, Akio, 203
multi-ethnicity *see* ethnic minorities
mura hachibu (ostracization), 117, 197
Murakami, Ryu, 110
Murayama, Prime Minister Tomoiichi, 46, 142–3, 203
Murphy, R., 101
Myanmar, 150

Nagasaki, 9, 154, 188
Nakakita, Ryutaro, 147
Nakasone, Prime Minister Yasuhiro, 32, 62, 63, 83, 95, 192, 203
Nanking Massacre (1937), 48, 50, 51–3, 146–8, 193
narikin, 108, 197
Narita International Airport, 27
National Police Reserve, 22
nenko see seniority wage system
New Deal, 13, 14, 198
Nikkeiren, 99
1955 system, 23–8, 30
Nishi, Haruhiko, 156–7
Nishimura, Shingo, 66
Nixon, President, 62, 95, 191
  on US relations with Japan during the Cold War, 160–1
No Regrets for Our Youth, 202
Non-Proliferation Treaty (NPT), 149
nopan shabushabu, 110, 197
North Korea, 55, 57, 58, 64–5, 156
  Japanese military force levels in, xi (map)
  missile tests and launching, 62, 64, 181, 193
  nuclear capabilities, 63, 64, 66, 181
  relations with Japan, 119, 181
North Vietnam, 58
nuclear accidents, 114–15
nuclear energy program, 114
nuclear power plants, x (map)
nuclear weapons, 58, 64–5, 65–6, 153–4
Nursing Care insurance program, 75, 83–5
nursing homes, 82, 83

Obuchi, Prime Minister Keizo, 67, 194
  five bridges to the twenty-first century speech, 179–85
ODA (Official Development Assistance), 53, 54
  charter, 148–50
Oe, Kenzaburo, 47, 143–4
OECD (Organization for Economic Cooperation and Development), 190
office ladies (OLs), 73
Official Development Assistance *see* ODA
Ohira, Masayoshi, 192
Ohtake, F., 86
oil prices, rise of (1973), 41, 43, 175, 191
Okinawa, 187
  and nuclear weapons, 153, 154
  returned to full Japanese sovereignty by US (1972), 59, 191
  US military bases in, 58, 180
Okinawa, battle of (1945), 59
Okinawans, 119, 187
Olympic Games (Tokyo) (1964), 43, 190
omoiyari yosan (sympathy budget), 59, 197–8
on, 81–2, 198

OPEC (Organization of Petroleum Exporting Countries), 43, 191
Osaka Stock Exchange, 178
outsourcing, 94
Ozawa, Ichiro, 63, 161–2, 204
  and five freedoms, 188–9
Ozu, Yasujiro, 203–4

Pakistan, 149
Pan-Asianism, 46, 47
part-time employment, 71, 72, 73, 92
patriarchy, 69, 80, 196
PCBs (polychlorinated biphenyls), 26
Peace, Friendship and Exchange Initiative, 142
Peace Memorial Museum (Hiroshima), 17
Peace Treaty *see* San Francisco Peace Treaty
peace-keeping operations (PKOs), 63, 161, 181, 193
Pearl Harbor, 17
pensions, 85, 86, 87, 173, 183
People's Republic of China *see* China
Perry, Commodore, 17
Philippines, 151, 152, 190
pill, birth control, 76, 164–5
Plaza Accords (1985), 106, 192
plutonium, 115
politics, 21–35
  changing logic of, 27–30
  and corruption, 25, 28, 30–1, 34, 96, 102, 127, 193
  decline of Socialist Party, 24, 27, 28, 2, 64, 203
  decline of radicalism, 27
  diminishing of importance of ideology, 28–9
  electoral reform, 33–4
  emergence of 'floating voters', 29
  focus on pork-barrel projects, 25
  and Iron Triangle of big business, LDP and government ministries, 21, 98, 99, 124, 197
  lack·of support by voters for reform, 29–30
  and LDP *see* LDP
  1955 system, 23–8, 30
  reform, 33–5
  tension between conservative and progressive political forces, 24
  and US–Japan security treaty *see* Security Treaty
  and Yoshida Doctrine, 22, 198
  see also individual names
pollution, 26, 191
'Pollution Diet', 26
pop culture, 56
population, 79, 190, 191, 193
pork-barrel public works projects, 24, 25, 34
pornography, 77, 78, 165–6

Power Reactor and Nuclear Fuel
  Development Corporation, 115
prices, 95, 105, 106
Pride (film), 16
private sector, 53
protectionism, 36, 41–2, 53–4, 91, 175
public day care centers, 75
public works, 25–6, 34, 35, 43, 102

Qemoy, 156

racism, 88 *see also* discrimination
radicalism, decline of, 27
Ramsayer, M. and Rosenbluth, F., 21
Rape of Nanking, The (Chang), 52, 146
Reagan, President Ronald, 62, 95, 203
recession (1990s), 34, 43, 52, 72, 74, 90, 91,
  96–7, 101, 106, 107, 193
Recruit scandal (1988), 31, 32–3, 34, 193
recruitment
  discrimination against women, 74–5
'red purge', 14–15, 198
Reischauer, Edwin, 11, 138
Rengo, 192
restructuring, 91, 93–4, 96, 97, 125, 127
retirement age, 87, 192
reverse course, 13–14, 15, 198
rice, 35
Roosevelt, President, 13, 17
Russia, xi, 10, 180
Ryukyu Islands, 119, 187
Ryukyuans, 187

Saburo, Ienaga, 49
Sagawa Kyubin scandal (1992), 31, 33, 34
Sakaiya, Taichi, 176–7
salaried workers, 176–7, 198
San Francisco Peace Treaty (1951), 22–3, 47,
  187, 190 *see also* Security Treaty
sangokujin, 88
Sato, Prime Minister Eisaku, 66, 95, 191
savings, 39, 95
SCAP (Supreme Command of the Allied
  Powers), 10, 11–12, 13, 14, 15, 16, 37,
  131, 198, 199
Schaller, Michael, 22
school system, 117
SDF (Self-Defense Force), 22, 88, 113, 198
  and Article Nine of Constitution, 12, 66,
    162–3
  establishment, 62, 190
  and new defense guidelines, 61
Second World War, 9, 45
  atrocities committed by Imperial armed
    forces, 140
  criticism by Oe of Japan's heightened sense
    of war victimization and call for
    apology, 46, 143–4
  focus on victimization by Japanese, 17,
    45, 48, 143

and Murayama's apology for atrocities
  caused by Japanese aggression, 46,
  142–3
and Pearl Harbor, 17
and war apology resolution, 45–6,
  139–40
security, 55, 58–67, 180
  and Article Nine of Constitution *see*
    Article Nine
  avoidance of relations with international
    community, 60, 161–2, 180–1
  calls to revise Constitution, 67
  defense budget and spending, 12, 40–1,
    62, 66, 192
  efforts in Cambodia, 63–4
  and Gulf War, 63, 161, 193
  and new defense guidelines (1999), 61,
    62, 64, 65, 157–9, 159–60, 180
  and North Korea *see* North Korea
  nuclear policy, 58, 64–5, 65–6, 153–4
  pacifist and defensive foreign policy, 60,
    161–2
  relations with United States *see* United
    States
  and SDF *see* SDF
  shedding reticence over and reassessment
    of defence posture, 61, 62–3, 63–4
  transforming of in 1990s, 61–3
Security Treaty (1951), 22–3, 28, 58, 65,
  153, 157, 159
  revision of and demonstrations against
    (1960), 23, 24, 25, 27, 58, 64, 135–7,
    156–7, 190
Self-Defense Force *see* SDF
self-sacrifice *see* *messhi hoko*
senile dementia, 79
seniority wage system (*nenko*), 39–40, 80,
  90, 92, 93, 176, 177, 197
Senkaku Islands, 65
sex industry, 77, 109, 117–18, 165–6
  and comfort women, 50–1
sexual assault, 77
sexual harassment, 77, 78
sexual slavery, 50–1
sexually transmitted diseases (STDs), 76
shareholders, 98
shinjinrui, 116, 198
Shintaro, Ishihara, 202
shipbuilding scandal, 30
Showa Denko scandal, 30
Showa era (1926–89), 104, 198, 201
single-parent families, 69, 164, 173
Smithsonian Museum (Washington), 17
social mores, 116–18
social security, 40–1, 68
social welfare policies, 41, 80, 83
Socialist Party of Japan (SPJ) (was JSP), 24,
  27, 28, 29, 64, 192, 203
Sohyo (General Council of Trade Unions of
  Japan), 24

sokaiya, 98, 198
Sokka Gakkai, 194
Sony, 38, 42, 203
South Korea, 64, 151, 156
  apology by Hosokawa for abuses during
    colonial rule, 193
  Nakasone's visit, 192
  relations with Japan, 119, 181
  US forces in, xi (map)
Soviet Union, 22, 155, 156–7
SPJ *see* Socialist Party of Japan
state intervention
  market-conforming methods of, 36,
    138–9
subway courtesy signs, 116–17
suicide, 109, 196
Sumitomo Corporation, 193
Sun Also Sets, The (Emmott), 44
Sunflowers, 108
Supreme Command of the Allied Powers *see*
  SCAP
Supreme Court, 12, 34
Supreme Truth Cult *see* Aum Shinrikyo
Suzuki, Prime Minister Zenko, 62
Swift, Graham, 2

Tachibanaki, T., 73
Taisho era (1912–25), 11
Taiwan, xi, 44, 47, 64, 65, 187
Takako, Doi, 192
Takeshita, Noboru, 32, 33, 83, 193, 204
Tanaka, Kakuei, 31–2, 33, 54, 188, 191,
  192, 203, 204
tatemae (public behavior), 3, 198
taxation, 71, 83, 85, 86, 87, 183
technology, 37, 38, 184
textbooks
  censorship and revision of, 45, 49–50,
    144–6, 192, 201–2
Thailand, 151, 152
Thatcher, Margaret, 203
Theater Missile Defense (TMD), 64–5
Time magazine, 82
tobashi, 102
Tojo, Prime Minister Hideki, 16
Tokaimura nuclear accident (1999), 114–15,
  194
Tokugawa era (1603–1868), 188, 196
Tokyo
  housing and land prices, 105, 106, 107,
    108
  Olympic Games (1964), 43, 190
  subway gas attack, 110, 193, 195, 203
Tokyo Stock Exchange, 178
Tokyo Story, 203
Toshiba, 42
Toyota, 42
Toys 'R' Us, 95
trade, 23, 99
  and bureaucracy, 185

with United States, 95, 192
and protectionism, 36, 41–2, 53–4, 91,
  175
trade unions *see* unions
training, 73–4, 101
truancy, 117
trucking firm scandal (1992) *see* Sagawa
  Kyubin scandal
Twilight Years, The (Ariyoshi), 81

ubasteyama, 80, 81, 198
ultra-nationalism, 11
UN Convention for the Eradication of All
  Forms of Discrimination Against
  Women (1985), 70
UN Security Council, 60, 63
unemployment, 90, 91, 93, 94, 109, 192,
  194 *see also* employment
unions, 13, 14, 15, 24, 28, 39, 40, 44
Unit 731, 48, 49
United Nations
  Japan joins, 190
United Nations Transitional Authority in
  Cambodia *see* UNTAC
United States
  abandoning of Bretton Woods system,
    44
  economy, 97
  elderly care poll, 82
  military bases in Japan, 23, 58–9, 135,
    156
  military force levels in Far East, xi
    (map)
  normalizes ties with China, 191
  occupation of Japan (1945–52), 9–17, 30,
    104, 127, 145
    absolving of Emperor Hirohito of war
      crimes by Americans, 15–16, 201
    aim of, 9
    ambivalence and impressions of, 16
    conservative shift in policies ('reverse
      course'), 13–14, 15, 198
    and demilitarization, 9, 12, 16, 22
    and democratization, 9–10, 12–13, 15,
      16, 134
    Dower on, 134–5
    and economy, 37–8
    ending of, 22
    and LDP, 24
    legacies of, 14–17
    and new Constitution *see* Constitution
      (1947)
    power of bureaucracy, 37
    promotion of growth, 37–8
    purge on left-wing sympathizers (red
      purge), 14–15, 198
    relationship between US and Japan
      during, 9, 16, 58, 135
    socio-economic reforms, 13
    and *zaibatsu*, 13, 14, 38

United States (*continued*)
  relations with Japan, 17, 23, 58–60, 61–3, 180, 202
    Ishihara on, 154–5, 202
    and military bases in Japan, 58–9
    Nixon on Cold War, 160–1
    over security *see* Security Treaty
    reliance on by Japan, 59
    strength of influence in Japan, 16
    and trade, 95, 192
  troops in Japan, xi, 58, 59
universities, 74, 184
UNTAC (United Nations Transitional Authority in Cambodia), 55, 63–4, 193
urbanization, 69, 103
Uruguay Round (1989), 34
US–Japan Security Treaty (1951) *see* Security Treaty

Viagra, 76
Vietnam, 149, 152
Vietnam War, 23, 27
von Wolferen, K., 21
voting
  decline in participation at elections, 29
  emergence of 'floating voters' in 1990s, 29
  participation, 126
  rural and urban voters, 34
  and women, 10, 12

wages, 40
  gap between men and women, 72–3
  seniority wage system, 39–40, 80, 90, 92, 93, 176, 177, 197
war apology resolution, 45–6, 140–1
War Bereaved Families of Veterans' Association, 45
War Crimes Tribunal, 15, 16–17, 49
wealth, and Bubble, 108
West
  catch-up-with goal of Japan, 26, 27

Whiting, R., 107
women, 68–78, 103
  and birth control pill, 76, 164
  comfort, 50–1
  difficulty in pursuing career and family responsibilities, 70
  discrimination in job recruitment, 74–5
  and education, 73–4
  and elderly care, 75, 81–2, 84, 171
  and employment, 43, 69–73, 74–5, 79, 88, 100, 128
  few concessions given to working, 71
  and *ie* system, 69, 196
  and low birth rate, 75
  low numbers in pursuing high-status careers, 72
  part-time and temporary work, 71, 72, 73
  powerful role in families, 68
  right to vote, 10, 12
  rights and Constitution (1946), 12, 69
  sexual exploitation of, 77, 165–6
  as shock absorbers of the economy, 43, 72
  stereotype, 68
  wage gap between men and, 72–3
World Trade Organization (WTO), 34

yakuza, 31, 33, 98, 107, 198
Yamamoto, Noriko, 81
Yayoi people, 187
yen, 44, 181, 190, 191, 192, 193
Yokoyama, 'Knock', 78
Yoshida Doctrine, 22, 198
Yoshida, Prime Minister Shigeru, 22, 30, 38, 62, 198, 204
Yoshida, Yasuhiko, 147
young, 116, 117–18

zaibatsu, 13, 14, 28, 197, 199
zaitech, 106, 199
Zemin, President Jiang, 180
Zhang, Premier, 65

SEMINAR STUDIES IN HISTORY

General Editors: Clive Emsley & Gordon Martel

The series was founded by Patrick Richardson in 1966. Between 1980 and 1996 Roger Lockyer edited the series before handing over to Clive Emsley (Professor of History at the Open University) and Gordon Martel (Professor of International History at the University of Northern British Columbia, Canada and Senior Research Fellow at De Montfort University).

MEDIEVAL ENGLAND

The Pre-Reformation Church in England 1400–1530 (Second edition)
Christopher Harper-Bill   0 582 28989 0

Lancastrians and Yorkists: The Wars of the Roses
David R Cook   0 582 35384 X

TUDOR ENGLAND

Henry VII (Third edition)
Roger Lockyer & Andrew Thrush   0 582 20912 9

Henry VIII (Second edition)
M D Palmer   0 582 35437 4

Tudor Rebellions (Fourth edition)
Anthony Fletcher & Diarmaid MacCulloch   0 582 28990 4

The Reign of Mary I (Second edition)
Robert Tittler   0 582 06107 5

Early Tudor Parliaments 1485–1558
Michael A R Graves   0 582 03497 3

The English Reformation 1530–1570
W J Sheils   0 582 35398 X

Elizabethan Parliaments 1559–1601 (Second edition)
Michael A R Graves   0 582 29196 8

England and Europe 1485–1603 (Second edition)
Susan Doran   0 582 28991 2

The Church of England 1570–1640
Andrew Foster   0 582 35574 5

STUART BRITAIN

Social Change and Continuity: England 1550–1750 (Second edition)
Barry Coward   0 582 29442 8

James I (Second edition)
S J Houston   0 582 20911 0

The English Civil War 1640–1649
Martyn Bennett   0 582 35392 0

Charles I, 1625–1640
Brian Quintrell   0 582 00354 7

The English Republic 1649–1660 (Second edition)
Toby Barnard   0 582 08003 7

Radical Puritans in England 1550–1660
R J Acheson   0 582 35515 X

The Restoration and the England of Charles II (Second edition)
John Miller   0 582 29223 9

The Glorious Revolution (Second edition)
John Miller   0 582 29222 0

EARLY MODERN EUROPE

The Renaissance (Second edition)
Alison Brown   0 582 30781 3

The Emperor Charles V
Martyn Rady   0 582 35475 7

French Renaissance Monarchy: Francis I and Henry II (Second edition)
Robert Knecht   0 582 28707 3

The Protestant Reformation in Europe
Andrew Johnston   0 582 07020 1

The French Wars of Religion 1559–1598 (Second edition)
Robert Knecht   0 582 28533 X

Phillip II
Geoffrey Woodward   0 582 07232 8

The Thirty Years' War
Peter Limm   0 582 35373 4

Louis XIV
Peter Campbell   0 582 01770 X

Spain in the Seventeenth Century
Graham Darby   0 582 07234 4

Peter the Great
William Marshall   0 582 00355 5

EUROPE 1789–1918

Britain and the French Revolution
Clive Emsley   0 582 36961 4

Revolution and Terror in France 1789–1795 (Second edition)
D G Wright   0 582 00379 2

Napoleon and Europe
D G Wright   0 582 35457 9

Nineteenth-Century Russia: Opposition to Autocracy
Derek Offord   0 582 35767 5

The Constitutional Monarchy in France 1814–48
Pamela Pilbeam   0 582 31210 8

The 1848 Revolutions (Second edition)
Peter Jones   0 582 06106 7

The Italian Risorgimento
M Clark   0 582 00353 9

Bismarck & Germany 1862–1890 (Second edition)
D G Williamson   0 582 29321 9

Imperial Germany 1890–1918
Ian Porter, Ian Armour and Roger Lockyer   0 582 03496 5

The Dissolution of the Austro-Hungarian Empire 1867–1918 (Second edition)
John W Mason   0 582 29466 5

Second Empire and Commune: France 1848–1871 (Second edition)
William H C Smith   0 582 28705 7

France 1870–1914 (Second edition)
Robert Gildea   0 582 29221 2

The Scramble for Africa (Second edition)
M E Chamberlain   0 582 36881 2

Late Imperial Russia 1890–1917
John F Hutchinson   0 582 32721 0

The First World War
Stuart Robson   0 582 31556 5

EUROPE SINCE 1918

The Russian Revolution (Second edition)
Anthony Wood   0 582 35559 1

Lenin's Revolution: Russia, 1917–1921
David Marples   0 582 31917 X

Stalin and Stalinism (Second edition)
Martin McCauley   0 582 27658 6

The Weimar Republic (Second edition)
John Hiden   0 582 28706 5

The Inter-War Crisis 1919–1939
Richard Overy   0 582 35379 3

Fascism and the Right in Europe, 1919–1945
Martin Blinkhorn   0 582 07021 X

Spain's Civil War (Second edition)
Harry Browne   0 582 28988 2

The Third Reich (Second edition)
D G Williamson   0 582 20914 5

The Origins of the Second World War (Second edition)
R J Overy   0 582 29085 6

The Second World War in Europe
Paul MacKenzie   0 582 32692 3

Anti-Semitism before the Holocaust
Albert S Lindemann   0 582 36964 9

The Holocaust: The Third Reich and the Jews
David Engel   0 582 32720 2

Germany from Defeat to Partition, 1945–1963
D G Williamson   0 582 29218 2

Britain and Europe since 1945
Alex May   0 582 30778 3

Eastern Europe 1945–1969: From Stalinism to Stagnation
Ben Fowkes   0 582 32693 1

The Khrushchev Era, 1953–1964
Martin McCauley   0 582 27776 0

NINETEENTH-CENTURY BRITAIN

Britain before the Reform Acts: Politics and Society 1815–1832
Eric J Evans   0 582 00265 6

Parliamentary Reform in Britain c. 1770–1918
Eric J Evans   0 582 29467 3

Democracy and Reform 1815–1885
D G Wright   0 582 31400 3

Poverty and Poor Law Reform in Nineteenth-Century Britain, 1834–1914:
From Chadwick to Booth
David Englander   0 582 31554 9

The Birth of Industrial Britain: Economic Change, 1750–1850
Kenneth Morgan   0 582 29833 4

Chartism (Third edition)
Edward Royle   0 582 29080 5

Peel and the Conservative Party 1830–1850
Paul Adelman   0 582 35557 5

Gladstone, Disraeli and later Victorian Politics (Third edition)
Paul Adelman   0 582 29322 7

Britain and Ireland: From Home Rule to Independence
Jeremy Smith   0 582 30193 9

TWENTIETH-CENTURY BRITAIN

The Rise of the Labour Party 1880–1945 (Third edition)
Paul Adelman   0 582 29210 7

The Conservative Party and British Politics 1902–1951
Stuart Ball   0 582 08002 9

The Decline of the Liberal Party 1910–1931 (Second edition)
Paul Adelman   0 582 27733 7

The British Women's Suffrage Campaign 1866–1928
Harold L Smith   0 582 29811 3

War & Society in Britain 1899–1948
Rex Pope   0 582 03531 7

The British Economy since 1914: A Study in Decline?
Rex Pope   0 582 30194 7

Unemployment in Britain between the Wars
Stephen Constantine   0 582 35232 0

The Attlee Governments 1945–1951
Kevin Jefferys   0 582 06105 9

The Conservative Governments 1951–1964
Andrew Boxer   0 582 20913 7

Britain under Thatcher
Anthony Seldon and Daniel Collings   0 582 31714 2

INTERNATIONAL HISTORY

The Eastern Question 1774–1923 (Second edition)
A L Macfie   0 582 29195 X

The Origins of the First World War (Second edition)
Gordon Martel   0 582 28697 2

The United States and the First World War
Jennifer D Keene   0 582 35620 2

Anti-Semitism before the Holocaust
Albert S Lindemann   0 582 36964 9

The Origins of the Cold War, 1941–1949 (Second edition)
Martin McCauley   0 582 27659 4

Russia, America and the Cold War, 1949–1991
Martin McCauley   0 582 27936 4

The Arab–Israeli Conflict
Kirsten E Schulze   0 582 31646 4

The United Nations since 1945: Peacekeeping and the Cold War
Norrie MacQueen   0 582 35673 3

Decolonisation: The British Experience since 1945
Nicholas J White   0 582 29087 2

The Vietnam War
Mitchell Hall   0 582 32859 4

WORLD HISTORY

China in Transformation, 1900–1949
Colin Mackerras   0 582 31209 4

Japan in Transformation, 1952–2000
Jeff Kingston   0 582 41875 5

US HISTORY

America in the Progressive Era, 1890–1914
Lewis L Gould   0 582 35671 7

The United States and the First World War
Jennifer D Keene   0 582 35620 2

The Truman Years, 1945–1953
Mark S Byrnes   0 582 32904 3

The Vietnam War
Mitchell Hall   0 582 32859 4

American Abolitionists
Stanley Harrold   0 582 35738 1

The American Civil War, 1861–1865
Reid Mitchell   0 582 31973 0